HOW TO DRAW
FANTASY FEMALES

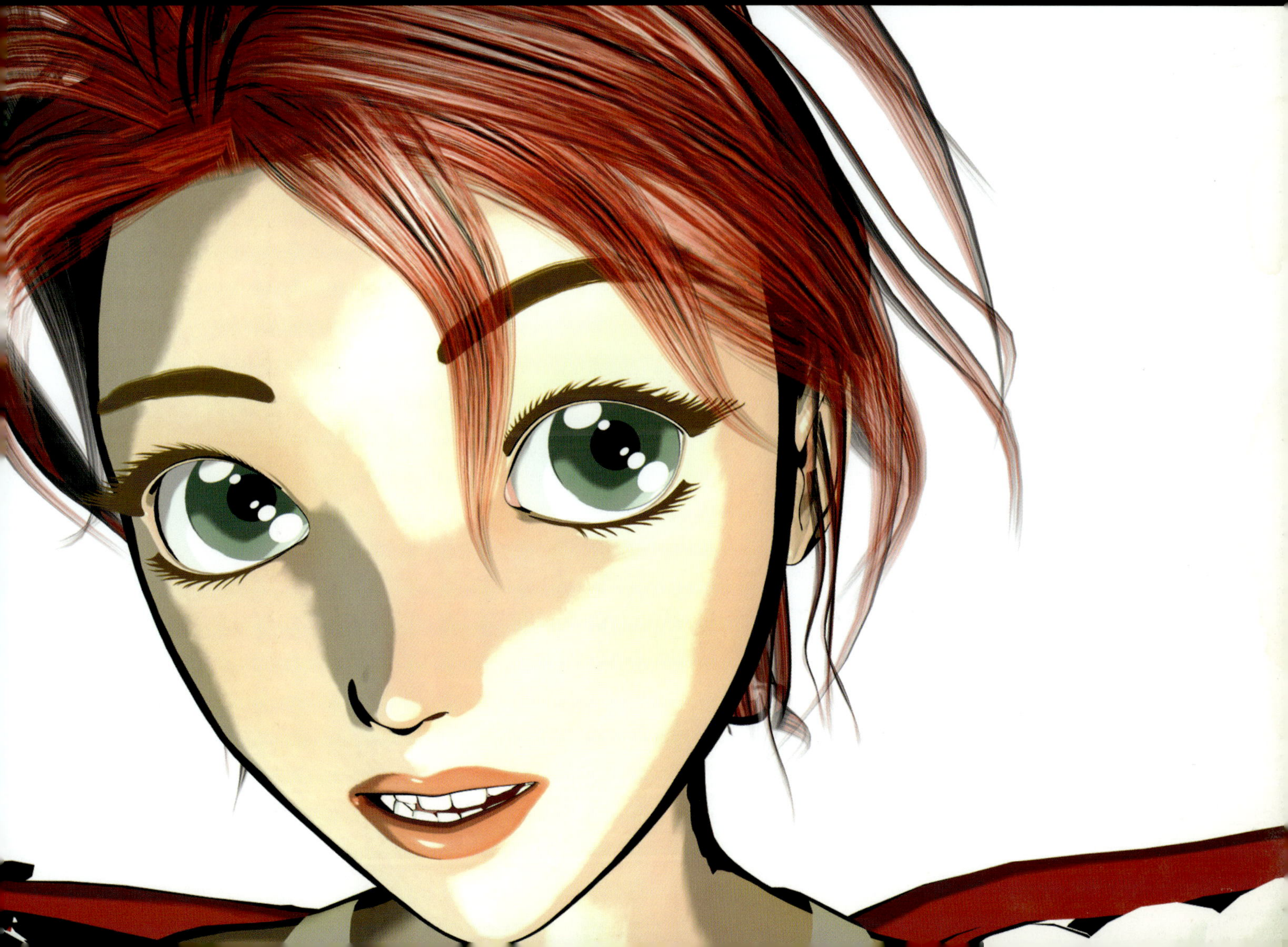

HOW TO DRAW
FANTASY

CREATE SEXY CYBERPUNKS, SEDUCTIVE SUPERGIRLS

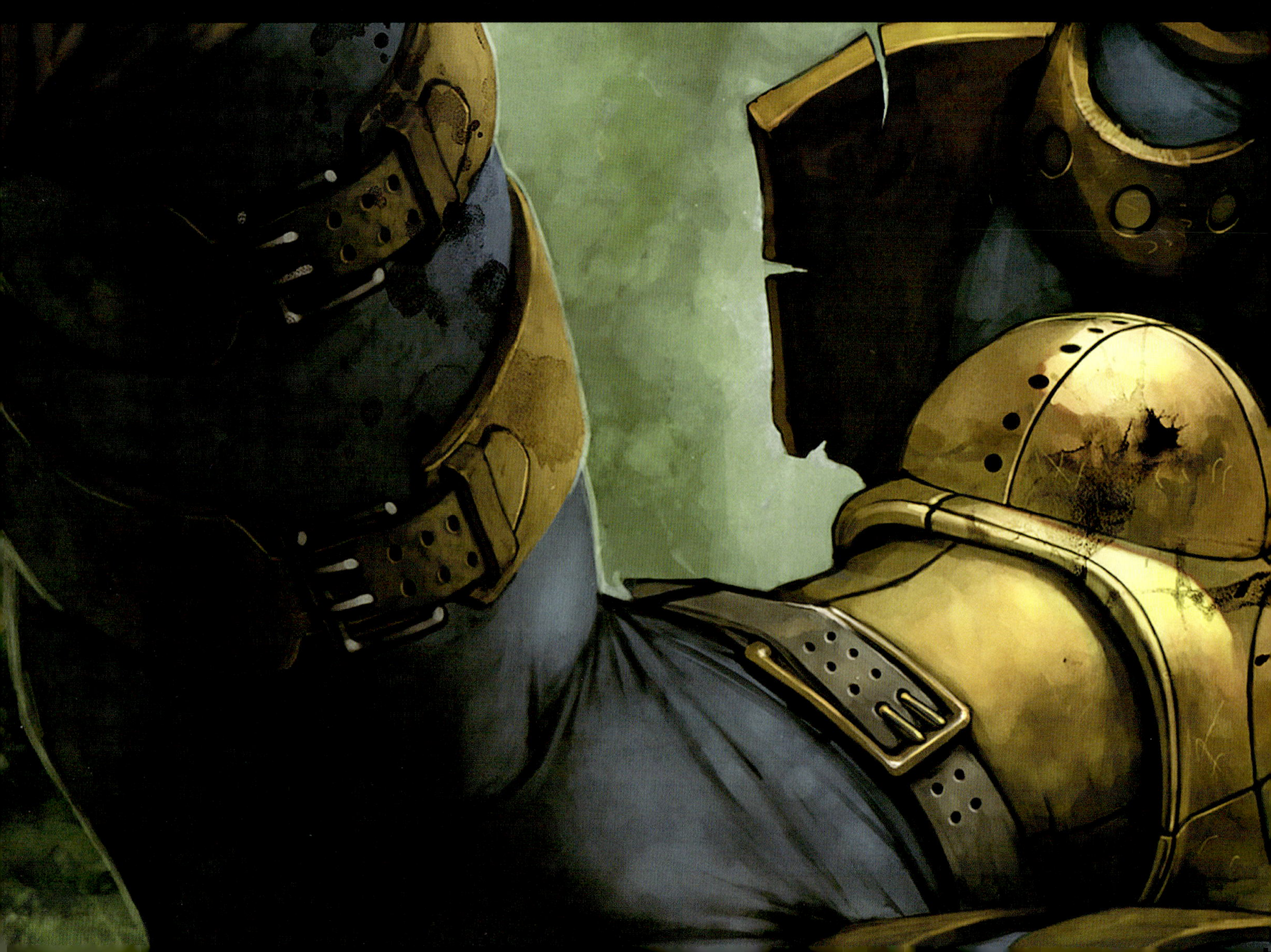

FEMALES

AND RAUNCHY ACTION HEROINES

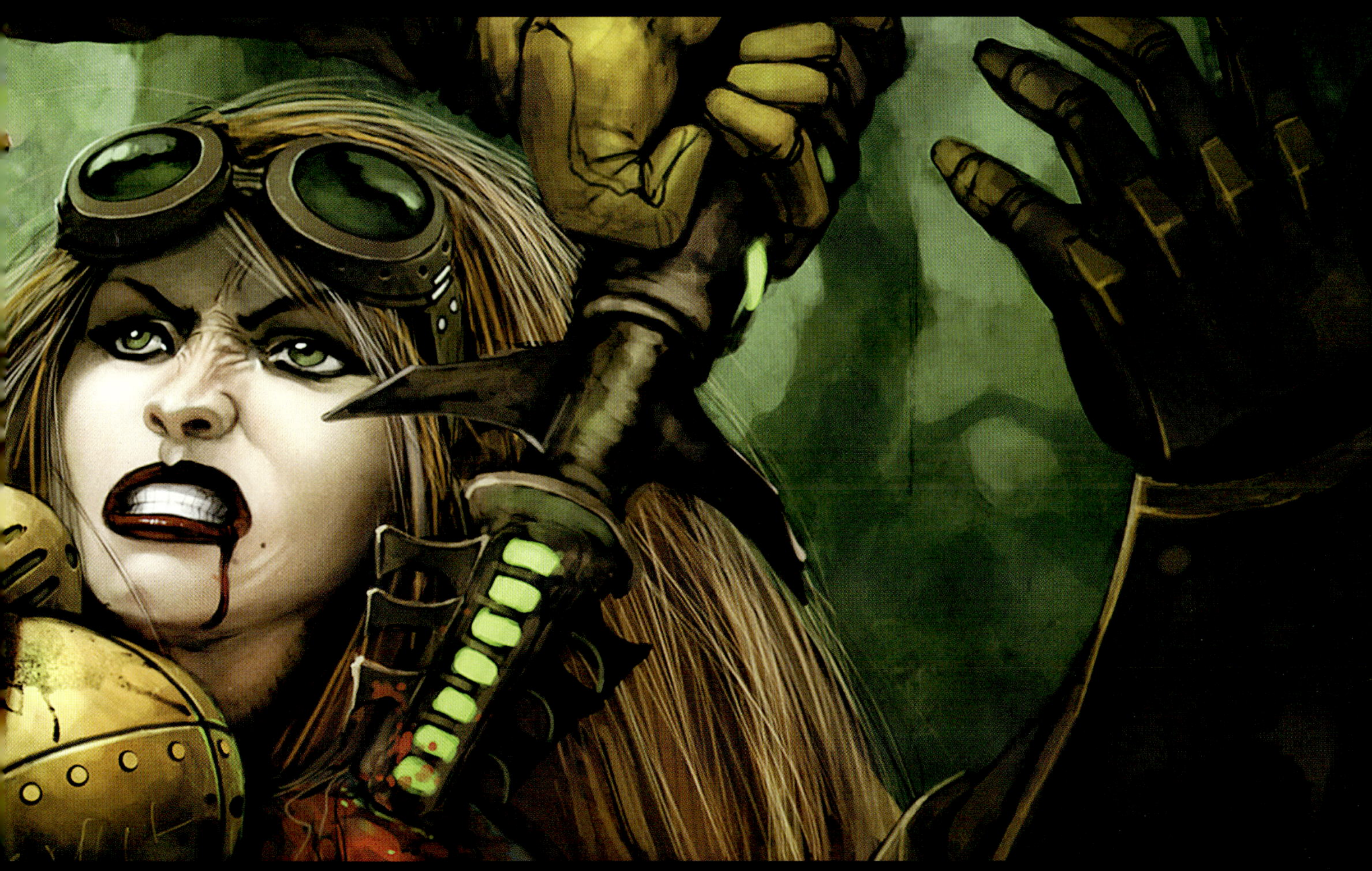

CHRIS PATMORE

BARRON'S

A QUARTO BOOK

First edition for the United States, its territories
and dependencies, and Canada published in
2006 by Barron's Educational Series, Inc.

All inquiries should be addressed to:
Barron's Educational Series, Inc.
250 Wireless Boulevard
Hauppauge, New York 11788
www.barronseduc.com

ISBN-13: 978-0-7641-3089-2
ISBN-10: 0-7641-3089-7
Library of Congress Control Number: 2005932034

Conceived, designed, and produced by
Quarto Publishing plc
The Old Brewery
6 Blundell Street
London N7 9BH

QUAR: TOB

EDITOR: Michelle Pickering
ART EDITOR & DESIGNER: Claire Van Rhyn
ASSISTANT ART DIRECTOR: Penny Cobb
PICTURE RESEARCHER: Claudia Tate
PHOTOGRAPHER: Martin Norris
INDEXER: Dorothy Frame

ART DIRECTOR: Moira Clinch
PUBLISHER: Paul Carslake

Color separation by Provision Pte Ltd, Singapore
Printed by Star Standard PTE Ltd, Singapore

9 8 7 6 5 4 3 2 1

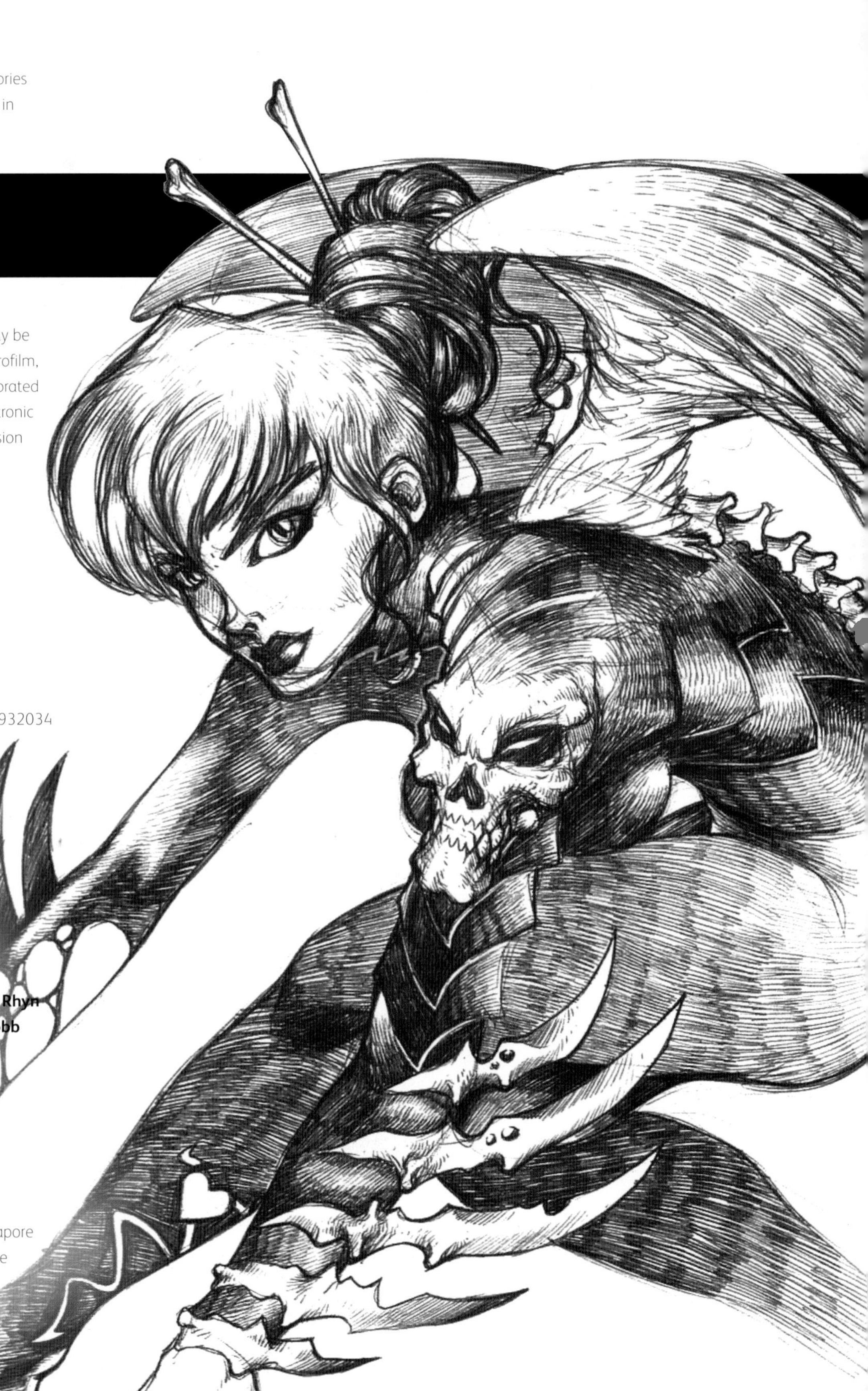

CONTENTS

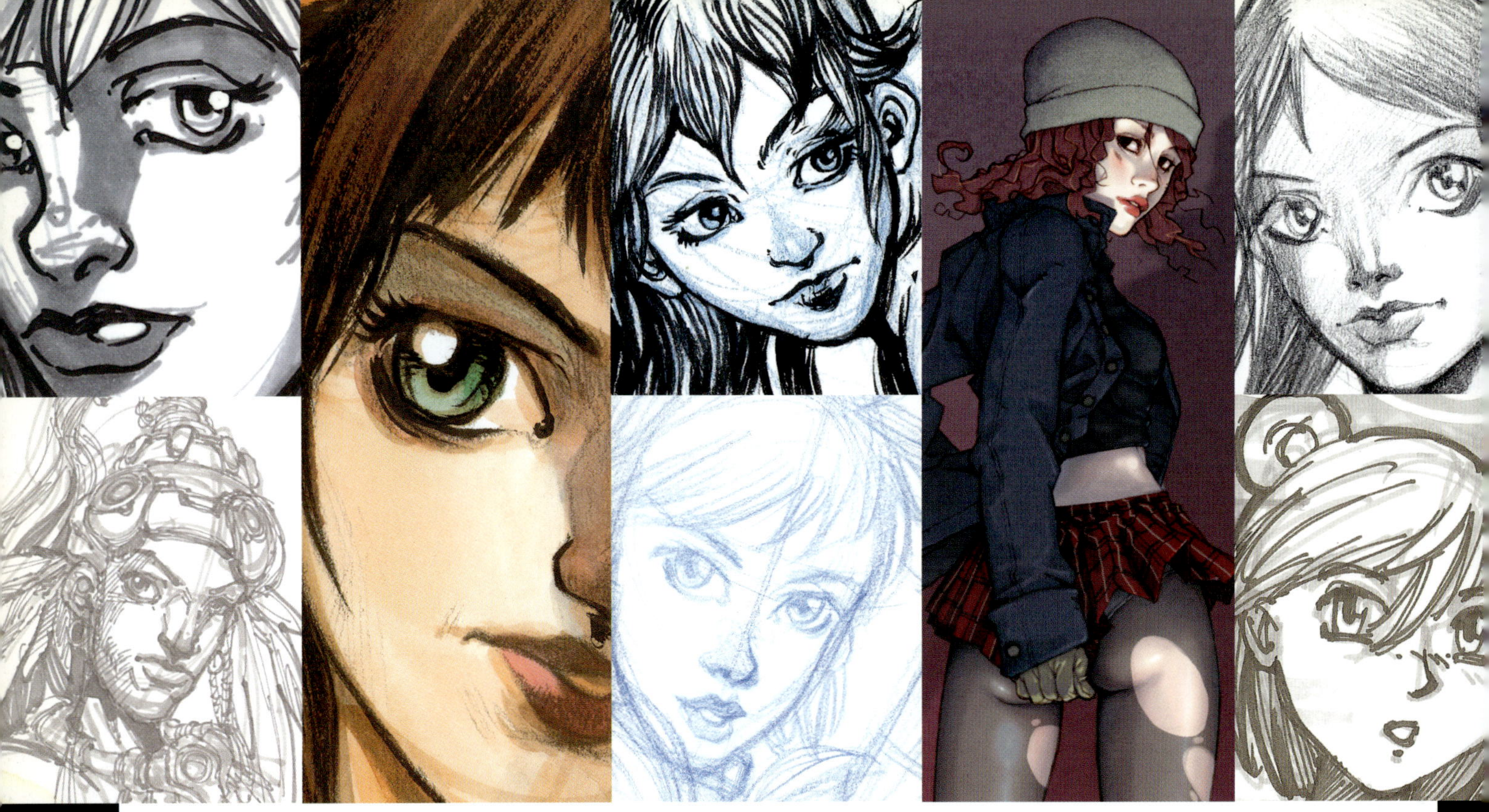

NOT JUST A PRETTY FACE

This book's purpose is twofold. First, it is a guide to creating and drawing females. Even though the commercial world of animation is abandoning its pencils in favor of computer-generated images, comics are still as popular as ever. For figurative artists, comics are the last refuge for their considerable talents. However, the competition and demands are heavy, not just for the quality of the linework and coloring, but also for strong characters in engaging stories.

That brings us to the second point. Rather than just concentrating on how to draw women (and/or girls), this book looks at ways of developing female characters with real personalities. Even if your main interest is just drawing, a fundamental knowledge of character development and storytelling will help bring life to the figures you create.

With this in mind, the first section of the book runs through the basics of getting started—equipment, anatomy, digital techniques, and how to create an inner personality for the body you are going to illustrate. Space does not allow for an in-depth exploration of

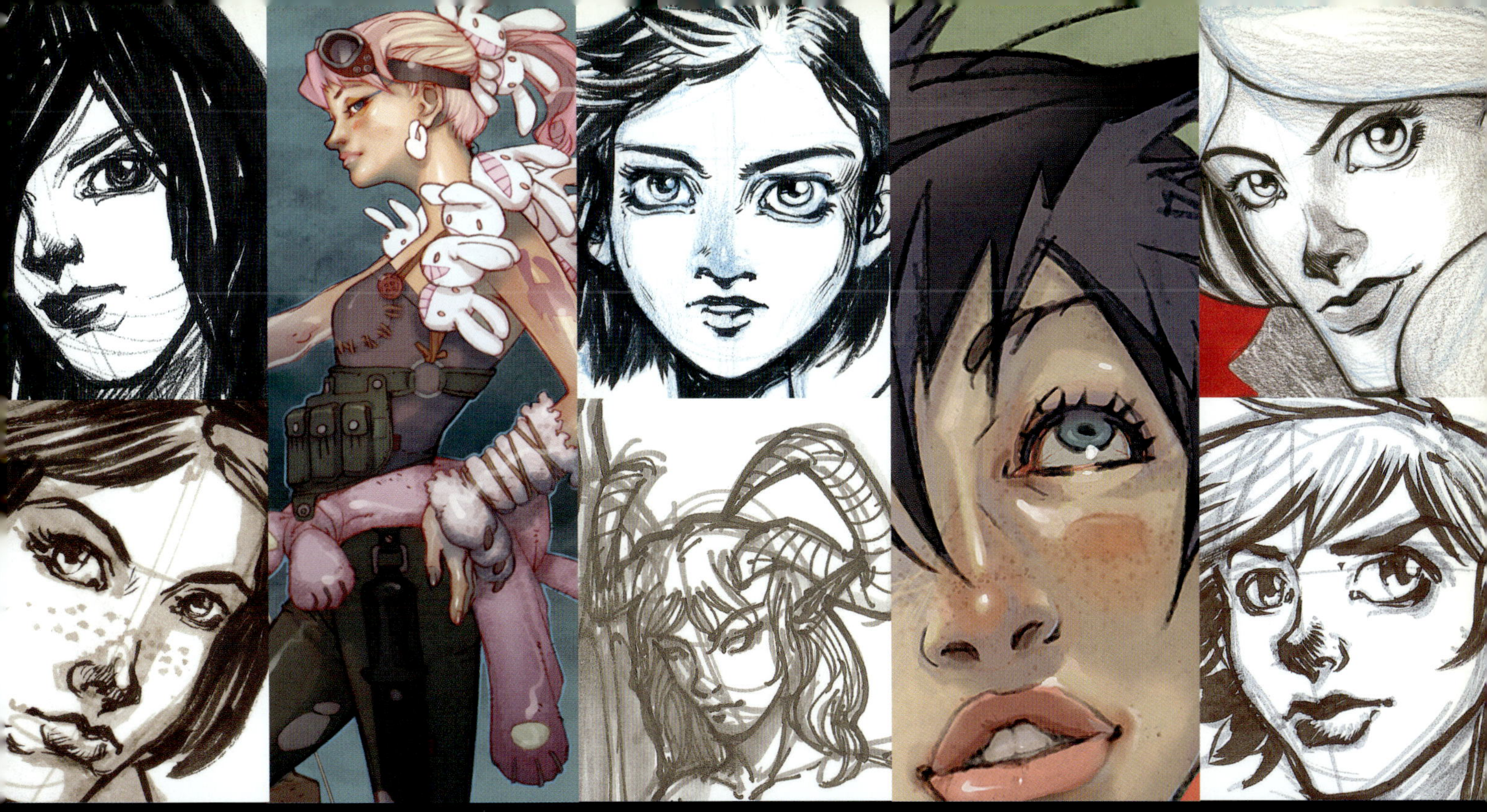

the subject, but it will be enough to get you working and developing your own ideas.

The second section is divided into a selection of character types. This is not a definitive list, but they do demonstrate a range of possibilities. They are drawn by more than 20 artists, both male and female, from around the world, who work in different styles and genres to bring divergent perspectives to the subject. Each character synopsis features a description of her personality, plus a brief tutorial of a technique used by the artist. The purpose of this section is to inspire and instruct.

Nearly all the works are a hybrid of traditional and digital methods, with most artists preferring to start with pencils and finish by coloring on the computer. For those who feel less confident with drawing, there are also some 3D examples created with Poser and/or DAZ Studio, indispensable software tools for anyone interested in figurative art. Featuring more than 40 examples of female characters, this book will inspire you to create interesting characters that glow with femininity and go beyond the stereotypical views often presented in the media.

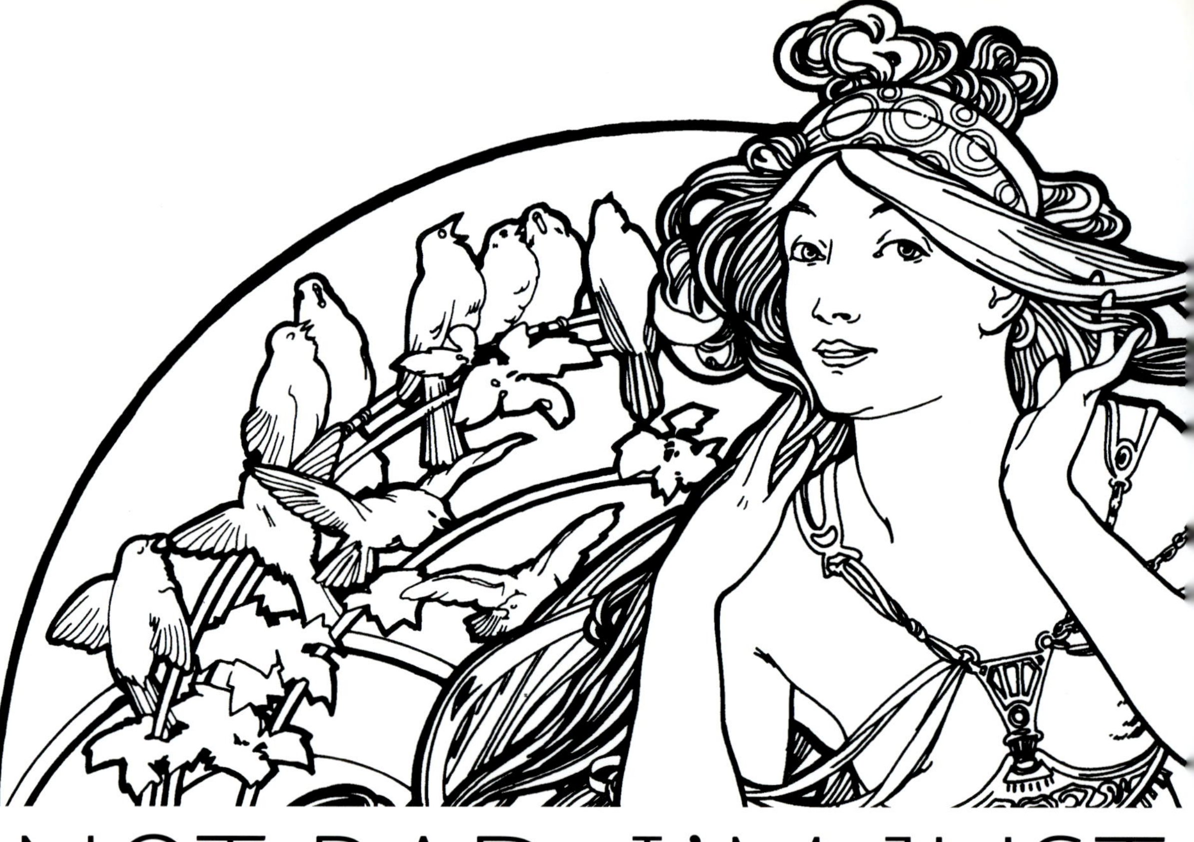

I'M NOT BAD, I'M JUST

Since humans first began drawing on cave walls, they have included the female form in their representations of the world. As humanity evolved and developed higher awareness, females were represented as the embodiment of all that was life-giving, from food to children. Women became an integral part of mythologies and religions, often portrayed as the power of the gods, or awesome entities in their own right.

Not all of these entities were pious, however, and most mythologies have their fair share of femmes fatales and man-eaters (literally). With art and religion being complementary in most of the ancient cultures, pictorial representations of goddesses adorned the walls and courtyards of temples. Because most of these temples were built centuries, and even millennia, before the Christian church introduced the concept of original sin and all the repression and guilt associated with it, the female form

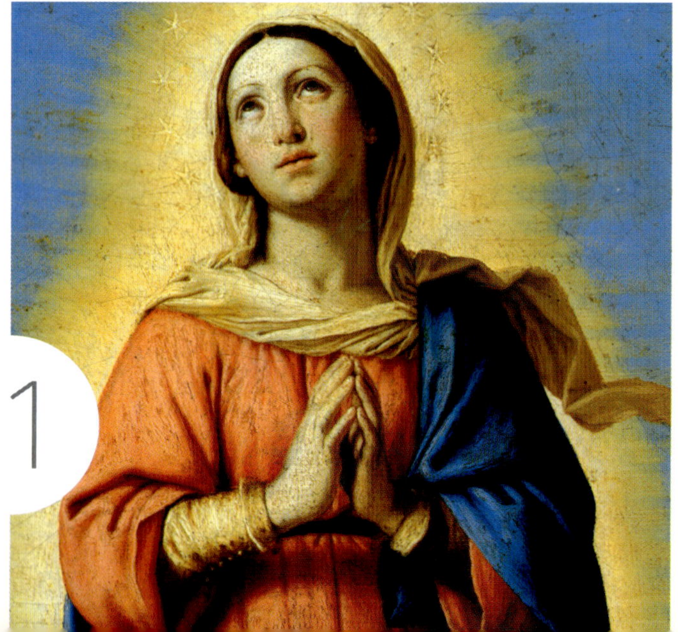

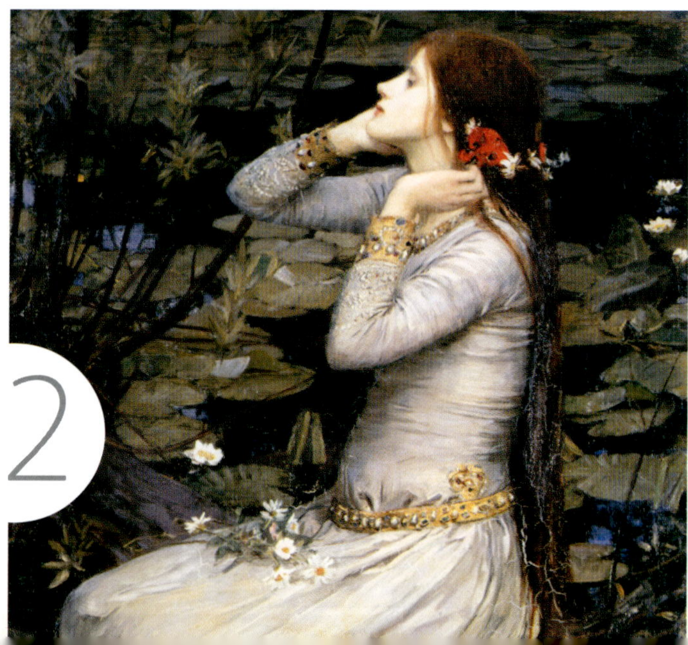

was represented in all its natural glory. However, some of the artists, or their patrons, did digress from worshipping God in female form to adoring the form itself and producing what is commonly known as erotic art—a trend that continued throughout history and not one this book is going to follow.

INTO THE TWENTIETH CENTURY

As the Christian church started to dominate Western culture, and infiltrate others, the role of women was subverted and their images in art were mostly reduced to portraits of the vain nobility, or representations of the Virgin Mary. There were, no doubt, exceptions, but it

(www.icecastle.org/artwork/index.htm has a great online gallery of works from all these artists.)

As society became better educated and more affluent, the demand for books and other printed materials increased, and many artists started producing graphic and commercial illustrations for magazines such as *The Studio*. Art Nouveau, which grew out of the Pre-Raphaelite and Arts and Crafts movements in Britain and other similar movements throughout Europe, produced some adventurous and elaborate images from diverse artists, such as Alfons Mucha, Aubrey Beardsley, and

storytelling tool, which was the preserve of the other new artform: cinema.

Movies were storytelling for the masses that even the illiterate could enjoy, and were creating a whole new breed of women who were adored by the public. They were larger than life and practically unobtainable, which is why they were known as screen goddesses, but there was one who was out of everybody's reach: Betty Boop.

Betty was an animated cartoon character created for one of animation innovator Max Fleischer's *Talkartoons* in 1930. Originally designed as a poodle, she was quite quickly redesigned as a human, with her floppy poodle ears

DRAWN THAT WAY

was not until the end of the nineteenth century that European art reintroduced the idea of allegory. Movements, such as the Symbolists and the Pre-Raphaelite Brotherhood, began to reexplore legends and myths in their works. Beautiful women were often an integral part of their compositions, and artists such as J. W. Waterhouse almost exclusively painted fantasy women. Other schools, such as the Orientalists and Romantics, also produced works featuring their ideals of womanhood.

Gustav Klimt, as well as the great book illustrators such as Walter Crane and Arthur Rackham.

A NEW CENTURY

With the newfound freedom that followed the end of World War I, illustrators started to produce simpler drawings of more risqué subjects. Photography was making its mark as an illustrative art and as a way of representing women, but very few artists used it exclusively as a

LADIES IN WAITING

1 In Western art, the Virgin Mary is always shown as pious, in contrast to the female icons of other religions (see pages 40 and 44).
2 Shakespeare's tragic female Ophelia by J. W. Waterhouse.
3 Betty Boop was the original animated "It" girl. Although moral, she was very sexy and fell victim to the censors.
4 Jessica Rabbit from Who Framed Roger Rabbit—*the fantasy female of many a grown man.*

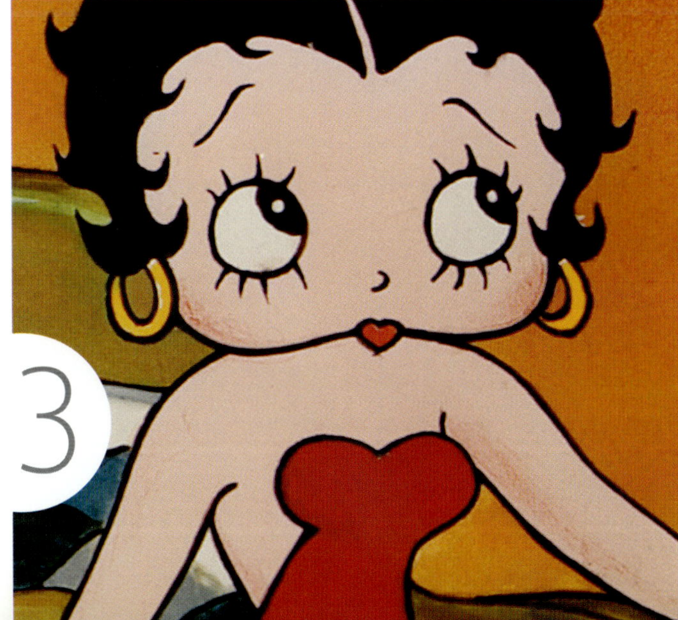

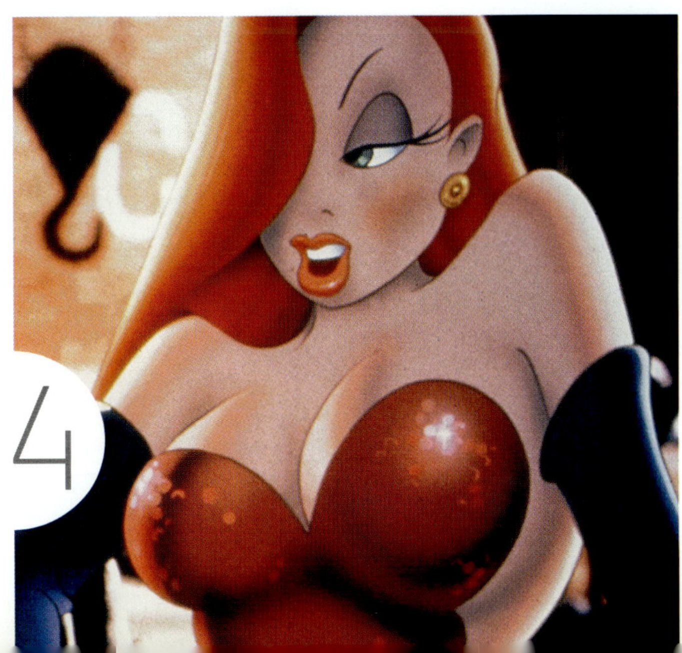

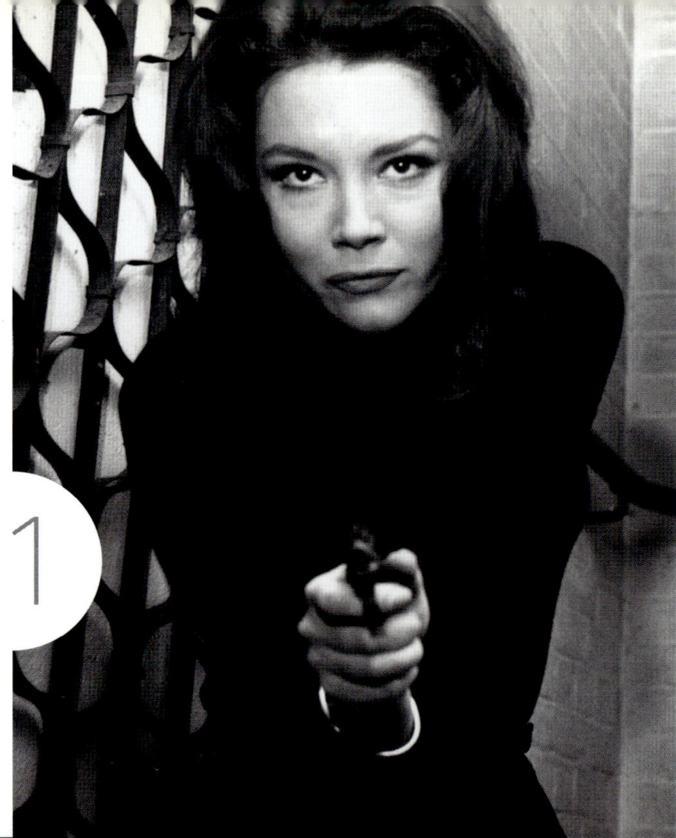

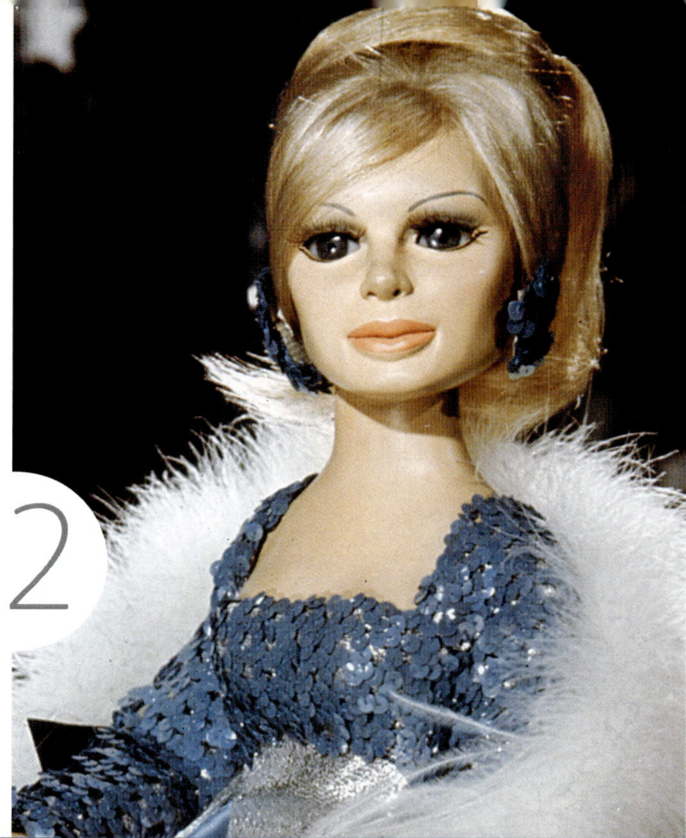

turning into hoop earrings. She was not called Betty Boop until 1932, when Dave Fleischer remodeled her into the sexy form she is best known for. Betty was a truly groundbreaking female character for her time because she was sexy and independent, rather than appearing as a support to a male. Her films also featured music by some of the best jazz musicians of the time, including "Minnie the Moocher" by Cab Calloway. Unfortunately, Betty soon fell foul of the film censors, with the enforcement in the 1930s of the Hays Code that specified what was and was not morally acceptable in screen entertainment, and her newfound demureness diminished her popularity. By 1939, she had disappeared from movie screens, until her guest spot in *Who Framed Roger Rabbit* in 1988.

WONDER WOMEN

It was not long before another strongly independent female character was to appear, this time in a comic book. Wonder Woman first appeared in Detective Comics' (now DC Comics) *All Star Comics* issue 8 in 1941. She was devised by William Marston, under the pen name Charles Moulton, as a reaction to the predominance of male superheroes. He used his character to champion women's causes, saying in a 1943 issue of *The American Scholar*: "Not even girls want to be girls so long as our feminine archetype lacks force, strength, and power. Not wanting to be girls, they don't want to be tender, submissive, peace-loving as good women are. Women's strong qualities have become despised because of their weakness. The obvious remedy is to create a feminine character with all the strength of Superman plus all the allure of a good and beautiful woman."

As the years passed, the character changed into a more domesticated version, mainly because of pressure from the (male) censors and the newly formed Comics Code Authority, who found Wonder Woman's sexuality and feminist views too subversive for the minds of America's youth. Women were meant to be weak, like Lois Lane—to be rescued, not do the rescuing. Luckily, the groundwork had already been done and the taste for strong, feminine heroes established, although most of these appeared in what were usually considered boys' comics. Girls' comics were something altogether different.

DC was producing romance comics for girls, filled with tales of young women with glamorous jobs, such as secretaries and nurses, who fall in love with doctors and pilots. They were supposed to be role models for postwar women looking to lead a life of domestic bliss. There were also the slightly more frivolous *Archie* comics aimed at teenagers and students, but the message was still the same.

It was not all polka-dot dresses and domestic bliss outside the world of comics, though. Other artists were creating images of a different type of ideal woman. Pinup art was in great demand for men's magazines, like *Playboy* and *Esquire*, because it could be a bit more daring than photography permitted. The master, and most popular of these artists, was Alberto Vargas. Apart from gracing the pages of the two previously mentioned magazines, his "Varga Girls" had their own calendars. They (or imitations of them) often adorned the sides of warplanes.

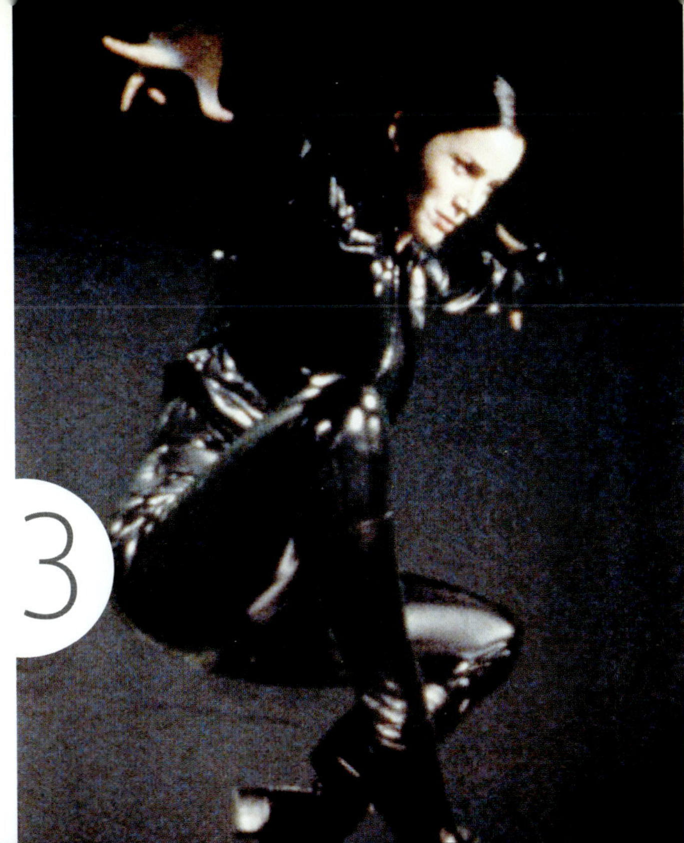

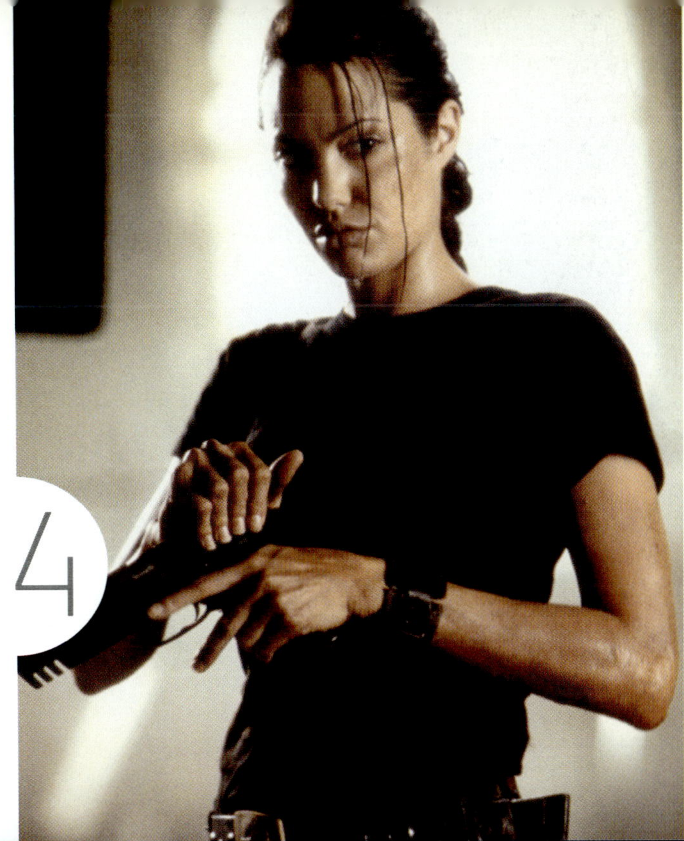

TAKE TO THE STAGES
*1 Emma Peel, from the 1960s cult TV
series* The Avengers: *sexy, lethal, and
very classy.*
2 Lady Penelope, Thunderbirds' *posh
British agent, who bears a resemblance
to singer Dusty Springfield.*
*3 Trinity, the high-kicking heroine of the
influential* Matrix *movies, combining live
and computer-generated action with
dazzling visual artistry.*
*4 Lara Croft has become the iconic
female action hero, in movies, games,
and comics.*

SWINGING SIXTIES ONWARD

As the 1960s progressed, there was a
revival in superhero comics, mostly
thanks to Marvel's stable of renegade
characters. Unlike Superman, Marvel's
heroes were not always seen as heroes,
and were often mutants or outcasts
shunned by society. Marvel's heroines
were treated as equals, with powers to
match their male counterparts and
the abilities to battle the most sinister
villains. DC created female versions of
their most popular properties (Supergirl,
Batgirl), but Wonder Woman was still in
a subservient position in the Justice
League of America to male counterparts
such as Superman and Batman.

In Britain, Modesty Blaise, the
enigmatic part-criminal, part-spy,
developed a huge following in her
daily newspaper comic-strip adventures.
Two other classy British ladies captured
the public's imagination around the
same era, this time on television:
Emma Peel in *The Avengers* and
Lady Penelope in *Thunderbirds*.
Both were intelligent, stylish, beautiful,
and ruthless and, luckily, on our side.
In the United States, Morticia Addams
(*The Addams Family*), (*I Dream of*)
Jeannie, and Samantha (*Bewitched*),
and their esoteric domestic lives, were
fulfilling fantasy female roles.

Meanwhile, in Japan, where manga
is an accepted part of cultural life,
comics with a diverse range of female
characters, from dizzy schoolgirls to
deadly assassins, were available. Manga
is even sorted into clearly defined styles
aimed at different genders and age
groups, such as "shojo" for teenage
girls or "josei" for women.

By the 1990s, girl power was in
full swing, and strong, independent
females were proving very popular,
especially among the growing number
of adult comic readers. There was
also an increasing number of stories
about ordinary life featuring nonheroic
characters, such as *Ghost World*, or
left-field characters such as Tank Girl.
This trend has continued into the
twenty-first century. Today, the most
popular female characters, such as
Buffy, Lara Croft, Trinity, and Amidala
(to name but a few), have become
multimedia stars, appearing on
screen (big and small), as well as
in video games and comics.

Check this out

**With so many dynamic female
characters appearing in the
various media over the years,
it has been impossible to give
a complete history in the limited
space available in this book.
A list of recommended reading
is at the back of the book on
pages 124–125, so you can
explore the characters and
their history in more detail.**

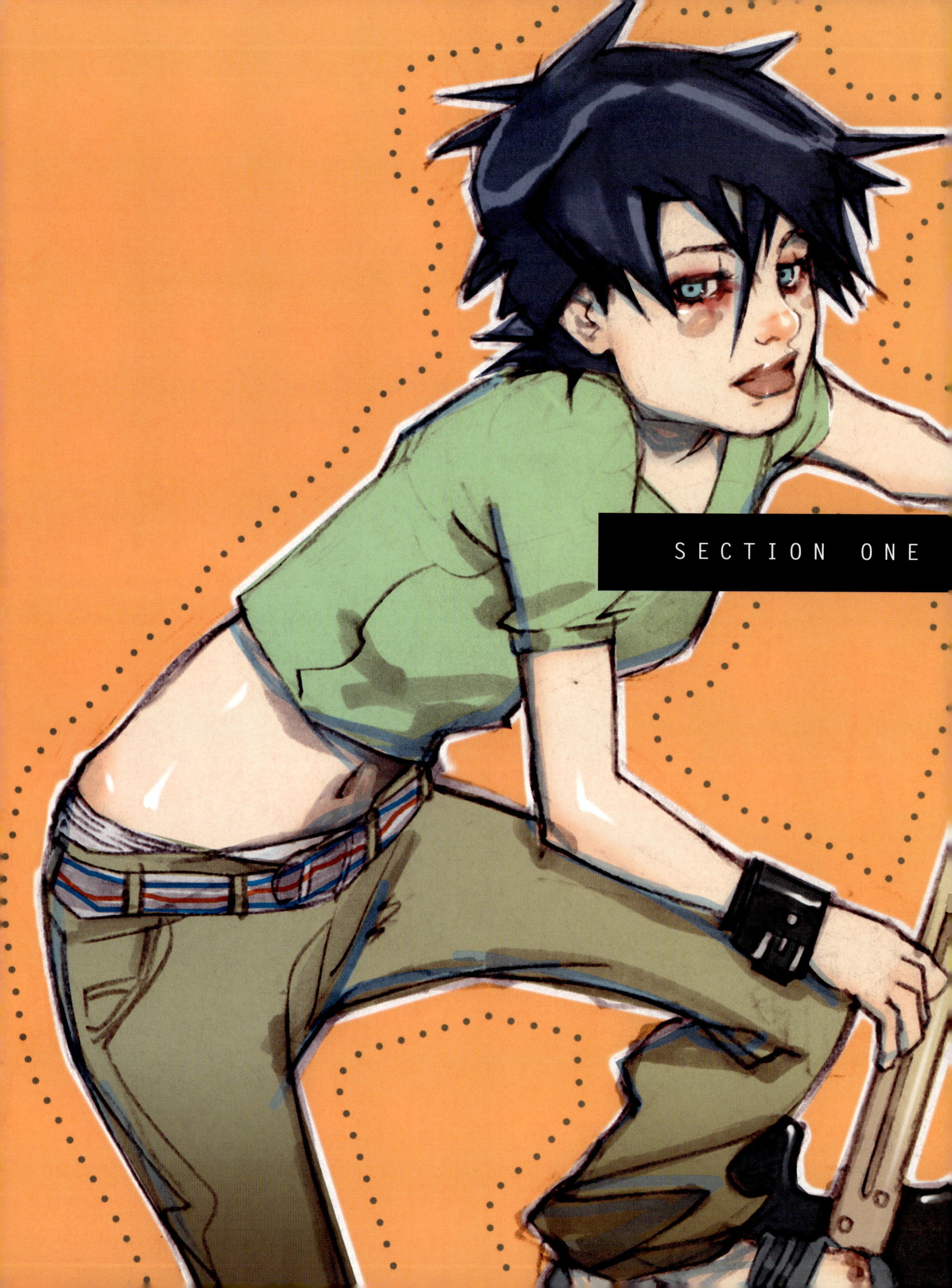
SECTION ONE

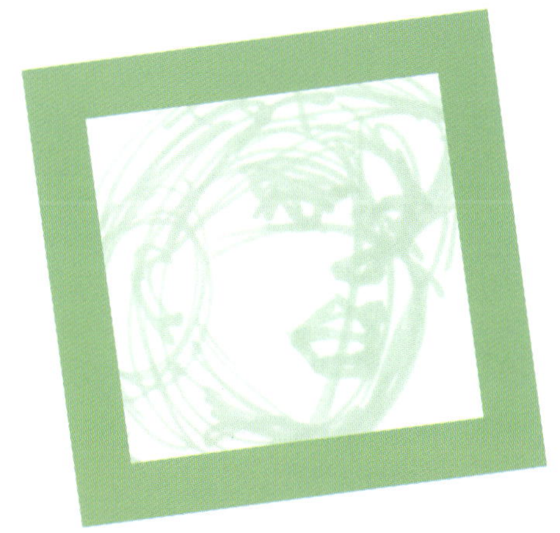

GETTING STARTED

This section takes you through the theory and practice of creating and developing female characters. When it comes to comics or animation, story is everything, so storytelling structure and techniques are outlined first. All the theory in the world will not make you a good storyteller, which is as much a natural gift as being a good artist or musician, but it will help prevent you from being a bad storyteller. Although creativity and expression are undoubtedly important, it is vital not to neglect the craft of drawing. Learning to draw from a book is about as practical as having a book that teaches you how to read, so if you are serious about figure drawing, you need to find a teacher who will not only guide you but correct you. You also need to practice—a lot. What you *can* learn from a book is how to use a computer. Some of the fundamentals of three of the most useful programs for artists are covered here.

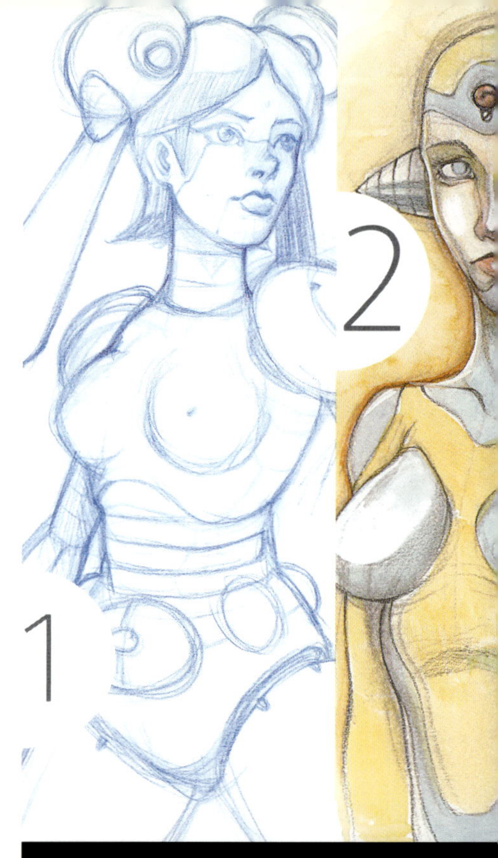

STORYTELLING

Writing and drawing are two different, although not mutually exclusive, disciplines. Both are used to convey ideas, one with words and one with pictures. A visual artist may be a good storyteller, whereas a writer is less likely to be good at drawing. For anyone serious about working as a sequential artist, it is important to learn at least some fundamental storytelling skills. The simplest way to learn about storytelling is to read a lot—not just comics, but as much variety as possible. There is no absolutely right way to tell a story, although there are wrong ways. If you do not captivate your audience, you can be pretty sure it is the wrong way. The trick to effective storytelling is often not what you say but how you say it. A good raconteur can make the most mundane occurrence seem exciting, whereas an unexpressive speaker can turn even capture by aliens into dross.

STRUCTURE

When developing a story, first you have to decide what it is about (the idea, the concept), then devise the who, what, and where of how to expound it. At its most basic, a story is divided into three parts: beginning, middle, and end—what is known in the movie business as a three-act structure. The beginning sets up the premise, the middle has conflict and action, and the ending is the climax and resolution. Supplementary to this, you can introduce a more complex form known as mythological structure or the hero's journey, which is particularly relevant to comic books.

HERO'S JOURNEY

The hero's journey uses the academic studies of Swiss psychologist C. G. Jung and American mythologist and folklorist Joseph Campbell, deconstructing stories and myths into a prescribed sequence of events carried by archetypal characters. This may seem like a rigid approach to storytelling, but the trick is not to use it to plan your story, but to analyze and improve it once it is written.

If you get an idea for a story, write it down as freely as you can, without

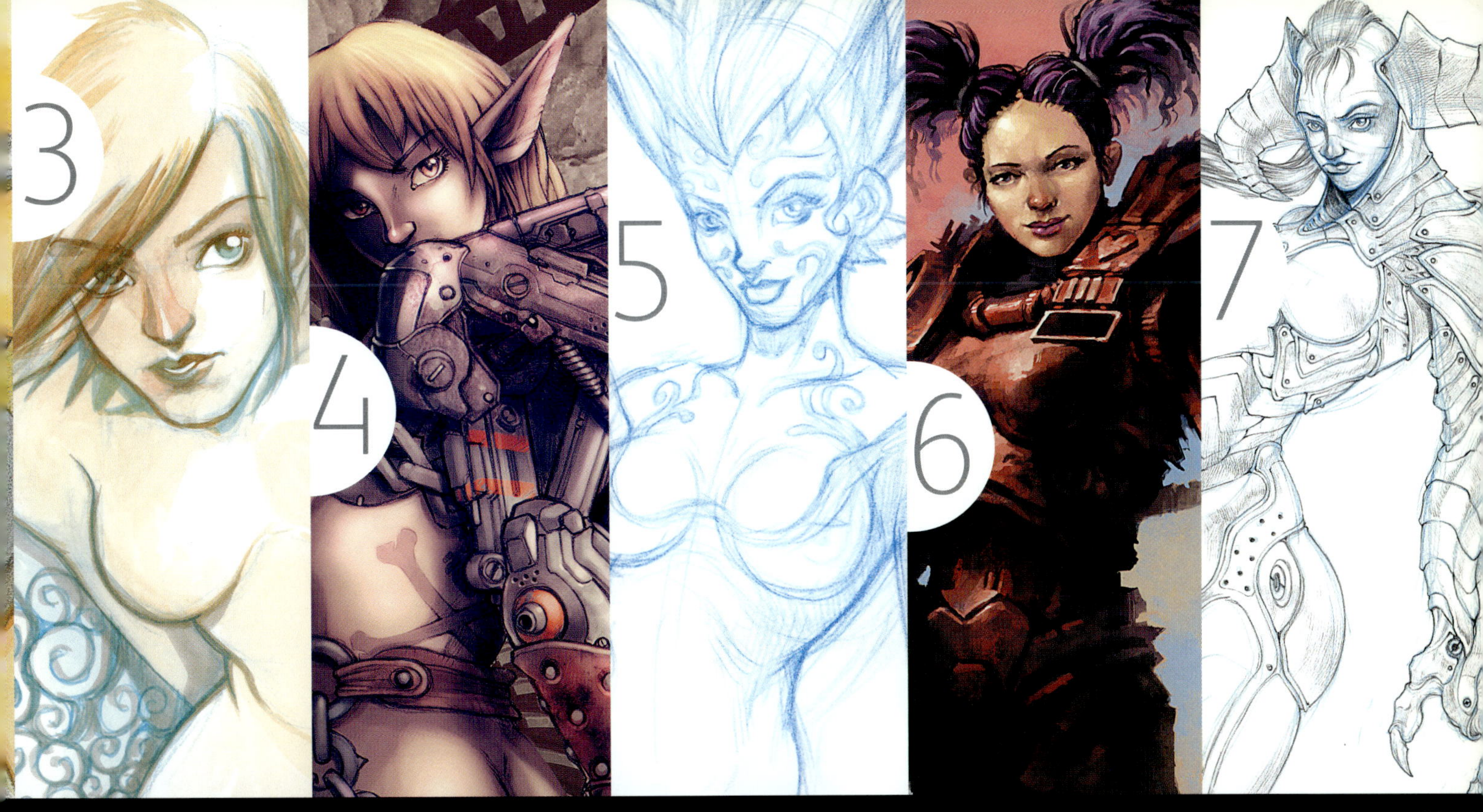

any thought to structure or even content. Once it is written, read it through and revise it into a reasonably comprehensible form. Now compare the structure with the hero's journey and check through the list of archetypes to see how many are present (see box, right). It is surprising how often inspired story ideas fit into this format, no matter what the genre. The beauty of the mythological structure is that it resolves the problem of whether a story is character or plot driven, because they are inextricably connected.

ARCHETYPE EXAMPLES

1 The hero always faces extreme physical danger during the journey.
2 The mentor is a strong figure with a clear moral compass.
3 The herald plays a key role in sending the hero on his or her journey.
4 The threshold guardian is a sinister force who tests the hero's worth.
5 The shape-shifter does not necessarily change physical shape, but may be a femme fatale with a hidden agenda.
6 The trickster is a comedic character.
7 The shadow represents all that is negative and must be defeated.

The hero's journey

CALL TO ADVENTURE
The hero is introduced to the reader in his or her ordinary world. A message or event invites the hero to embark on an adventure that will involve completing an important task.

REFUSAL OF THE CALL
The hero initially refuses the call to adventure, but a significant meeting with his or her mentor changes the hero's mind.

THRESHOLD TEST The hero is faced with a test at the start of the journey, often encountering future allies and enemies.

CRISIS The hero undergoes an ordeal that tests his or her physical endurance and mental resilience.

CLIMAX The hero succeeds in the task and returns to the ordinary world having undergone profound personal growth.

The archetypes

HERO The lead character whose story is being told.

MENTOR A benefactor who guides the hero and imparts knowledge to him or her.

HERALD The person who announces the hero or brings the message that sets the hero on his or her quest.

THRESHOLD GUARDIAN
A person, or even an object, that blocks the hero's path. It can be a subtle force, such as self-doubt.

SHAPE-SHIFTER A person who is not what they appear to be.

TRICKSTER The comic relief who breaks the tension by playing the fool or causing chaos.

SHADOW The character or thing that the hero has to defeat, even if it is the hero's own neurosis.

FEMALE ROLES

If you have already skipped ahead to the next section with all the pictures (it was probably what enticed you to part with your money in the first place), you have seen a diverse range of female characters. There is everything from homebodies to home wreckers, from angels to demons. Each has an individual look and personality, as well as a unique role to play in the story. So how do we define female roles and separate them from those of the male of the species?

On the previous page you will find descriptions of the seven main archetypes found in the mythological story structure (the hero's journey), which are all roles that can be fulfilled by females—from the hero to the shadow, the protagonist to the antagonist. In fact, some of these roles suit females far better than they suit men, such as the mentor (women are innately nurturing), the herald (women have the power to inspire men to perform great acts), and the shape-shifter (the femme fatale). Of course, being archetypes, they can be represented not only by males and females, but also by any animate being or object. One of the reasons for working with archetypal characters is to avoid creating stereotypical ones, which unfortunately is easier said than done. Conversely, creating personalities that are obviously against type can be equally counterproductive.

EMOTION AND PHYSIQUE

The way females are represented on the page, verbally or visually, will be influenced by your attitude toward the gender and any conditionings you may have accumulated over the years. Men and women will definitely approach the portrayal of female roles in different ways. For example, for most males, the female mind is one of the great mysteries of the universe, yet women understand each other no matter how complex and emotional an issue is.

At the risk of making a generalization, emotion is the crux of the female role, whereas the male is more mental or physical. This is not to say that either gender is incapable of displaying all of these traits, but to make female characters believable, they should be motivated by emotions.

Physically, men tend to portray women in what they consider to be the ideal form, usually involving long legs, narrow waists, and big breasts. Women, however, are more likely to endow their characters with physical characteristics they find lacking, or dislike, within themselves, or they create "plain" women with great personalities or talents.

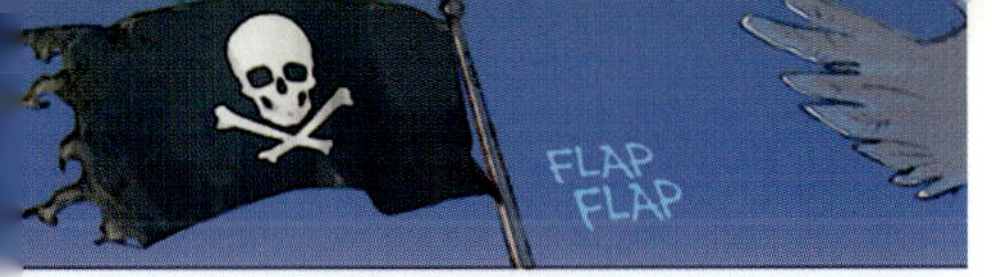

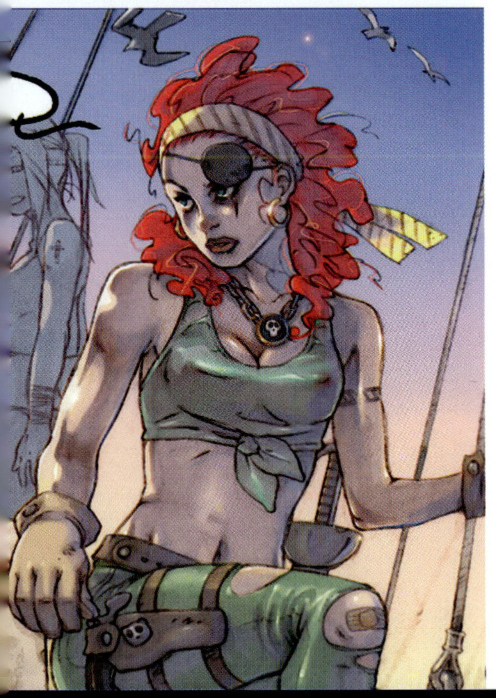

ON THE HIGH SEAS

Female characters do not always have to be good girls. A ship full of swash-buckling female pirates combines strength and femininity to great effect.

FEMININITY

What sets women apart from men is that almost indefinable quality known as femininity—just as everyone has a different interpretation of what beauty is, so do they with regard to what femininity is. Forbearance, generosity, gentleness, nurturing, and gravity are aspects of the feminine nature that may be considered weaknesses by today's standards, but they are the qualities that can overpower most men without the need to resort to muscle power.

Don't make your female characters look and behave like men, with breasts. Focus on their inner strengths to make them brave, and teach them martial arts, or find unique idiosyncrasies to make them dangerous.

Make your women heroic. Make them strong, sexy, and beautiful. Make them shy or wacky or intelligent. Make them any shape you like, but make them feminine, and your stories will take on new dimensions and really show what "girl power" is.

WARRIOR

Historically, there are few female warriors whose heroism is remembered today, but those who are (Joan of Arc, Boudicca) are legendary—and, of course, there is Xena.

FUTURISTIC

It would be impossible to predict the future role of women. They could be political leaders, like Amidala, or creatures of pleasure, like Barbarella, or simply cyborg breeding machines.

SORCERESS

The innate intuition of women and their ability to attune their bodies with the cycles of the cosmos make them ideal for magical roles, even if they go bad— like Willow in the Buffy series.

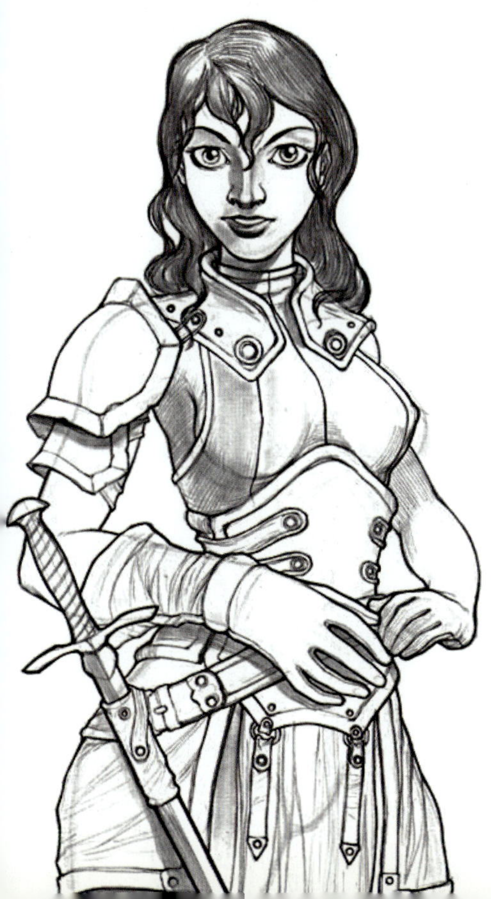

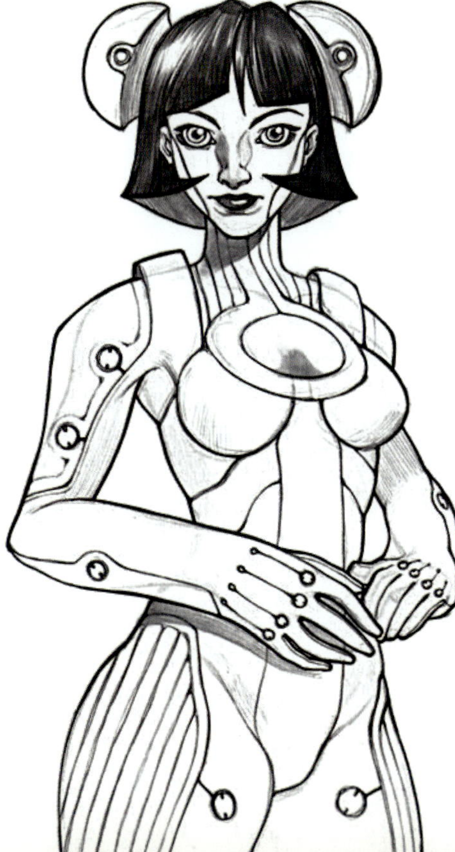

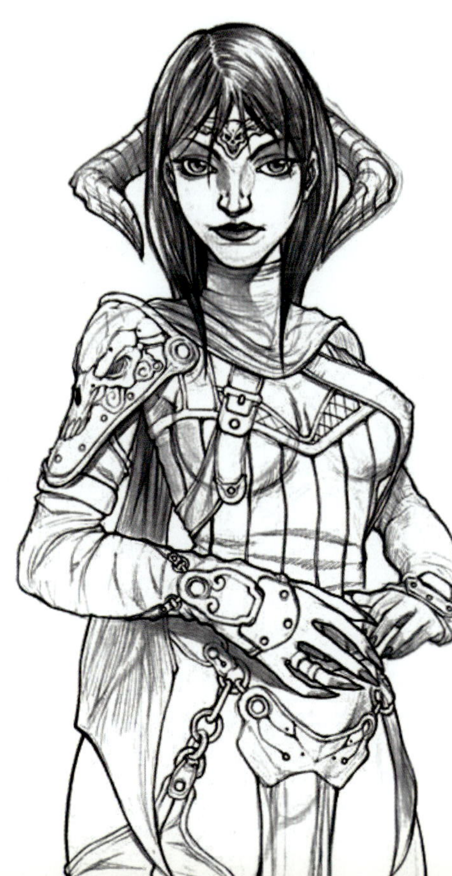

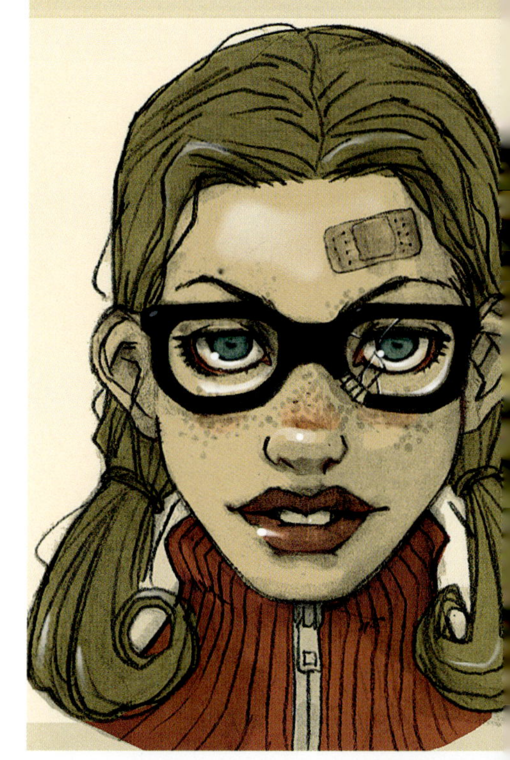

GEEK OR GODDESS?
Every picture tells a story. Using the profile sheet opposite, create two different histories for the character in this image— for example, one fantasy and one "real" world.

BACK STORY

In comics and graphic novels, it is not uncommon to establish a character or fantasy world by telling some of the back story, or history, that led to the place where the story begins. To bring your characters and environments to life, you need to invent a life for them. Your stories are taking place at a particular time in a character's life, which unfolds with the telling. There is also a huge back story that has molded them into the personalities they are, and you have to know every detail of that history. When working with superheroes, revealing their history may help in suspending disbelief, but you need to credit your audience with the intelligence to go with your ideas without having to spell them out.

CHARACTERS

One of the simplest ways of developing a back story for a character is by devising a profile sheet. This lists all the personal information about the character, and will help you make him or her believable and avoid continuity errors. It will assist not only with the storyline, but also when it comes to drawing the character.

There are essentially two approaches to creating characters: drawing them first and then adding the personality traits, or vice versa. Both methods work, and the one you choose really depends on your preferences. It is good practice to use both techniques, and devising characters from written concepts is a good discipline, especially if you have a visual bias and want to work with other writers.

All this background information may never actually appear in the story, but considering it will add depth to the characters and possibly help to resolve problems in plot and characterization. There is no better way to undermine your credibility as a storyteller than by introducing a deus ex machina solution. Let your characters be spontaneous, but not irrational.

ENVIRONMENTS

It is not just your characters that need back story, but also the environment in which they live. If you are devising your own world, for sci-fi or fantasy stories, you have to consider everything about it, from its geography, chemistry, physics, and biology to its sociology and culture. You have to question and rationalize every decision you make; if you do not, there will be plenty of geeks out there who will question them. If you create a desert planet, for example, where do the inhabitants get their food and water? Do they need it? If not, why not? How do they survive? Where do they live? Then you have to relate one thing to another. If such and such does this, why does this happen? And so on. You get the idea.

It is not just fantasy worlds that need attention to detail; real worlds need even more. If you are using actual places, they have to be represented as accurately as possible. Hollywood is great at messing up the geography of cities, even if it is only the inhabitants of that city who know. Your story and characters will have more credibility if you show cities as they really are.

▼ JUST HANGING AROUND
It is essential that there is some synchronicity between your characters and their environments, such as using related materials for buildings, costumes, and weapons.

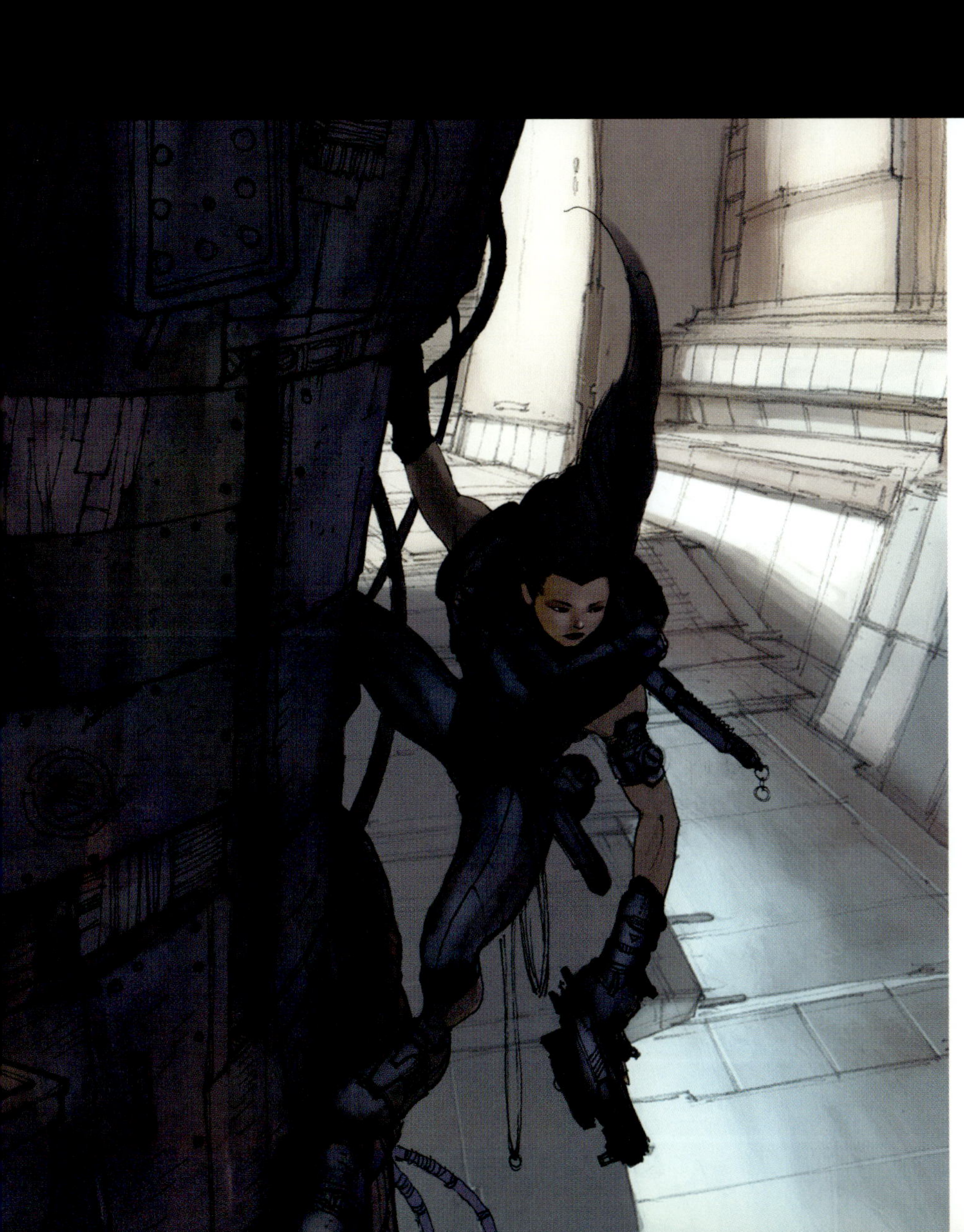

Character profile

This example of a profile sheet is by no means a definitive list. You can adapt it to your story's genre, adding and deleting categories as necessary. The more you can write about the character's history, the better. Try doing it as a role play by interviewing the character.

PERSONAL DETAILS
Archetype / Name / Age / Date of birth / Sex

APPEARANCE
Height / Weight / Physique / Hair color / Skin color / Eye color / Distinguishing marks (natural or inflicted) / How they were acquired

CLOTHING
Style / Material / Accessories (hat, jewelry, etc.) / Weapons and their use

FAMILY
Mother's name / Father's name / Place of birth / Details of birth (events, etc.) / Siblings (names and relationships)

EDUCATION
School (name and type of school, level of schooling) / Special teachers or subjects / Languages / School friends and relationships

OCCUPATION
Type of work / Economic status / Special skills

BELIEFS
Religion or spiritual path / Politics / Ambitions / Other philosophies

PERSONALITY
Motivations (needs/wants) / Weaknesses or flaws / Strengths / What causes fear / What causes anger / What causes happiness / Lessons to be learned

FAVORITES
Color / Food / Drink / Music / Art / Hobby / Sport

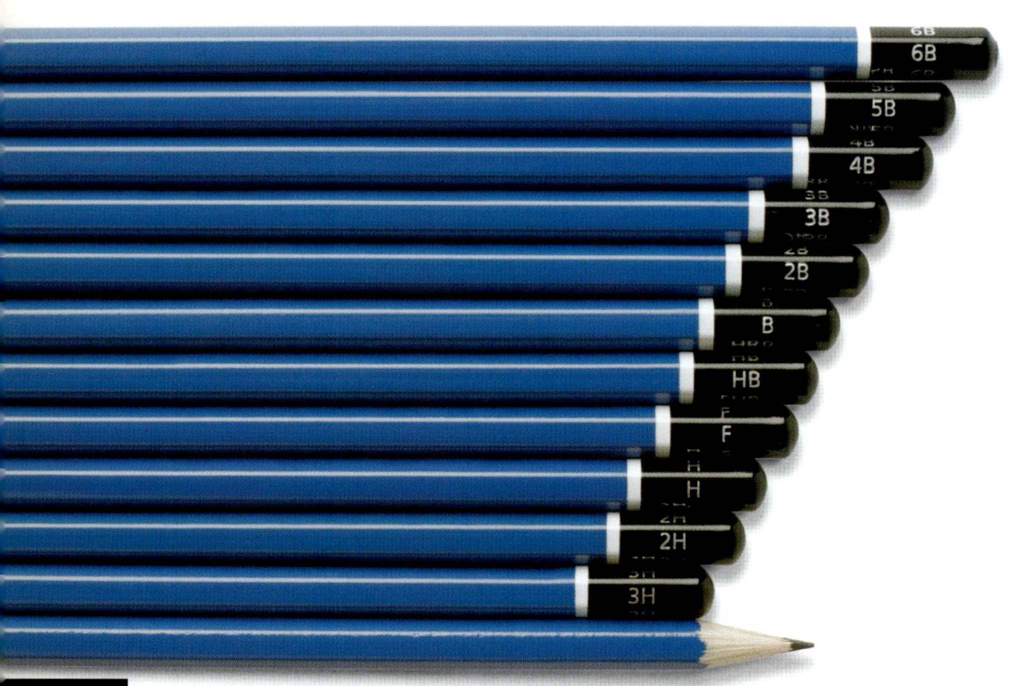

◄ PENCILS

Experimenting with a full set of pencils, from very faint hard (H) pencils to soft black (B) ones, will let you find the grade that suits you best.

▼ PENS

Pens can be roller-point, fine point, chisel tip, or even simple ballpoint. They can have fat, thin, round, square, or even triangular barrels. The important thing is that they are comfortable in your hand and suit your drawing style.

ART MATERIALS

Despite all the advances in digital technology, nearly all illustrators like to start with the artist's fundamental tools of paper and pencil. Even if it is just for jotting down ideas as rough sketches, nothing beats the immediacy and tactile pleasure of graphite on paper.

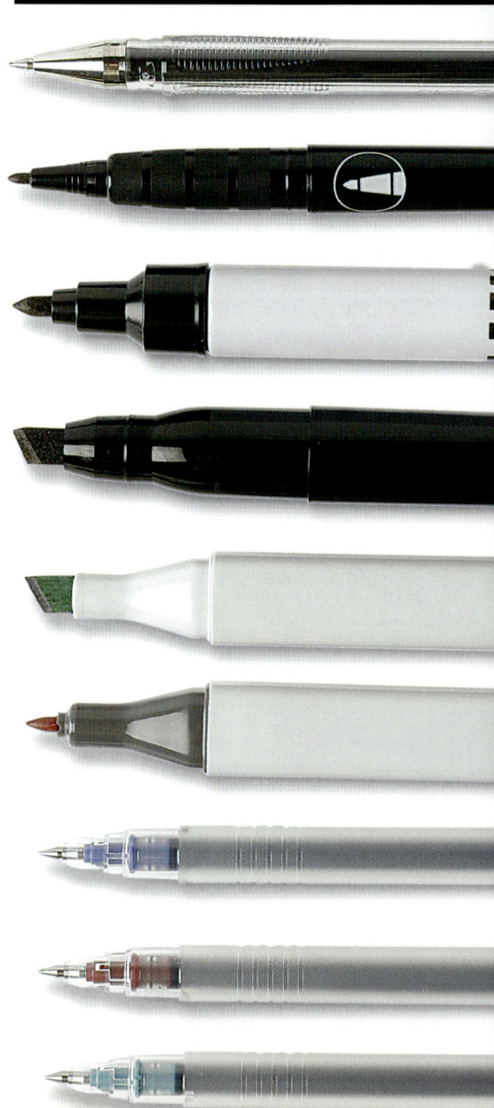

DRAWING

The first thing you need to buy is a good range of pencils and some notebooks and sketchpads of different sizes—spiral-bound ones are good. You can carry them with you in your pocket or bag, to make scribbles whenever inspiration strikes. The sketchpads should be of decent-quality paper, like those you find in art supply stores, whereas notebooks can be cheap, lined reporters' pads, just for writing your ideas and stories in.

For finished drawings, you will need some large sheets of heavy paper or, better still, art board, such as Bristol board or CS10 board. Whenever possible, you should work as large as you can, which will give you the chance to add more detail (if that is your style). It is also easier to hide little anomalies when the work is reduced in size for printing. If you intend to scan your linework at home, you may have to limit yourself to letter (A4) sized paper, because larger format scanners are expensive (see page 23).

A full range of graphite (lead) pencils, from a 5H through HB to 5B, should be in your studio kit, either wooden ones or mechanical (propelling) ones with replaceable leads. A single mechanical pencil is useful when you are on the road, so that you do not need to carry a sharpener or other metal objects that may cause alarm. A non-repro blue pencil is also useful for drawing structural lines as the basis of your final drawings. Erasers are invaluable.

INKING AND COLORING

Comics rely on consistently black lines and fills. For this, you can use anything from a traditional Japanese brush or reed pen to a modern technical pen, such as a Rapidograph. Any of the pens and markers available at your local stationery or art suppliers will give excellent results, although you may have to try several before you find one with which you are comfortable. Brushes and dip pens with india ink are extensively used, but practice on photocopies before attempting to finish an important drawing. Ink and pens do not have the luxury of an undo command that you get with digital tools, and it is better to avoid having to correct with Wite-Out or similar products if possible.

Inks, paints, brushes, and airbrushes are still used for coloring images, although most people work digitally now. Apart from the advantage of easily correcting mistakes, most images end up on a computer before going to print anyway. Working with paints, your choice will be determined by the effect you want to achieve. Water-soluble products, such as poster paint, gouache, watercolor, acrylics, or drawing ink, are preferable to oils, but it always comes down to your preference.

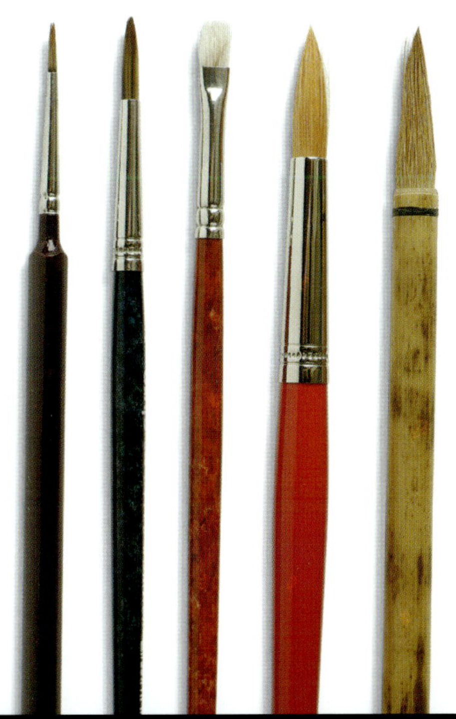

Workspace

Whether working traditionally or digitally, you need to create a proper workspace for yourself. This means a desk with a decent chair, a good light source, both natural and artificial, a drawing board, and storage space. A light box can be useful, too. If you are working with liquids, such as paints and inks, try to keep them separate from your dry goods, such as paper, and even more important, your computer, because liquids and electricity just do not mix.

▲ BRUSHES

Fine sable brushes are useful for inking, and bristle and thicker sable brushes are great for painting. The Japanese brush (far right) requires practice to use effectively, but will give flowing lines.

▼ INKS AND PAINTS

Try to keep your paints water based. Acrylics can be used similarly to oils and come in jars or tubes. Inks come in bottles. Gouache comes in tubes and watercolors in tablet form. Be aware that the color you see on your palette will dry differently when applied to your paper.

▲ PAPER

No matter which paper or board you choose to draw on, if you intend to color it, make sure it will support your chosen coloring media.

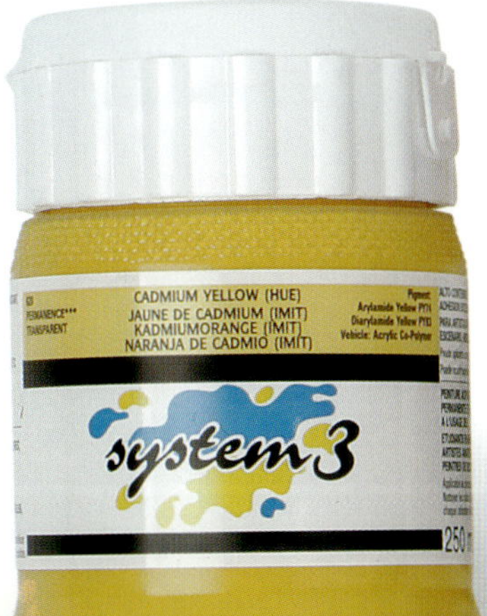
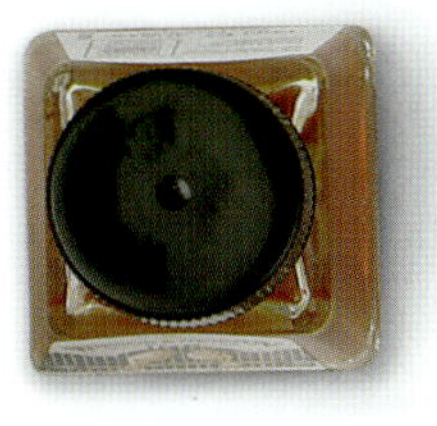
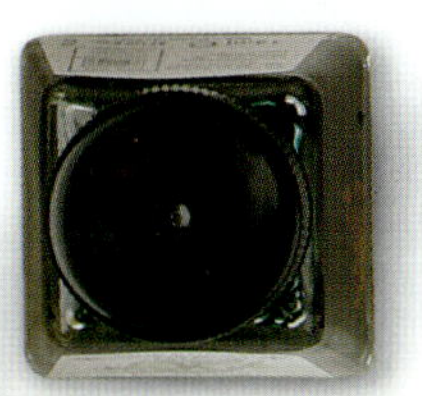
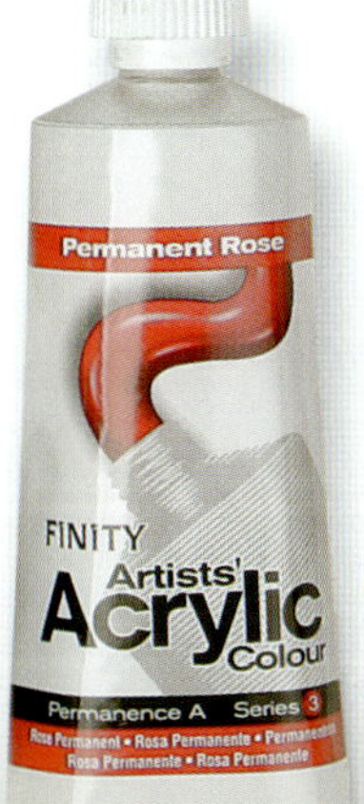
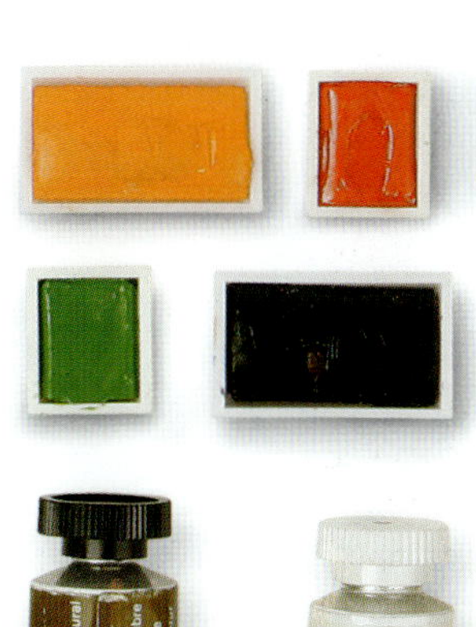
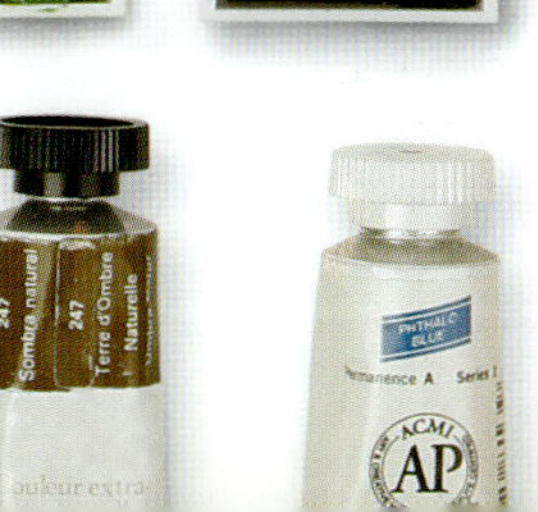
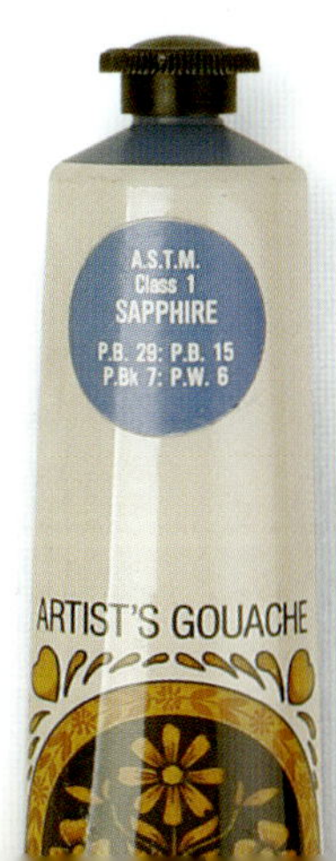

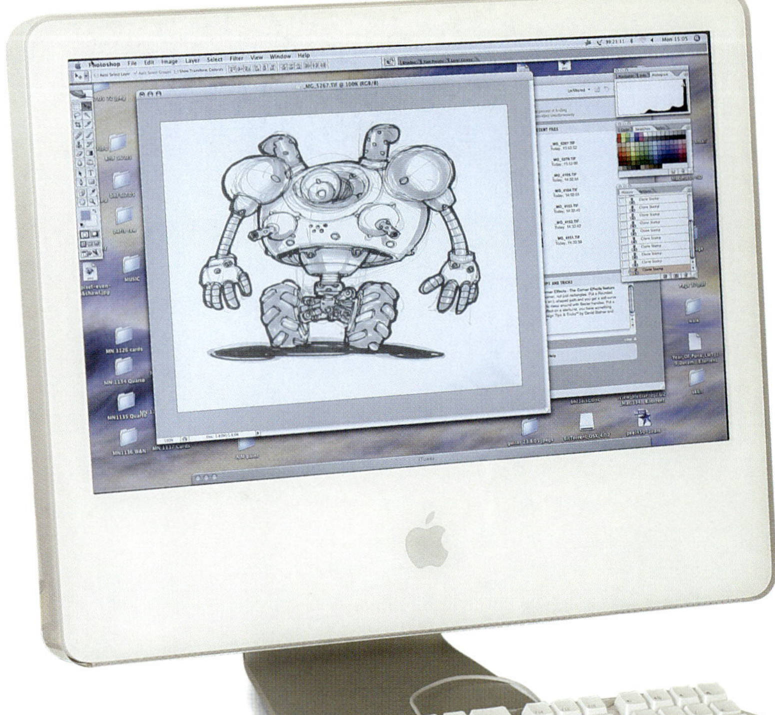

MONITOR

If absolute color accuracy is an issue, get a CRT monitor; if desktop space is your concern, it has to be a flat screen. This technology has improved so much in recent years that the sacrifice of color fidelity is minimal compared with the gains in space.

HARDWARE

There is no escaping the use of computers and other digital devices in the creation of commercial art, which is essentially what we are talking about: art that sells. As with the art materials listed on the previous two pages, to make the most of computers and software, skill and imagination are required. A lot of people fall into the trap of thinking that applying digital filters to a picture makes it art. However, even though digital tools will let you experiment with techniques quickly and safely, they have to be supported by real artistic skills. So what digital tools will you need?

LAPTOP

If you are on the move a lot, buying a laptop makes sense. With larger screens and more powerful processors, today's portables outperform the desktop workstations of not so long ago.

COMPUTER

First, you need a computer. This will either be an Apple Mac (the creative's choice) or a Windows PC. The argument that Macs are too expensive or not powerful compared with Windows is no longer valid, as is the issue of compatibility, because most creative and design software originated on Macs is completely cross-platform. In terms of ease of use, quality, and reliability, Macs are excellent, virtually virus free—and they look great. Ultimately, the choice is yours, because you are the one who has to use it. Whether you decide on a desktop or a laptop will be dictated by your personal working habits. Desktops will always be more powerful and have greater storage capacity than laptops, although that gap narrows with each hardware release.

Always keep in mind, though, that although having all the latest technology is wonderful, you can produce the same work on older, secondhand computers as you can on the latest top-of-the-range power towers. Remember: computers are just tools.

INPUT PERIPHERALS

The first of these is a scanner, to digitize your pencil or inked drawings. These come in two sizes: letter (A4) and A3. Ideally, you should get the larger model, because this will let you scan large drawings in one piece, but they are very expensive, costing more than the computer itself. A letter (A4) model can be purchased very cheaply, especially if it is just for scanning linework.

The other indispensable input tool is a graphics tablet and stylus. The stylus is a penlike pressure-sensitive device, and is a more natural way of drawing and coloring than using a mouse. Tablets also come in a range of sizes and costs.

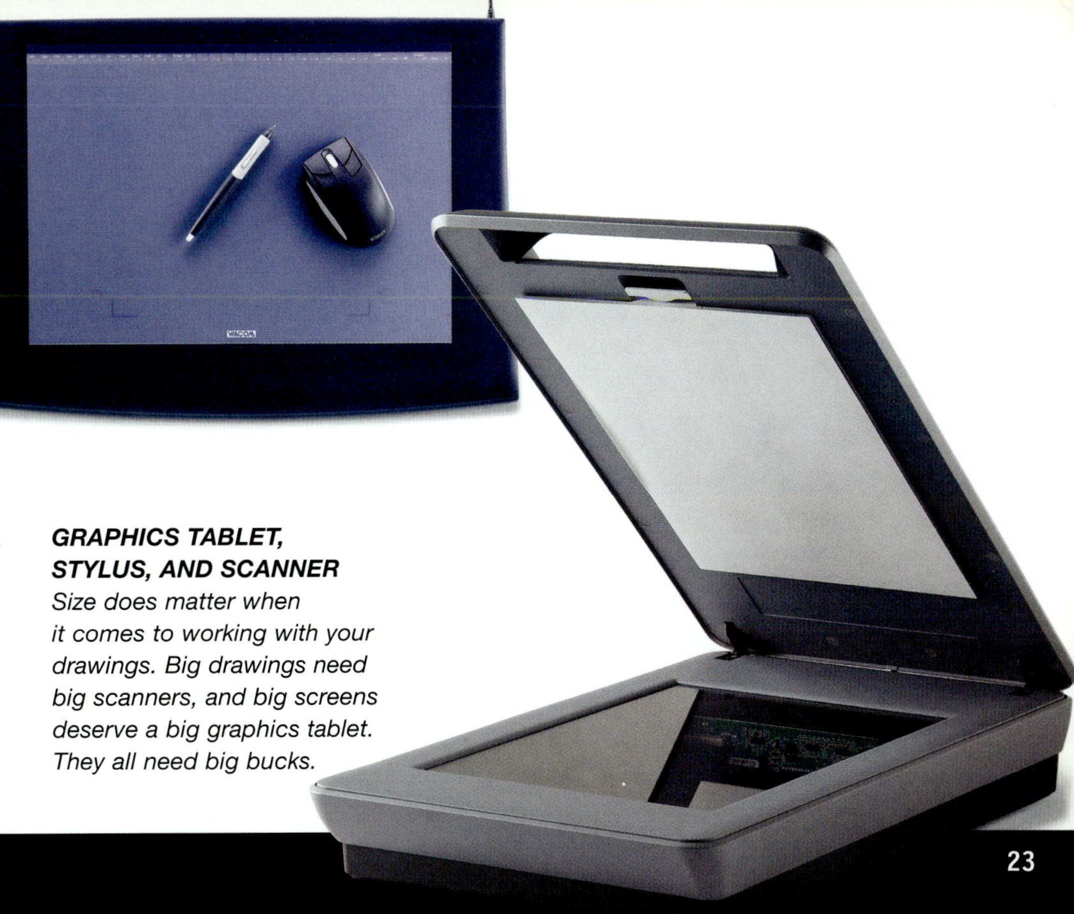

***GRAPHICS TABLET,
STYLUS, AND SCANNER***
Size does matter when it comes to working with your drawings. Big drawings need big scanners, and big screens deserve a big graphics tablet. They all need big bucks.

Mac versus Windows PC

When buying a computer and peripherals, remember that you get what you pay for. That secondhand PC bargain will be no good when the components stop working or extra memory cards have to be added to get the **functions you need for your work. For ease of operation, stability, and build quality, you simply cannot beat a Mac for the price— and remember, they really do look very cool.**

PRINTER
Ink-jet printers can produce amazing high-quality prints, at a price. Used properly, they can be used to proof your digital artwork.

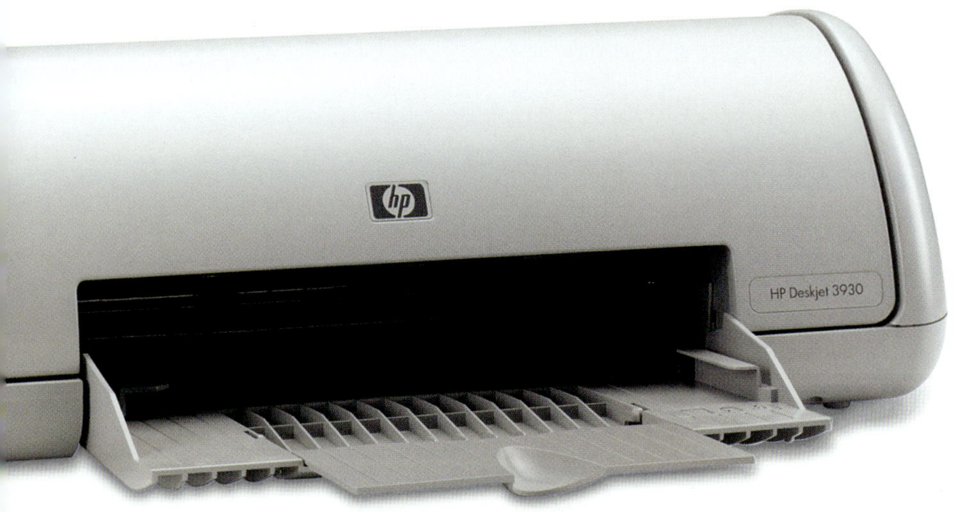

PRINTER

The other piece of hardware you will need is a printer. Although not as important as a scanner or graphics tablet, a printer is the best way to see your finished work, rather than just on screen. You have a choice between laser and ink-jet. When it comes to color, ink-jets are definitely more affordable and the quality is excellent, depending on the type of paper you use. The big trap with ink-jets is the cost of the supplies. Replacement ink and quality paper can cost you almost as much as the original printer price. A printer that has separate cartridges for each color will be more economical, especially if you use a lot of one color. A3 printers will set you back more than a letter (A4) one, but you can always use it for producing limited edition prints to sell.

Laser printers are much faster than ink-jets and the cost of consumables is much lower per print, although the initial outlay is high but constantly dropping. If you intend to self-publish short runs of your comics, a laser printer is definitely the better option. Of course, if you intend to work only in black and white, monochrome lasers are your best choice.

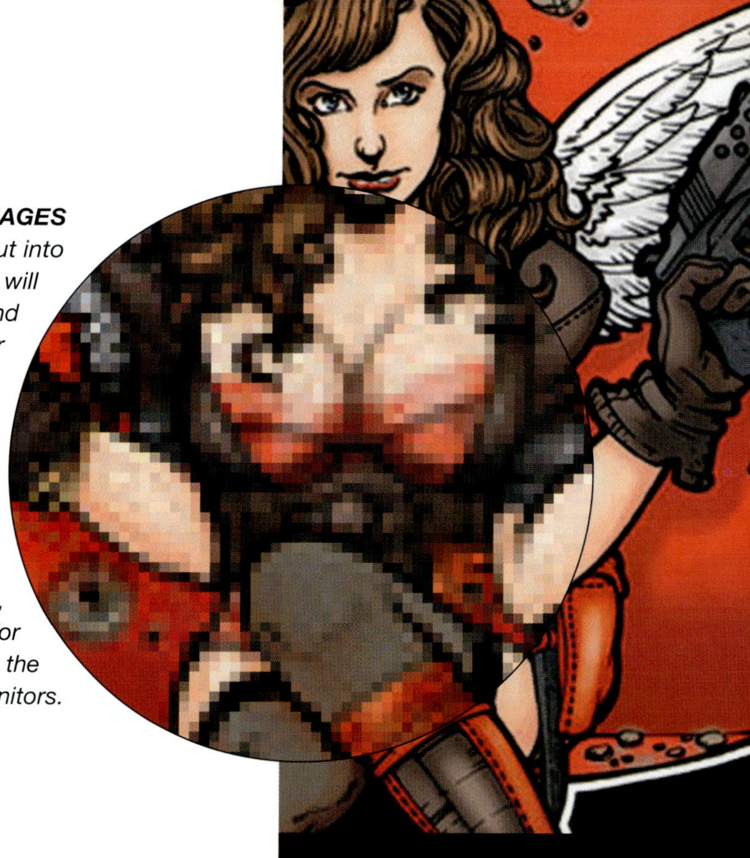

▼▶ PIXEL IMAGES
The more pixels you put into the picture area, the sharper it will be. Something that appears big and sharp on your screen can appear very small on the printed page, or very pixelated if you print it any larger. Examine the deterioration in print quality of the three images below: 300 dpi (1), 150 dpi (2), and 72 dpi (3). The standard resolution for printed artwork is 300 dpi (1), whereas 72 dpi (3) is sufficient for online display because 72 dpi is the standard resolution of monitors.

SOFTWARE

If you are working digitally, you are going to need software for producing your finished images. Computer drawing and painting packages are divided into pixel- and vector-based varieties, and combinations of both. Each program has its merits and drawbacks, and the one you choose will depend on personal preference and the style of art you are producing. If you intend to design your own comic layouts or create 3D characters and animations, you will need additional software. The software outlined here includes the standard programs used by professionals, but there is lots of alternative software, such as Shareware and Open Source, that is cheaper than the major commercial packages and will still do the job.

PIXEL-BASED SOFTWARE

Pixel-based software uses small amounts of data to represent a pixel (picture element) on-screen. The most popular pixel-based image-editing software is Adobe Photoshop. Others, such as Corel Draw and Deneba Canvas, which incorporate vector tools, also have their dedicated adherents. For those preferring a more natural look to their images, Corel Painter is in a league of its own, with its ability to simulate oils, watercolors, and every other traditional media.

Pixel-based programs are entirely resolution dependent. This means that the output quality of your image will depend on the number of pixels per inch you allocate to the original image. A standard printed image (such as those in this book) has 300 dpi (dots per inch), which affects the size of the finished file. A letter (A4) sized full-color TIFF will be about 30MB.

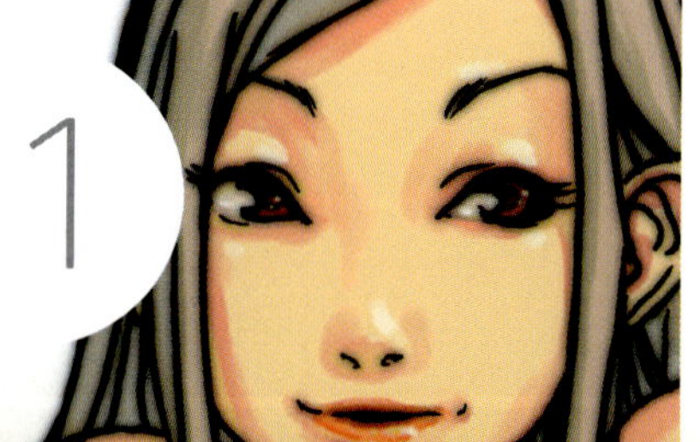

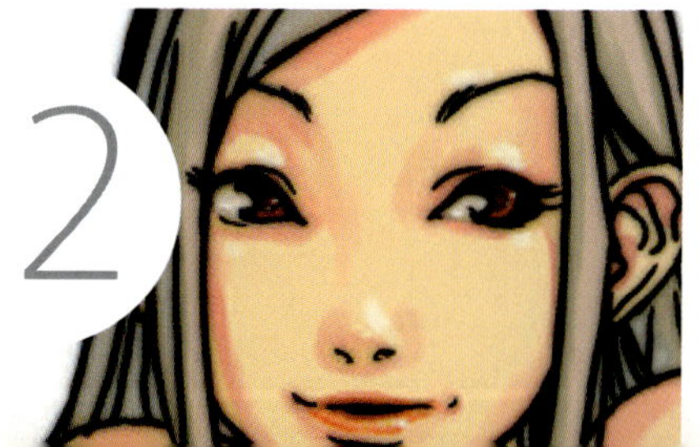

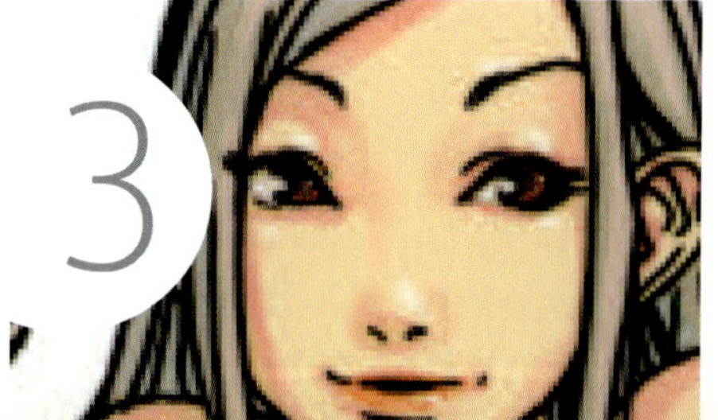

VECTOR-BASED SOFTWARE

Vector illustration software, such as Adobe Illustrator and Macromedia Freehand, use mathematical equations and PostScript language to produce their drawings. As a result, they create very small files whose images can be enlarged to any size without loss of quality. The images produced with these programs are more hard edged than pixel-based ones, making them an excellent choice for comics, especially if you want to use large areas of flat color. These are best output using PostScript-equipped laser printers, although recent software releases do work well with inkjets. Illustrator and Freehand are the two market leaders, but if you want to explore vector-based natural media, have a look at Expression from Microsoft.

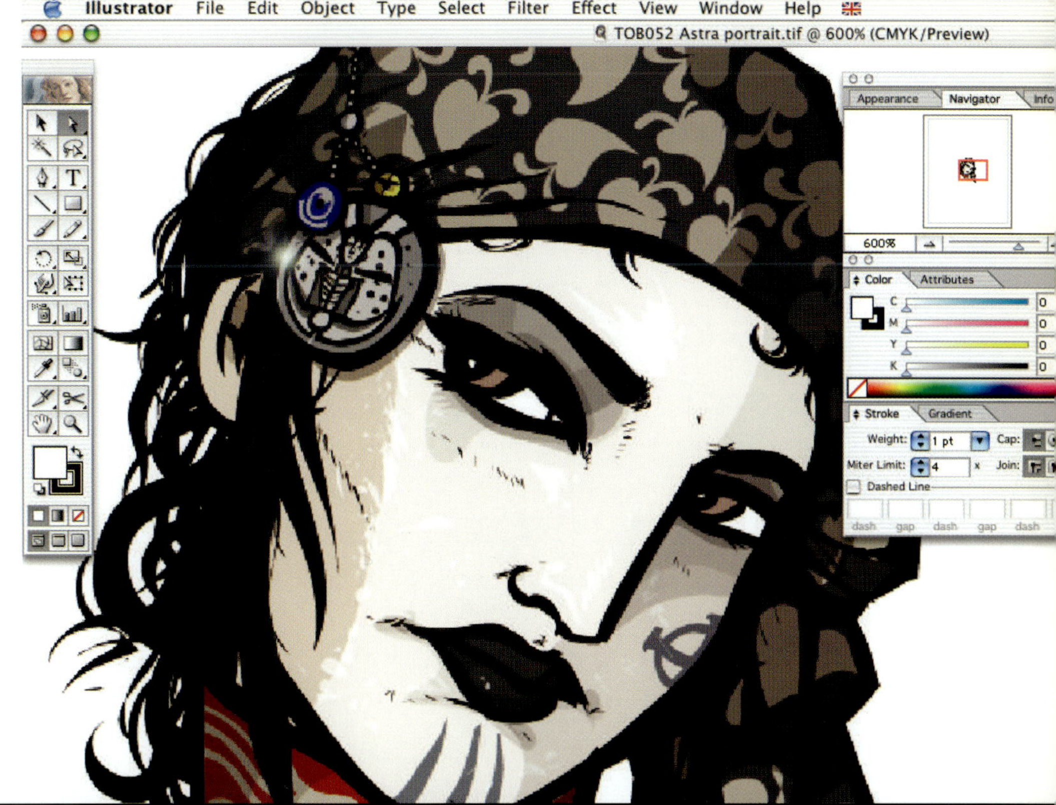

3D CHARACTER SOFTWARE

There is one other piece of software that is indispensable for character artists and that is Curious Labs Poser. Originally designed as a digital version of the artist's wooden mannequin, it has developed into a creative tool in its own right. The advancement in 3D technology and an international network of users and content creators has seen it become one of the major programs for creating fantasy females in 3D. This was taken to new heights with the arrival of DAZ 3D's Victoria character. DAZ now produces a huge collection of female, male, and animal characters, as well as a range of clothes and props. They also produce their own program to rival Poser, DAZ Studio, along with 3D landscape generator Bryce.

All the 3D females in this book were created with Poser, DAZ Studio, and readily available characters. Both these programs are also capable of producing 3D animations. Even if you are not interested in 3D, Poser is still an excellent reference resource for characters, poses, and camera angles when producing drawings, because they hold their poses for as long as you need.

LAYOUT PROGRAMS

If you want to produce your own comics, you may also need a page layout program, such as QuarkXPress or Adobe InDesign. These are certainly not essential programs to have, but they will make your work easier. Adobe has an excellent bundle that includes Photoshop, Illustrator, and InDesign, which will give you everything you need at a competitive price.

▲ VECTOR IMAGES
Adobe Illustrator produces images with very precise lines and flat colors that can be easily edited.

▼ 3D IMAGES
Poser is the easiest way to get started in 3D, especially if you want to specialize in character and figurative illustrations, without having to know a lot about 3D modeling.

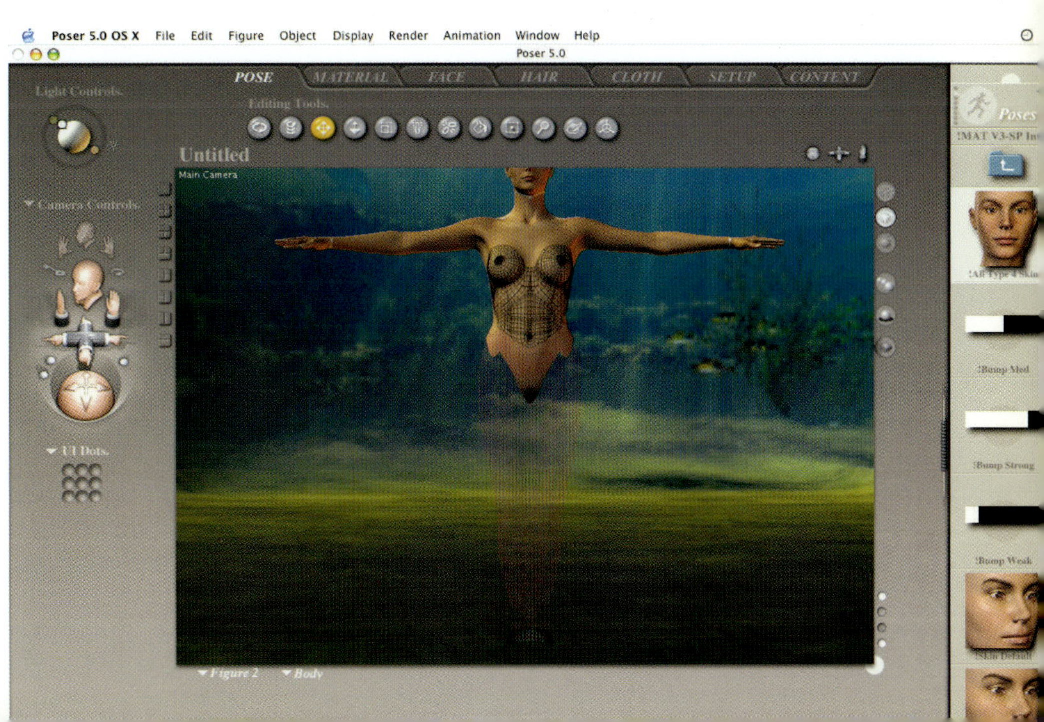

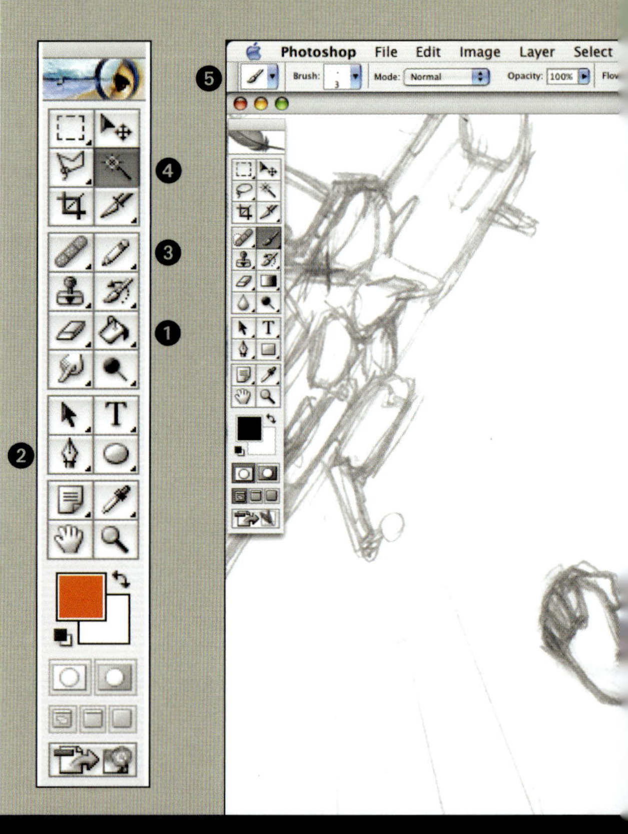

PHOTOSHOP

Adobe Photoshop is such a ubiquitous part of the digital toolkit of artists that it has become a verb. Images are no longer retouched but "Photoshopped." Although it was originally designed for the Mac as a digital darkroom for scanned images, it was quickly adapted as a standalone painting program and promoted into the dominating position it still holds today. Chances are you are already familiar with its functions, but you may still find some useful tips here. There is room to provide only a brief overview of some of Photoshop's basics in this book; refer to a manual or online help for more information.

CAPTURE

Assuming that you are originating on paper or board, you will need to scan your linework to get it into a format you can use in Photoshop. Most scanners supply a plug-in that will let you capture or import scans directly into Photoshop, although some come with standalone applications. There are lots of different approaches to scanning that serve their advocates' purposes, but the important thing to start with is scanning at the highest optical resolution your scanner permits, and never below 300 dpi.

When it comes to scanning, you have a choice of three modes: line (bitmap), grayscale, or color. Line is best used for black-and-white images that have already been inked, and you definitely need to use a resolution of not less than 600 dpi. Bitmap will generally ignore any lines that are less than 50 percent black, so any light pencil, or non-repro blue, construction lines will disappear. If you are going to color the image, you can change it to the color mode later.

Grayscale is best for pencil drawings that you are going to ink digitally. This will capture the full tonal range of your pencils, and because it is serving only as a template, it can be discarded afterward. Using grayscale to scan inked artwork that is to be colored can leave white artifacts on the edges where they overlap the color (anti-alias).

Most scanners capture color in the RGB (red, green, blue) color space, although professional reprographic scanners can capture CMYK (cyan, magenta, yellow, black). If you are capturing ink or pencil images, it is best to avoid using color mode to scan them because it captures more data than you need and can complicate matters later. If you want to scan hand-colored images at home … don't, at least not if you intend to use them for print. Unless you have a properly calibrated, color-matched system, you will find that what you see printed does not look like what you spent so long creating.

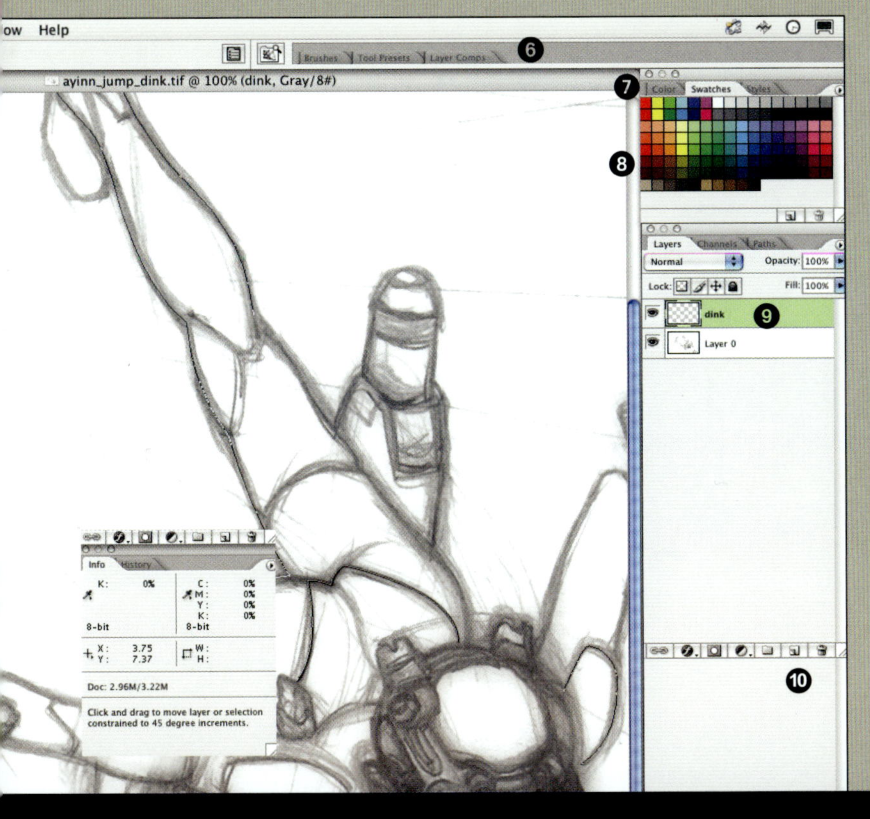

Photoshop interface

The layout of Photoshop and the principal tools you will need to ink and color drawings digitally.

1 **Paint Bucket and Blend**
2 **Pen**
3 **Brush and Pencil**
4 **Magic Wand**
5 **Tools options**
6 **Drop-down palettes for brushes and other tools**
7 **Palette menu button**
8 **Color Swatches palette**
9 **Layer and Paths palette; green shows active layer**
10 **New Layer button**

TOOLS

For digital inking, you can use the Brush or Pen tools—your choice will be partly dictated by your hardware, but also by your hand. If you have a graphics tablet, the Brush tool is the better choice. Once you are used to drawing with a stylus, it will create clean, natural-looking lines like a real ink pen or brush. However, if you only have a mouse, the Pen tool is your best option. One advantage of the Pen tool is that it uses vectors to create the lines, producing smooth curves that remain editable, and that can have fixed-width strokes applied to them. However, if you want to work with vector lines, Adobe Illustrator or Macromedia Freehand are better options.

When working in Photoshop, take advantage of the Layers option because this will make editing easier. Create a new layer over the top of the scanned pencil drawing, ensuring it is set to Transparent, give it a logical name, such as "ink," and work on this layer. Your pen lines will be found in the Paths palette. You will need to save them, rather than leaving them as "work path." You can also save separate paths for each object. Establishing good working practices like this will make your job much easier.

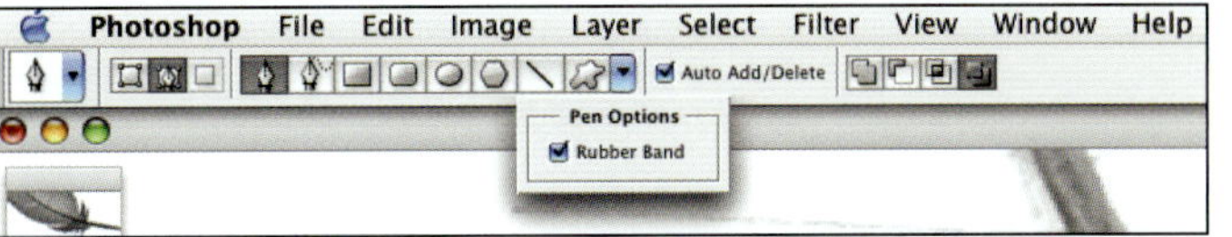

▲ PEN OPTIONS

Setting the Pen options to use Rubber Band lets you see exactly where a path is being created as you do it. You will also need to select the other options shaded here, especially when working with a mouse.

▲ MAKING PATHS

To create a path with your mouse, click at a suitable point (such as a corner), then at another point (as shown), holding down the mouse button and dragging to create a curve. Repeat until you return to your starting point or reach the end of the line. The lines can be fine-tuned by adjusting the "handles" at the click points.

▲ NAMING PATHS

Once the path has been completed, go to the Path palette, double-click on "working path," and give it a relevant name. If you want to keep various objects separate, you will need to create a new path from the palette's menu.

MASKS

Masks are a very useful feature with which you should familiarize yourself. These work like digital Frisket, a film used by airbrush artists to block areas that are not to be colored. Photoshop masks work in the same way and can be applied to individual layers.

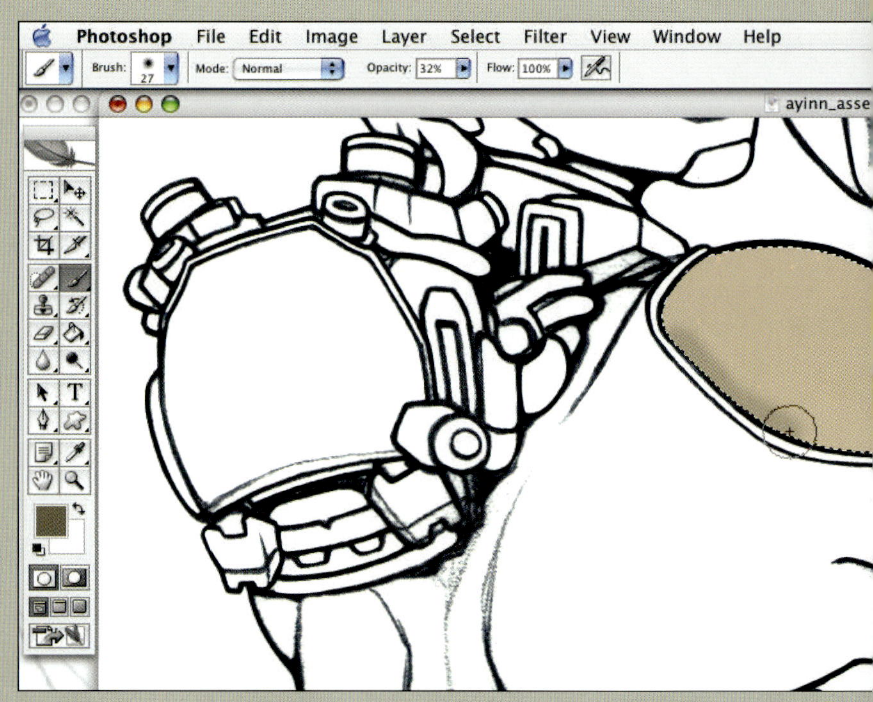

▶ QUICK MASK

A quick way to mask an area is to use the Magic Wand tool. Simply click in the relevant area, as with the Paint Bucket, applying the same tolerance rules (see opposite). This will create a selection that will be the only active area on the layer, so you can use a large Airbrush along an edge and keep it contained to where you want it.

CHANGING PATHS TO LINES

Once you have drawn paths over your pencil drawing, you need to add black lines to the drawing. Start by making a new layer in the Layers palette, so as not to make the lines part of the original drawing. Make sure the foreground color is set to 100 percent black.

② ▼ *From the Brushes menu, select an appropriate brush size for the line.*

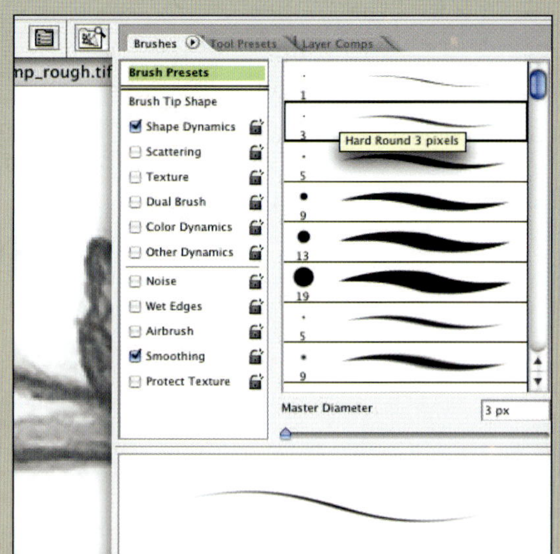

① ◀ *From the ensuing menu, select "Brush."*

③ ▶ *Select a path, then "Stroke Path" or "Subpath" from the Path palette's menu.*

④ ▶ *This will apply a three-pixel line along the selected path. To add a thicker line, change the brush size and repeat the procedure.*

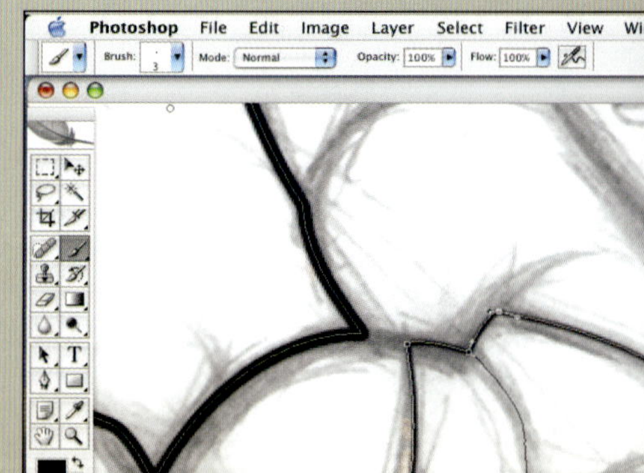

COLOR

Once you have "inked" your drawing, you will want to start coloring it. If you have been working in grayscale, you will have to convert to a color mode. For printing, you will need to work in CMYK; work in RGB if it is for screen only. The main disadvantage with CMYK is that a lot of Photoshop filters work only in RGB mode.

Another thing to be aware of are your black lines. If you have inked in grayscale, once you convert to CMYK, it will create a composite black (known as process black or rich black) made up of the four process colors. The advantage of this is that, when the linework is placed over the color, you will not get "show through"—something that happens if you place just 100 percent black over color. This is because the black ink is the last to be printed. If you are placing lettering in your image, use 100 percent black rather than process black because this will make it easier for a printer to produce different language texts.

To color your images, the main basic tools you will need are the Paint Bucket (Fill), Brush, Eraser, and Magic Wand. Whether you use other tools, such as Blur, Smudge, Dodge, Burn, and Sponge, will depend on the effects you want to achieve. Be adventurous, because interesting effects can be discovered through making mistakes. The History palette will help you repeat an effect.

Remember to make use of layers. You can allocate one layer per color, or one layer per object. Assigning a color to its own layer makes it easier to alter that color at a later stage. On the other hand, if you want to add effects to a particular object, assigning it its own layer will help. There are lots of filters and effects in Photoshop to enhance your images, but use them with discretion, rather than just because they are there.

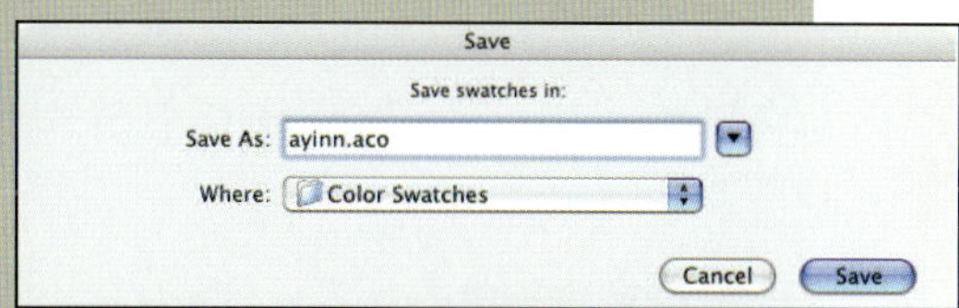

◀ MULTIPLY LAYER
In the Layers palette, set the blending mode to Multiply. This will make the white area act as if it is transparent, while retaining the black lines and any shading. This is mostly for working with scanned ink drawings, because digitally inked images would already be transparent.

▲ COLOR SWATCHES
When working with a character over a series of drawings, it is a good idea to create a palette of colors that can be loaded at any time, to keep your coloring consistent. Choose Save Swatches from the Swatches palette menu and give it a recognizable name. To bring the swatch into a job, simply use Load Swatches from the same menu.

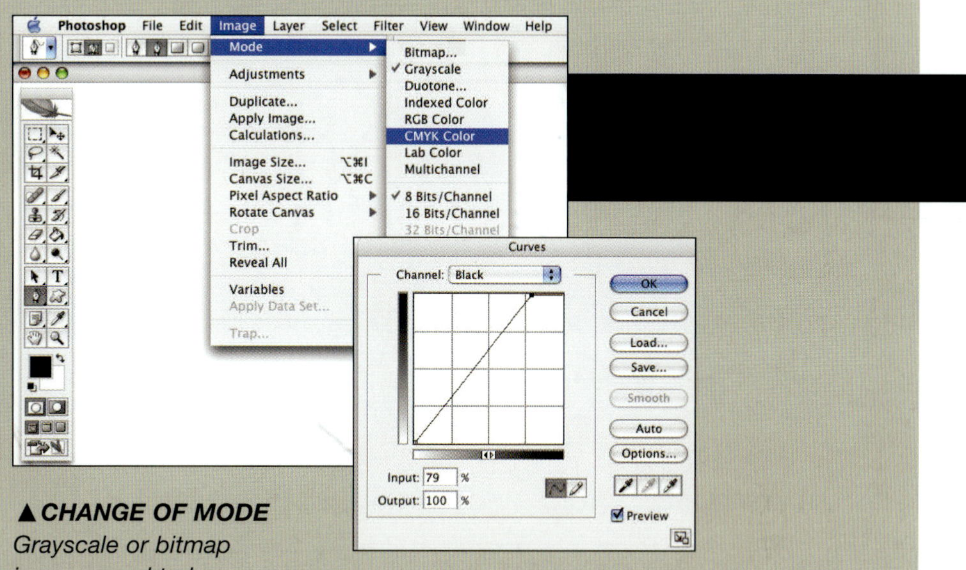

▲ CHANGE OF MODE
Grayscale or bitmap images need to be changed to a color mode: CMYK for print or RGB for screen (or for using particular filters and effects).

▲ CURVES
Blacks are converted to CMYK or RGB equivalents. If you are working with process colors, adjust the curve for the black channel of the linework layer to bring it up to 100 percent, as shown.

▶ PAINT BUCKET FILL
The fastest way to get color into your image is with the Paint Bucket. Create a layer for the color or object and select All Layers in the tool options. The amount of Tolerance you set will depend on your linework. In this example, there are some pale pencil lines left to add tone, so setting the Tolerance high ensures that all the area is filled. Anything missed can easily be touched up with a few "brushstrokes." When using the Paint Bucket, it is important to check that there are no gaps in the lines between areas of two different colors. Otherwise both areas will be flooded with one color.

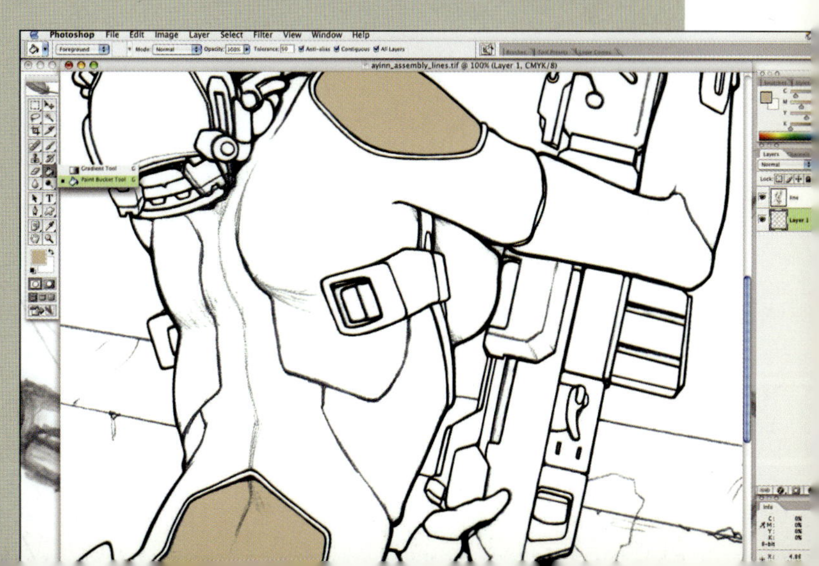

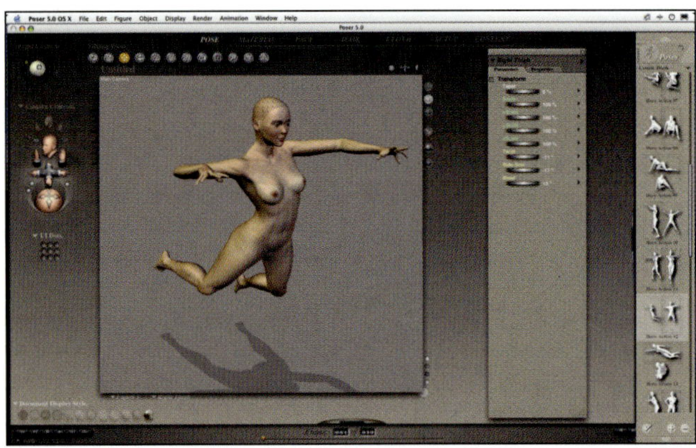

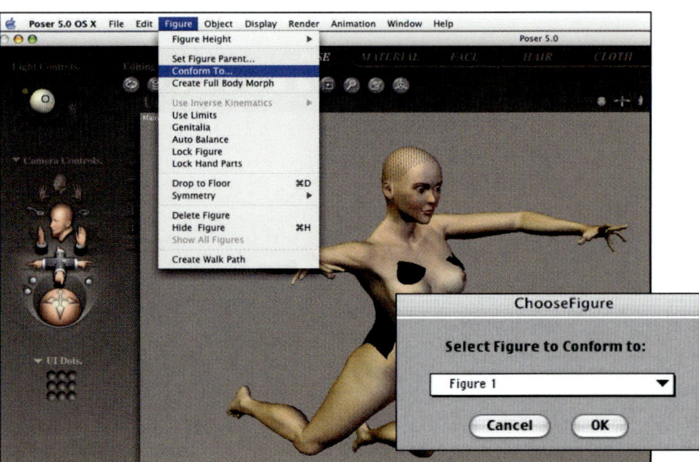

POSER AND STUDIO

If you were allowed only two applications for creating artwork on your computer, one would definitely be Adobe Photoshop and the other should be Curious Labs Poser or rival DAZ Studio. Not only do the latter serve as virtual modeling agencies, but they are also capable of producing stunning stills and impressive 3D animations. Scattered throughout the next section are examples of characters created with both programs, but here is a quick rundown of what each will do.

WHAT THEY DO

Although Poser and Studio are both complex 3D programs, they do not require any knowledge of Boolean operations, NURBS, metaballs, splines, polygon count, or even texture mapping. The software was designed to be used by artists, with Poser originally created as a digital version of the wooden mannequin, a character that is still present in the software. With a huge range of anatomically correct models available, as well as anime, fantasy, and cartoon characters, and a virtual menagerie of animals, you can now build any type of scene and use it as a drawing reference. Poser and Studio both come with figures (also known as content). Poser comes with a bigger selection and a bigger price tag, whereas Studio offers only two of DAZ's most popular characters (Victoria and Michael), but is free.

Poser and Studio both operate in similar ways, in that you take a model and modify it, add clothes, props, and environments, pose the elements, and render the final picture or animation. The main difference, apart from the price, is the interface. Poser's is a legacy of GUI genius Kai Krause, whereas Studio's is more pedestrian and utilitarian.

Both programs have their pros and cons, but if you just want to use one of them as they were originally intended, as a digital mannequin, then Studio's "price," coupled with DAZ's well-established and popular content, would make it the first choice. Studio also offers an ever-growing number of plug-ins to extend the program's basic functions into an even more professional tool. Poser, on the other hand, does have a long development history that gives it the edge in other ways, apart from its well-known reputation, such as its more complex animation-editing functions and the ability to grow and style hair on Poser's own models.

▼ FACE LIFT

Every aspect of Poser's built-in figures' faces can be adjusted in the Face room. You can even add photos of your own face, or of your friends, and map them onto the figures.

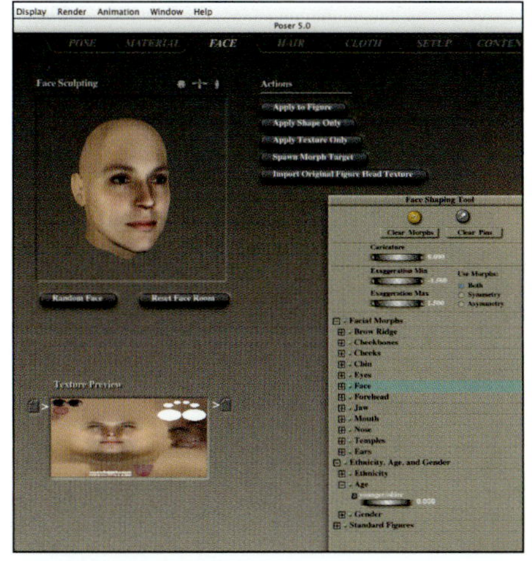

Poser interface

The Poser interface is different from most other graphics software, but is logical and easy to use once you are familiar with its functions.

1 Light controls: For adding and editing lights.

2 Cameras: Select one of the preset cameras or create additional ones for animation.

3 Camera control: The camera's movements (track, dolly, pan, and tilt) are controlled from these icons by clicking and dragging the mouse.

4 Animation timeline: Scenes can be animated using keyframes on the timeline (see page 49).

5 Parameter controls: All the elements that make up the picture can be controlled from this palette by dragging the scroll wheels or typing in appropriate numbers.

6 Adds a single figure to the scene.

7 Adds additional selected figures to a scene, including clothing and props.

8 The main picture window or camera view used for the image. It can be altered to any proportion. The finished size can be adjusted at the render stage.

9 A variety of display modes that affect how quickly the image redraws on screen.

10 Palette containing all the preset figures, poses, lights, and so on. Trivia: Poser 5's figures are named after the Robinson family in *Lost in Space*.

11 Editing tools: For moving and modifying body parts and props.

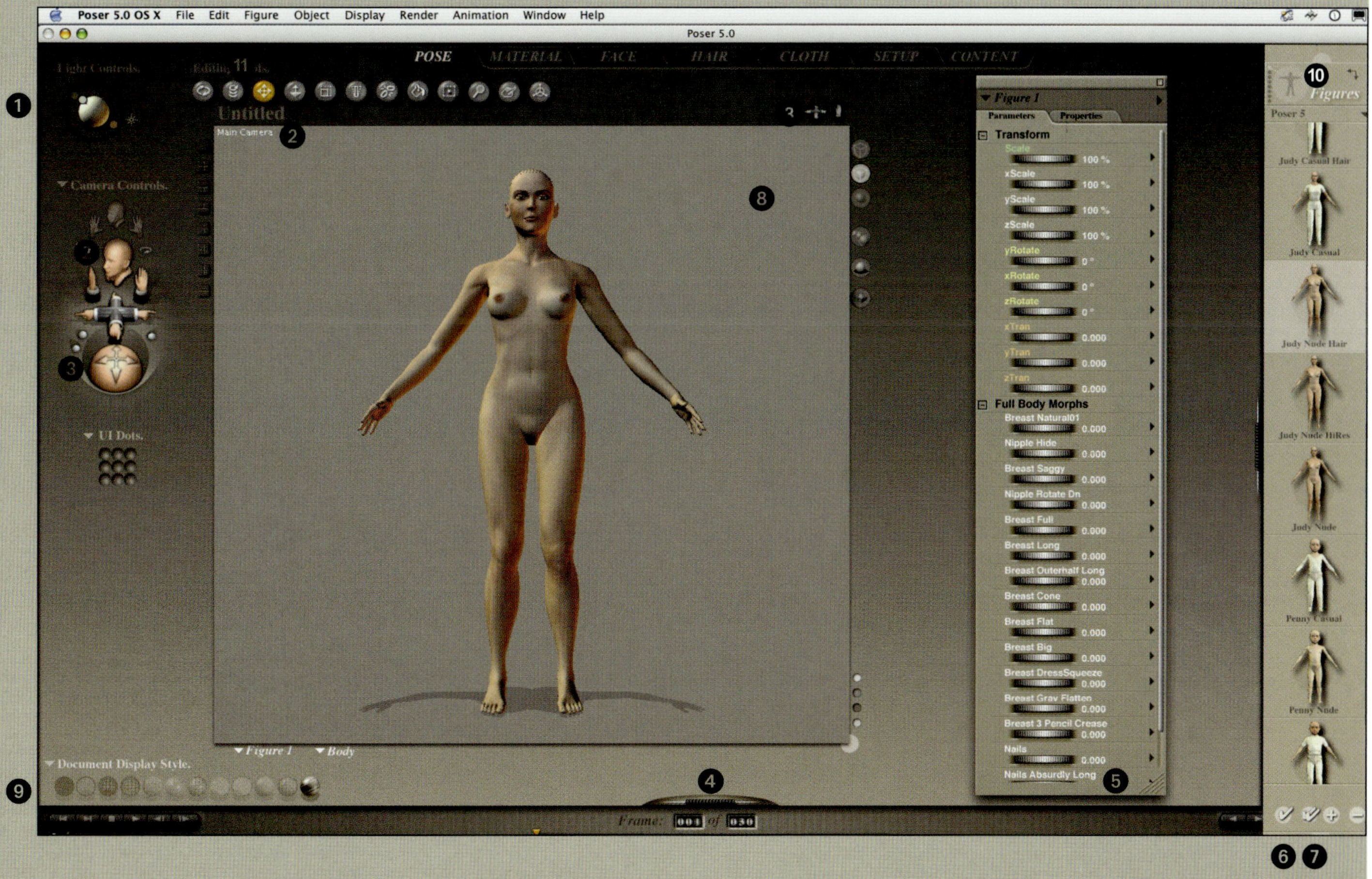

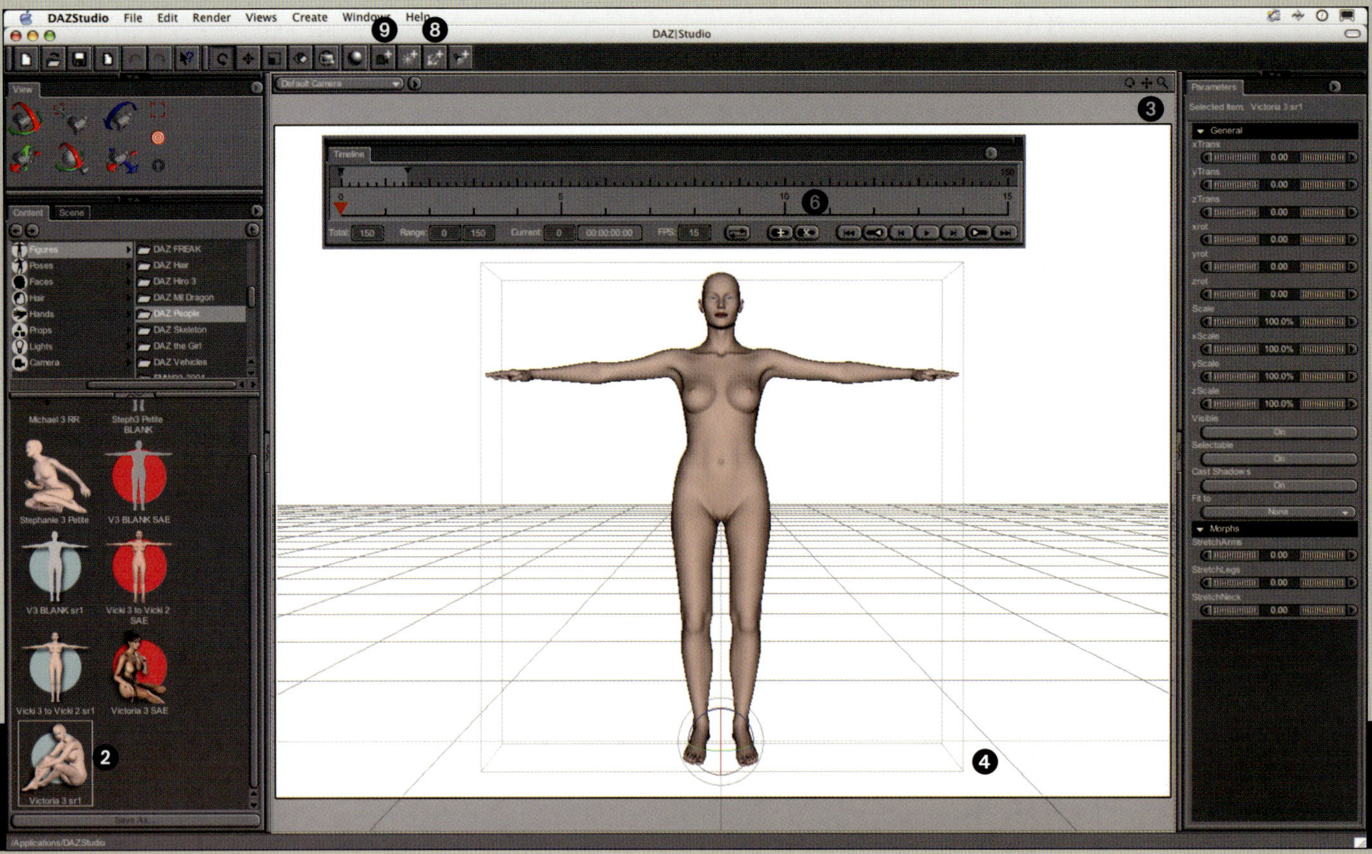

Studio interface

In comparison to Poser, Studio's interface is stark, but it is uncomplicated and it works.

❶ Content: Hierarchical menus make finding figures and props easy. If you are running Poser as well, it will share the resources so everything is not duplicated.

❷ Previews of the selected figures, props, pose, and so on.

❸ Camera movements: The icons clearly show what each one does.

❹ The viewing window's size can be adjusted in the preferences and works on common screen ratios such as 4:3 and 16:9.

❺ Parameter controls: Adjust the figures by dragging the sliders or typing in numbers.

❻ The timeline palette for animation uses keyframes. The palette can be hidden away when not in use and activated from the Windows menu.

❼ For adding new lights.

❽ The main picture window or camera view used for the image. It can be altered to any proportion. The finished size can be adjusted at the render stage.

❾ For adding new cameras.

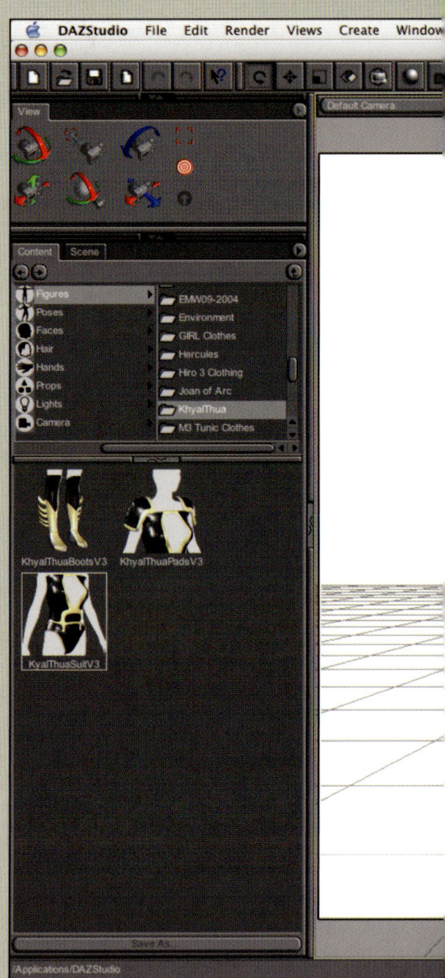

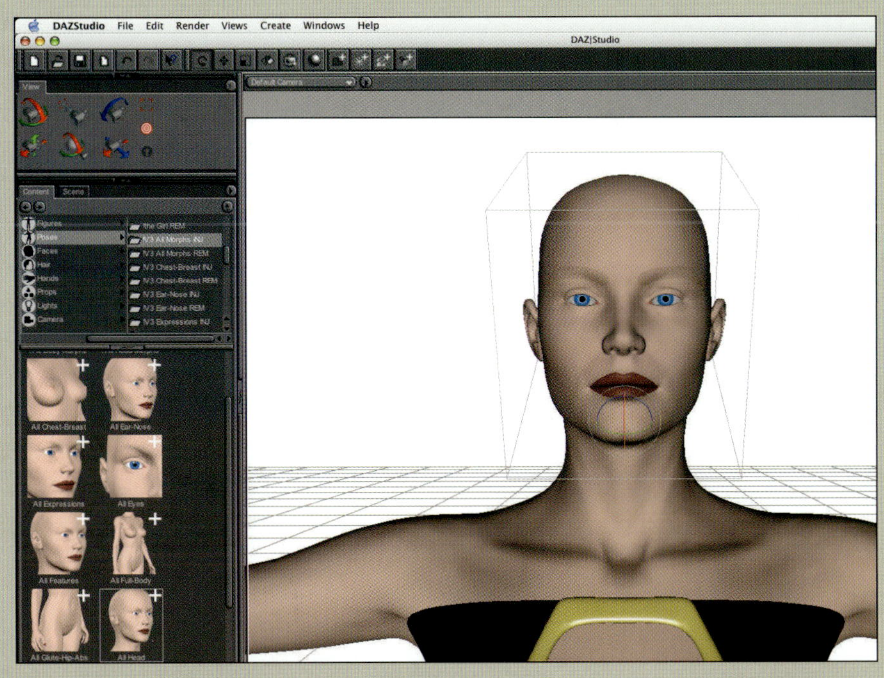

◄**FACE FACTS**

The basic Victoria model that comes with Studio will serve you well for most tasks, but if you want to start creating highly individualized characters, you will have to buy some additional morph packs (shown here) to alter the look of the original, and texture maps to get different skin tones. Victoria is the most popular female character available, and as such there is a massive library of clothes and props available for her on the Internet. If you intend to use Poser or Studio to create your fantasy females, you should join DAZ's Platinum Club to get at least 30 percent discount off their products.

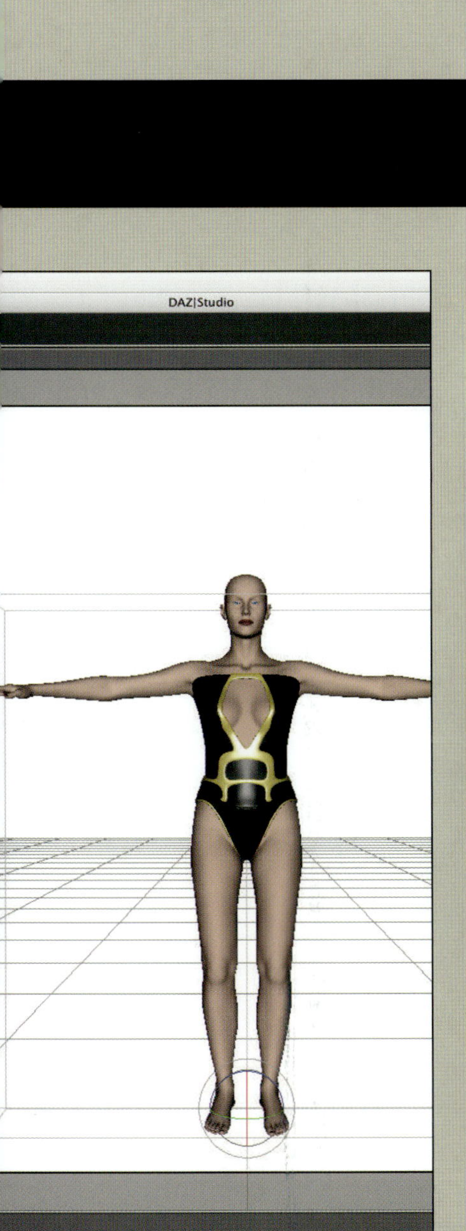

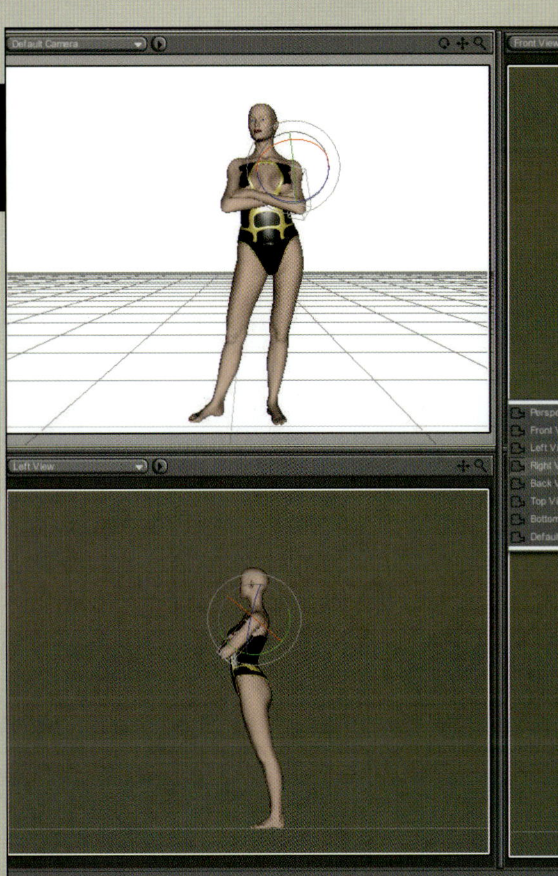

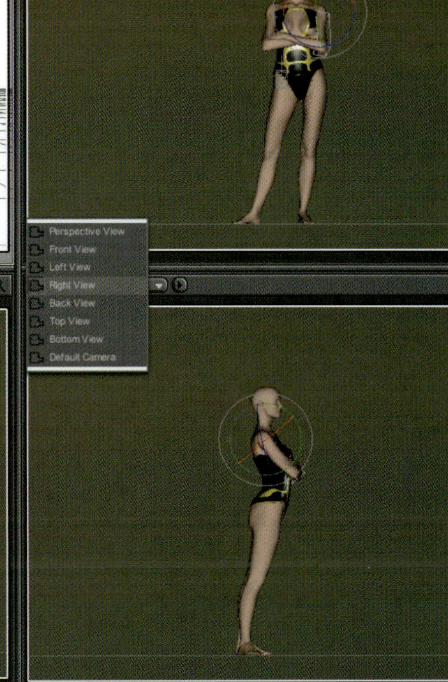

◄**FIT**

The important function of attaching clothes to figures (called "Conform" in Poser) is called "Fit to" in Studio. As long as you have the clothing item selected in the scene, you can select the character you want to attach it to from the menu in the Parameter controls.

▲ **DIFFERENT VIEWS**

When posing characters, it is a good idea to take advantage of the split screens, so that you can see from all angles exactly how the pose is developing without having to move the main camera. Using the sliders is much better than direct manipulation as long as you can remember which are your x, y, and z axes.

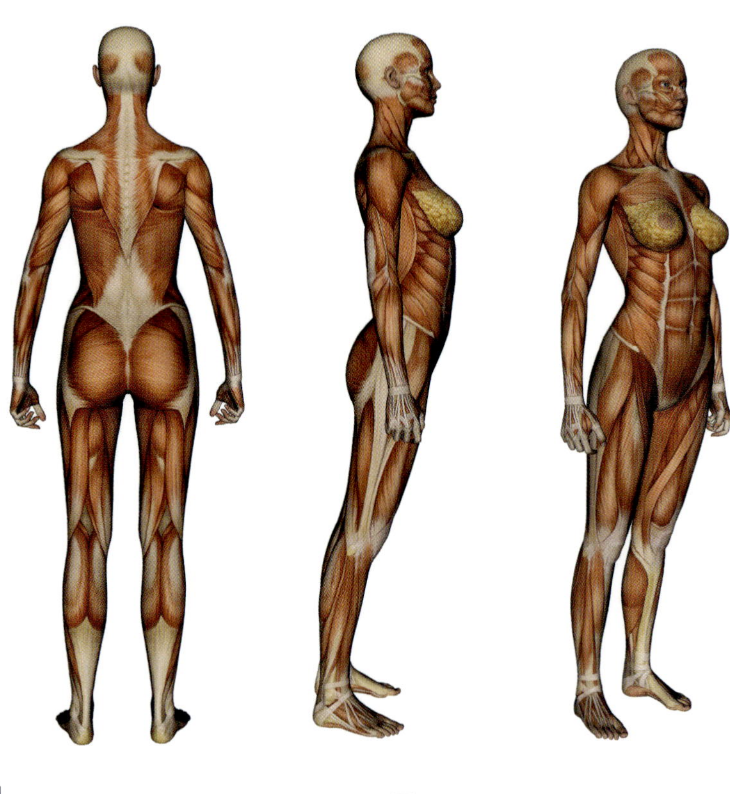

ANATOMY

Apart from the obvious differences between male and female bodies, there are other anatomical variations that you need to be aware of. Most of this information is generalized and based on ideals, but as you are dealing with fiction, all the characters can be perfectly proportioned and free from defects—unless you decide to incorporate them. Excluding the primary sex characteristics, secondary ones, such as women having less body hair, are not that important to artists. More important are the structure of the skeleton and the musculature, because women are constructed differently—and no amount of exercising can alter this fact.

FLESH AND BONES

Although it is not necessary to know the names of all the bones in the human skeleton, you should make yourself familiar with its construction. Knowing how joints work, where the bones are placed, and how they support the muscles will give your drawings a foundation to build on. The principal difference between the female and male skeleton is the size and shape of the pelvis (hips), which in women is designed for the very important job of carrying children (before, during, and after birth). The muscles of the thighs and buttocks are also larger for the same reason. The

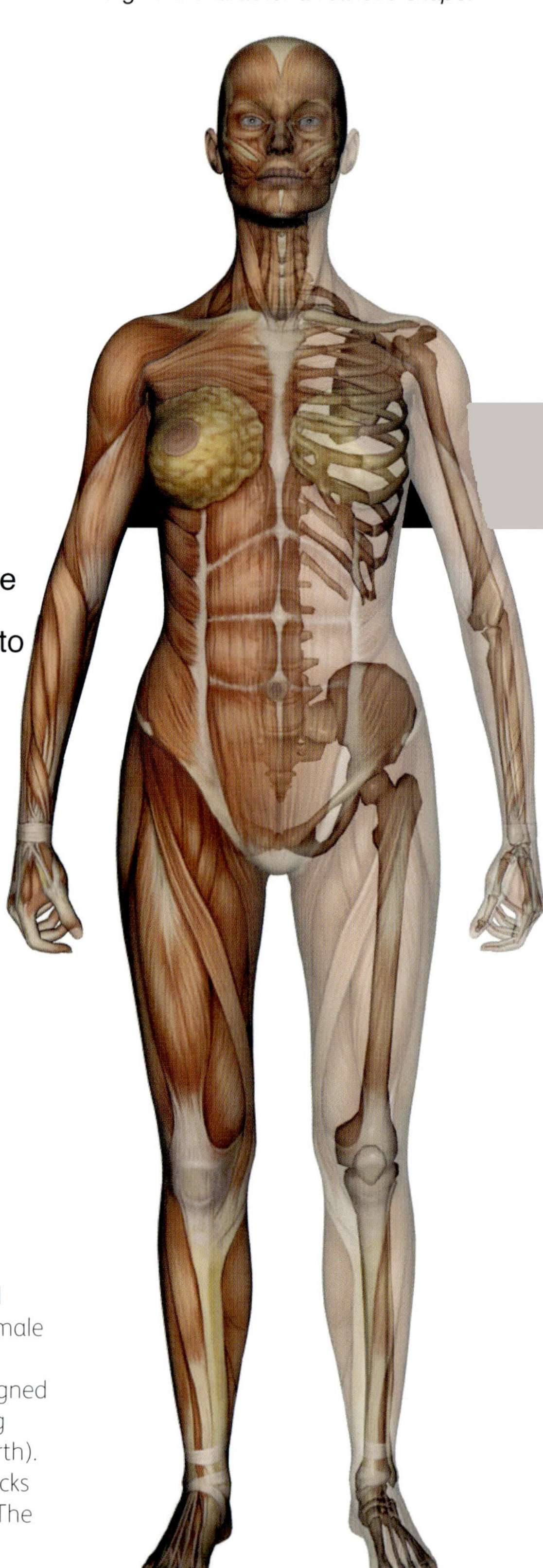

◄▼ MUSCLE TONE

Seeing how the muscles are joined to the skeleton and give the body form will help you construct your characters. You do not need to remember the names of all the muscles and bones, just where they are and what they do. Some idea of how far the muscles can be pumped up or reduced will also help to give a character a realistic shape.

shoulders and rib cage are smaller on women, as are the bones in general.

Although many supermodels like to show off their bones, fantasy women do look better with some flesh on them. They are also more interesting to draw. That does not mean they have to have superhero muscular bodies, but they need to have some shape. Women's muscles are naturally smaller and more straplike than the male equivalents (apart from the thighs/buttocks already mentioned). Again, speaking generally, the female form is more delicate. The jaw is less pronounced and the neck more slender, the waist is higher, and the navel is situated lower. Wrists, hands, ankles, and feet are all comparatively smaller. Hands, in particular, are deceptively hard to draw convincingly, with each hand containing 27 bones.

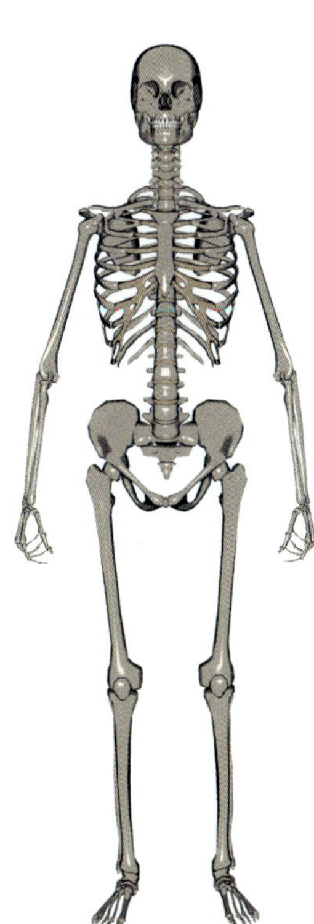

◄ SKELETON
The important part of understanding the structure of the skeleton is knowing where the joints are, how they work, and how much movement they will allow.

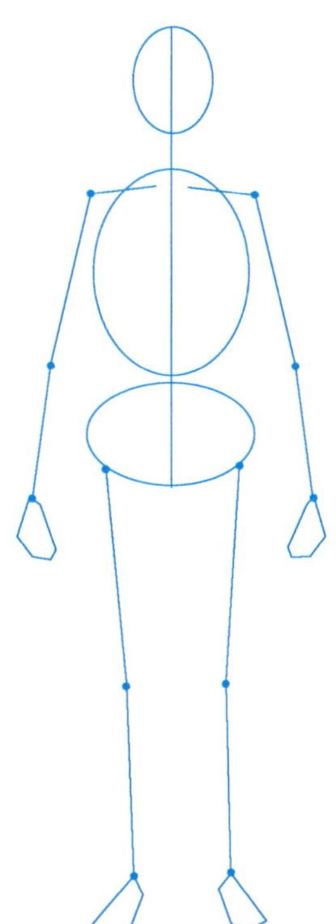

► STICK FIGURE
Making a simple stick figure, properly proportioned, of course, is a good place to start constructing your character, especially when drawing from your imagination. Use a non-repro pencil to hide it in the final drawing.

PRACTICE

Humans come in all shapes and sizes. If you are serious about working in figurative art, you need to make yourself familiar with this diversity, and the best place to do this is at a life-drawing class. There is no substitute for working with real models and getting feedback on your work. Failing that, you can always try asking friends and family to pose for you. It does not mean you have to get them to undress, because it is just as important, if not more so, to learn how clothes fit and fabrics fall.

Alternatively, you can use Poser or DAZ Studio. The anatomical illustrations, including the skeleton, on these pages were created using these programs. Although the models in these programs are no substitute for the real thing, they can hold a pose for considerably longer, especially jumping in the air, and will assume any position without complaint.

Another option is to buy one, or more, of the large number of books on anatomy for artists. Some break down every component of the body with drawings made from different angles. These books can be expensive, however, and given that DAZ Studio is free, the software route may be a better one.

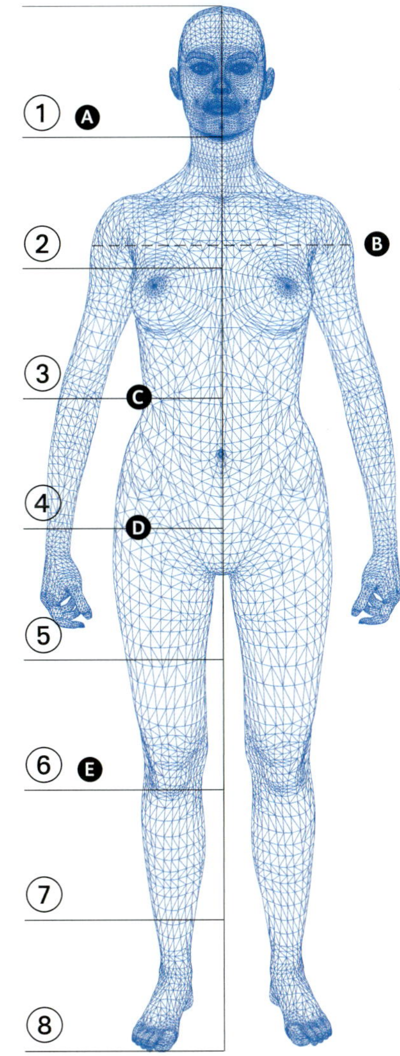

Proportions

Getting the right physical proportions for your characters is important; otherwise they will not look right (unless you are drawing in the manga chibi/super-deformed style). The standard measurement is eight heads high, with the head height taken from the crown to the bottom of the chin. This measurement is used for other proportions, as shown in the diagram at left. The ideal adult is measured as eight heads (male and female), and heroic figures are drawn as nine heads high.

A *The head unit. For a woman 5 feet 8 inches tall, the head would measure 8¼ inches high.*
B *At the widest point, the body measures two head units.*
C *Waist and elbows align. The waist is usually no less than one head unit wide.*
D *Midpoint. The hips/buttocks are measured as 1½ head units. The crotch is ⅓ unit below the midpoint.*
E *Bottom of the knee.*

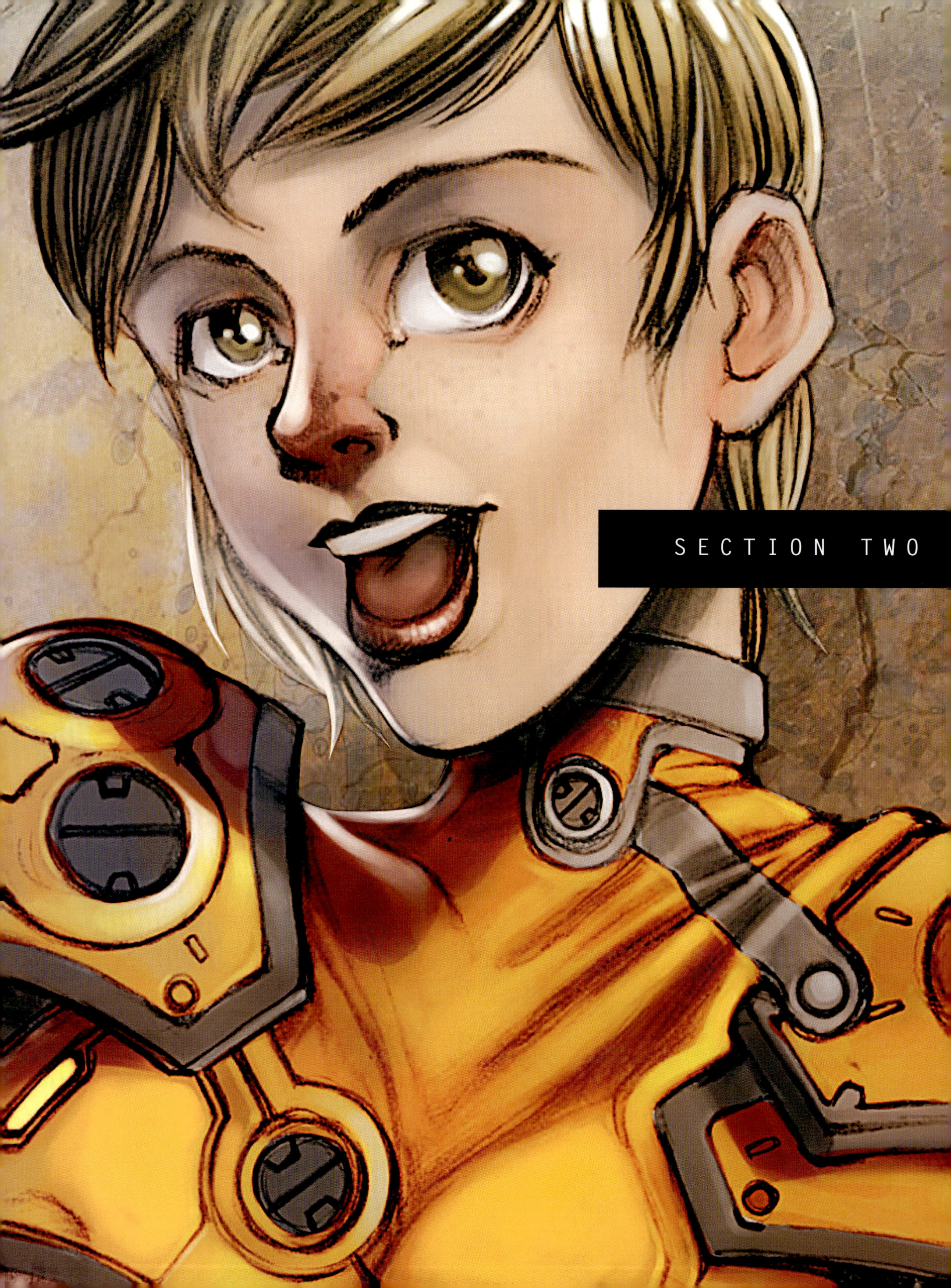
SECTION TWO

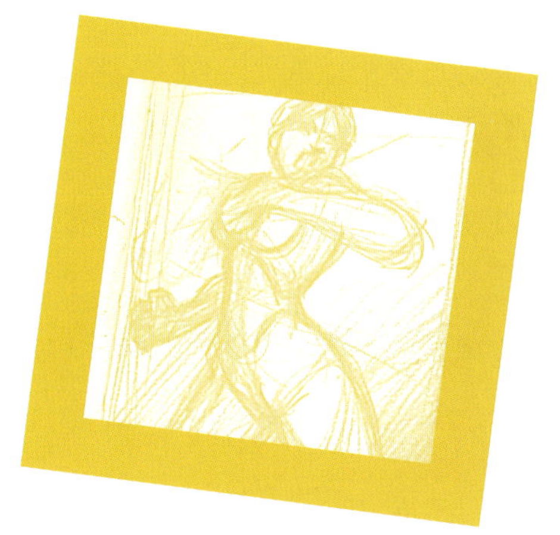

THE CHARACTERS

Getting the right tools and creating the proper work environment will help make the creative process easier, but remember that they will not make you creative. That is the job of this section of this book—to inspire you and get those creative juices flowing. The characters have been divided into nine different genres or types. This is by no means a definitive list, and some of the characters could just as easily belong to one group as another. However, this is not about classification and labeling; it is about showing diversity and the range of possibilities for creating female characters that can go beyond stereotypes. Each character features a personality profile that gives a little insight into who she is and what she does. Different artists, both male and female, from around the world have created these characters using a variety of influences, styles, and techniques, which are explained in practical, illustrated steps. Follow their examples and start creating your own characters and developing your own unique style.

Who is she? Zed, a driver-for-hire with some nefarious clientele, has been given the job of transporting this strange, silent girl to an unknown destination. She was put in the back of his car cuffed and chained, with a bag on her head, and he was told to drive and await further instructions. **What does she wear?** She arrives wearing jeans, T-shirt, and sneakers, which she eventually discards when her wings fully unfurl. **What does she do?** Mostly, she sits silently in the car as Zed, fearing the worst from this job, starts to open his heart to her and recount the good and bad things that have happened to him since he fell into the criminal life. **What happens to her?** As the situation worsens on the journey, her supernatural powers start to manifest. She easily frees herself from her shackles but does not attempt to escape. Zed cannot understand why she is not leaving him or if he really saw her flying with angel wings.

GUARDIAN ANGEL

Illustrations by Simon Valderrama and Silvia Fusetti

Making your own character

Angels are not gods or goddesses, but messengers of God. They are ethereal beings that appear in all cultures and religions, which means they can take on any appearance according to the area in which they manifest. Apart from acting as messengers, angels are often assigned specific functions, such as angel of mercy, guardian angel, or angel of death. Zed wants to know which of these his captive angel is. What type of angel would you create?

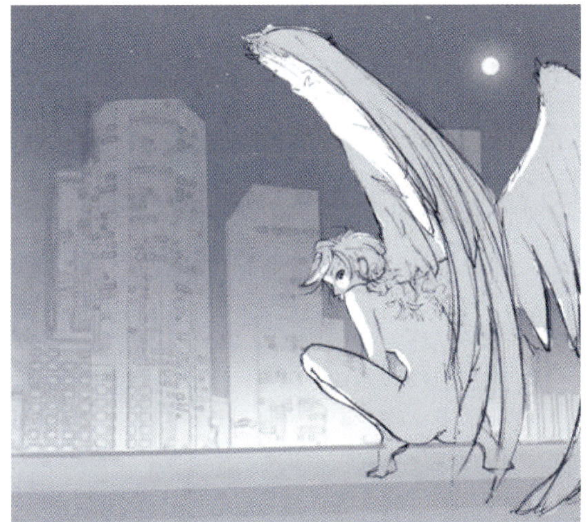

◄ Background
To make the cityscape, a scanned photograph was used as reference and the Stylize>Find Edges and Median filters applied in Photoshop. The drawing was finished using a stylus and graphics tablet, and then digitally colored.

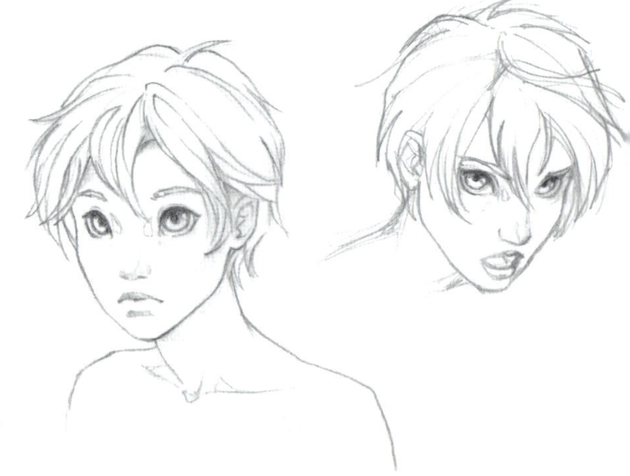

► Concepts
Initial pencil sketches explored different drawing styles and ways of expressing personality. The influence of manga/anime styles is evident in the use of large eyes and minimal linework, helping to create an impression of innocence.

You will need

- Bristol board or drawing paper
- Pencil and eraser
- Black marker pens with various tips
- Macintosh or Windows PC
- Scanner
- Graphics tablet and stylus
- Adobe Photoshop

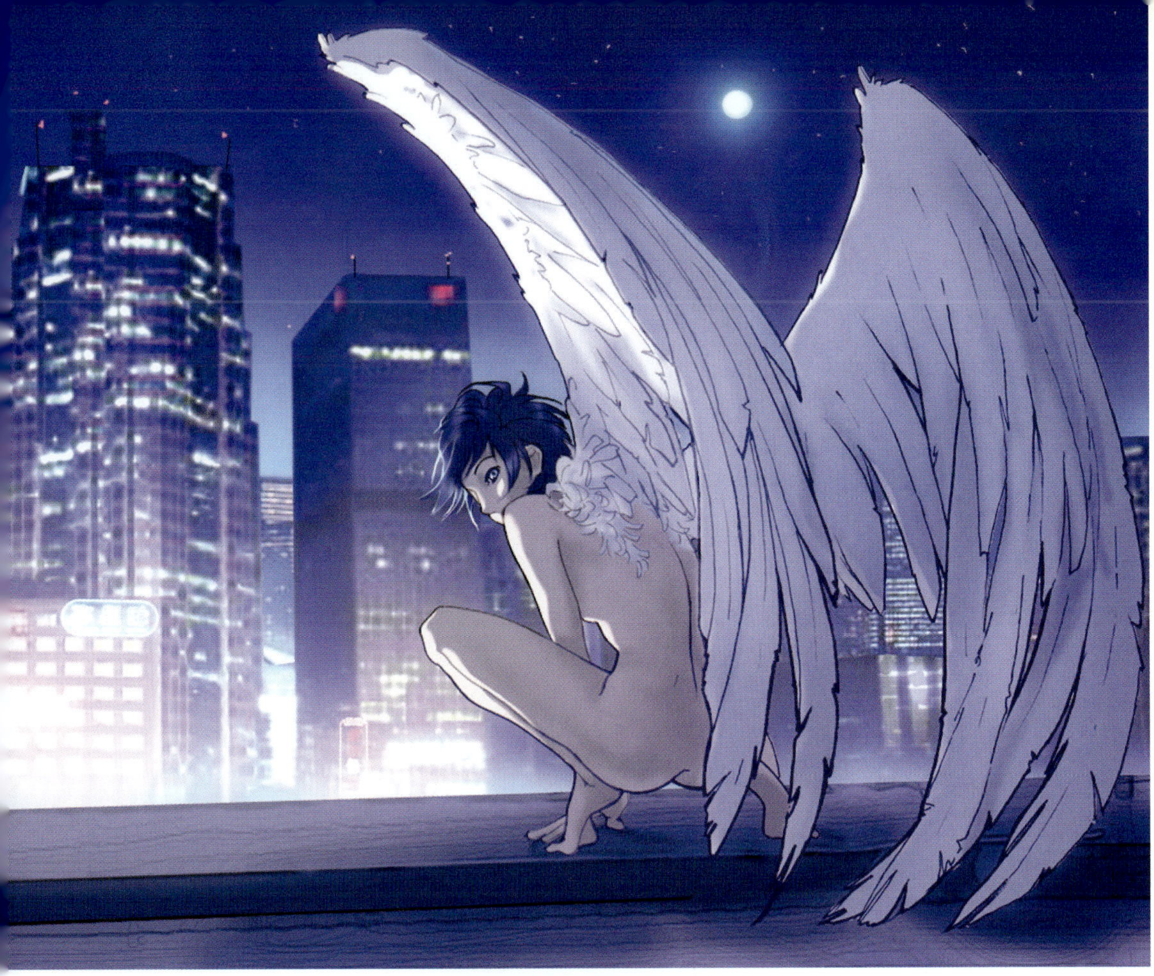

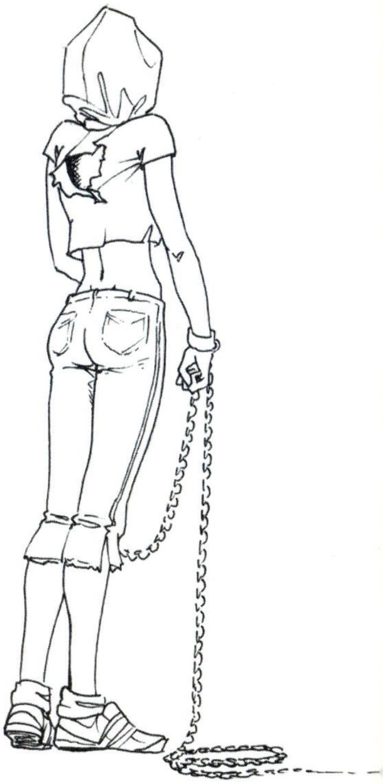

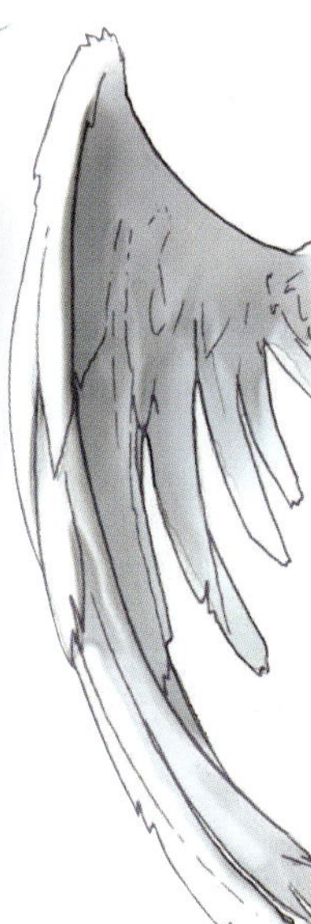

▲▼ Angel delight

Sketches of the character in key moments of the story serve as useful references when it comes to creating the final piece, whether for animation or a comic book.

▼ Angel face

Building on the earlier concepts, a sketch was made with more detail and shading using a soft (2B) pencil. A soft, dark gray marker pen was then used to strengthen the main lines while retaining some softness to the edges. This was then scanned into Photoshop for coloring.

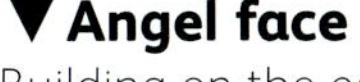

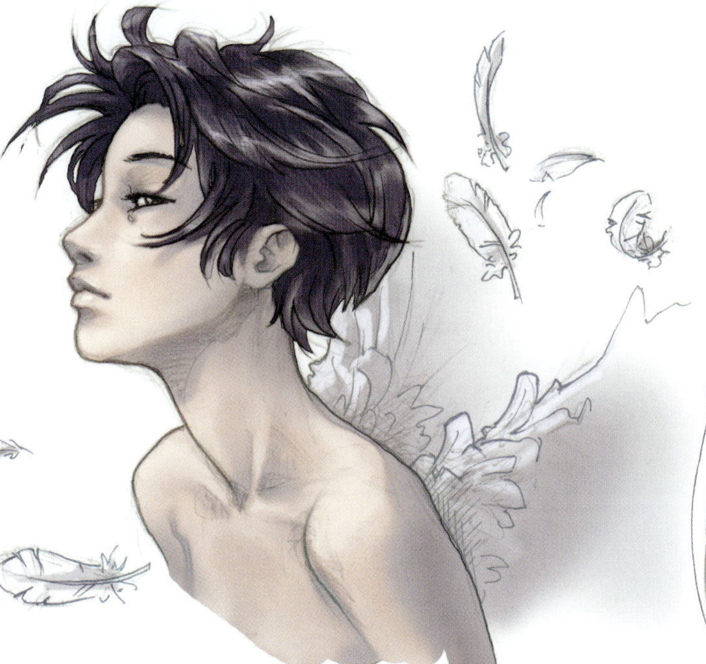

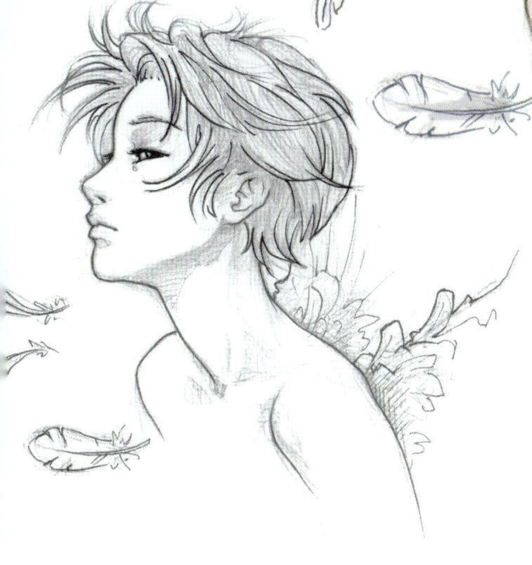

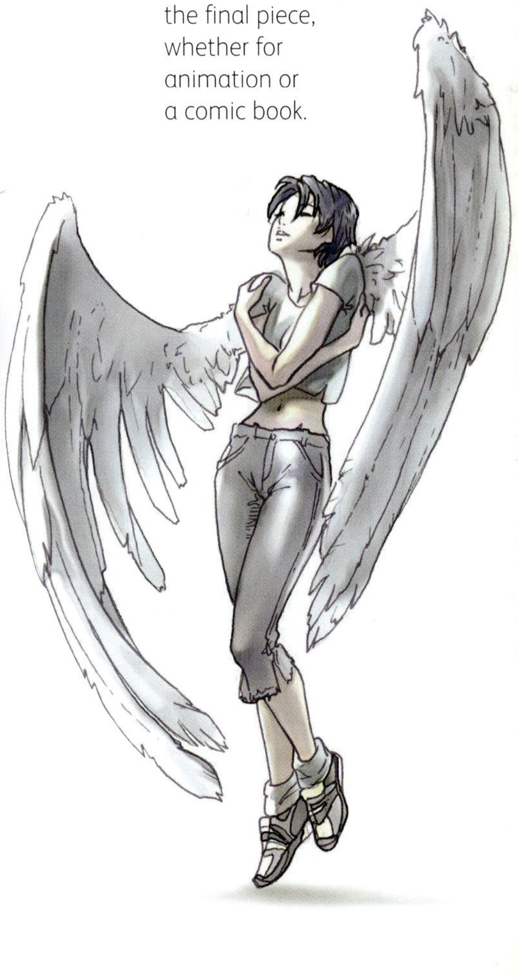

▲ Color palette

The artists wanted a character of delicate beauty who appeared both vulnerable and strong, so a palette of pastel and muted colors was used to convey a sense of femininity. This was further enhanced by building layers of tone using airbrush and watercolor brushes in Photoshop.

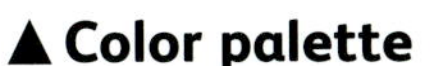

Who is she? Kali is one of the pantheon of Hindu goddesses. She is the mother of the universe, both loving and fearsome. She is an aspect of the mother goddess Durga, who is in turn an aspect of Parvati, the consort of Shiva, the lord of the universe and the destructive power of the Hindu trinity. **What does she wear?** A garland of human heads and usually a skirt of severed arms. She is adorned with a golden crown and other ornaments on her arms and legs. **What does she do?** She appears when her devotees call to her, and protects them by destroying their enemies. **How does she do it?** Using the weapons she carries, or simply by opening her mouth and consuming the enemies.

Mother Goddess

Making your own character

Kali is one of the more popular of the Hindu pantheon, among contemporary writers anyway, probably because of her powers of destruction. She has been in movies such as *Indiana Jones and the Temple of Doom* and was animated by Ray Harryhausen in *The Golden Voyage of Sinbad*. When using an existing personality, especially a religious one, it is a good idea to do as much research as possible, not only into their appearance but also into all aspects of their history and character. You also need to decide exactly how you want to portray the deity, and if you want to risk offending anyone.

You will need

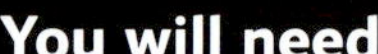

- Paper
- Pencils and pens
- Watercolor brushes
- Ink and Luma dyes

▼ Eternally bad

This picture was originally produced for the cover of *Eternally Bad* by Trina Robbins, a collection of stories of "goddesses with attitude." The picture caused an adverse reaction among sectors of the Hindu community because of its portrayal of Kali in a bar, but it could be argued that it is a matter of interpretation. As Kali is the destroyer of evil, her consumption of alcohol and tobacco could be for that end (just as Shiva does), as well as overcoming chauvinistic male attitudes.

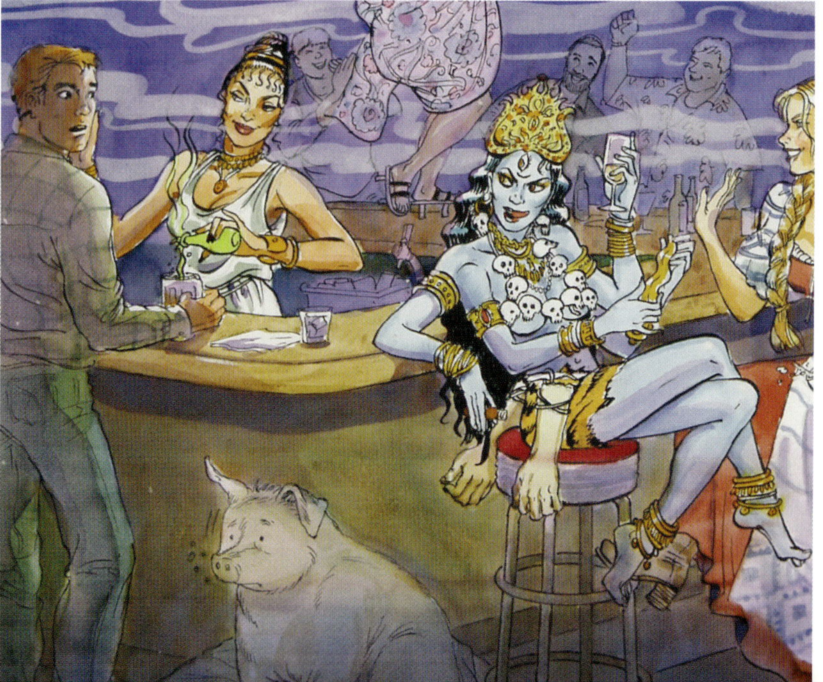

▶ Expressions and body language

In this early proposal for the book cover of *Eternally Bad*, Kali's four arms are visible but her other defining attributes are not there, making her a rather generic interpretation of a Hindu goddess. The artist relied on a mirror to capture the nuances of the characters' expressions while sketching. Acting the role and playing with body language and posture will help bring your characters to life.

Eternally Bad illustrations by Mary Wilshire

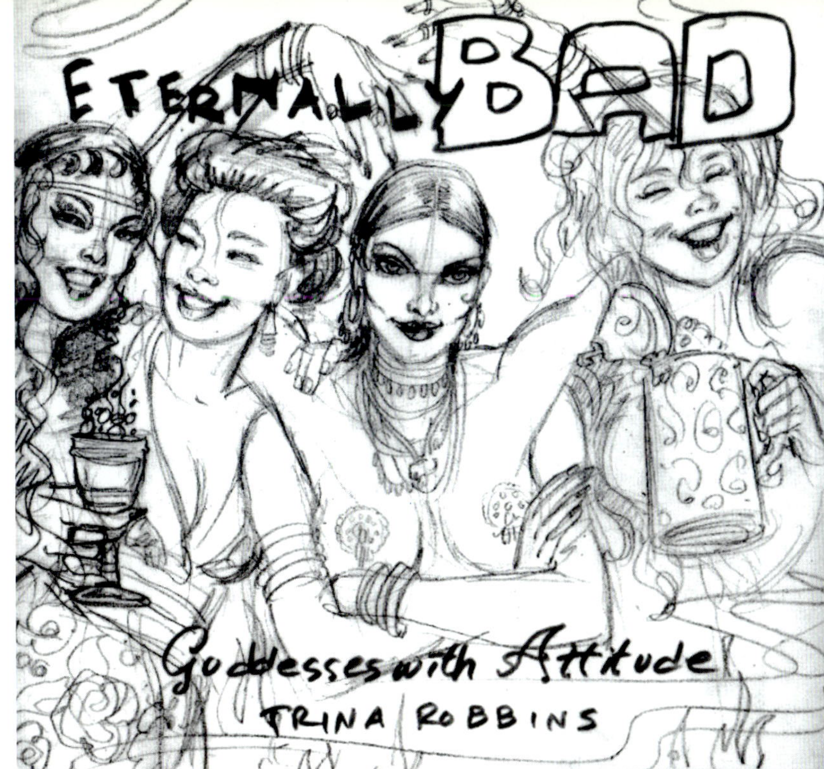

▼ Pinup Kali

Pictures like this are very popular with Hindus for decorating altars, temples, and homes, and provide useful reference for creating your own interpretation of this type of female character. Although fearsome and ferocious in battle, and often shown with a face that conveys that aspect, Kali is still a mother goddess whose beauty is sublime, as this portrayal demonstrates.

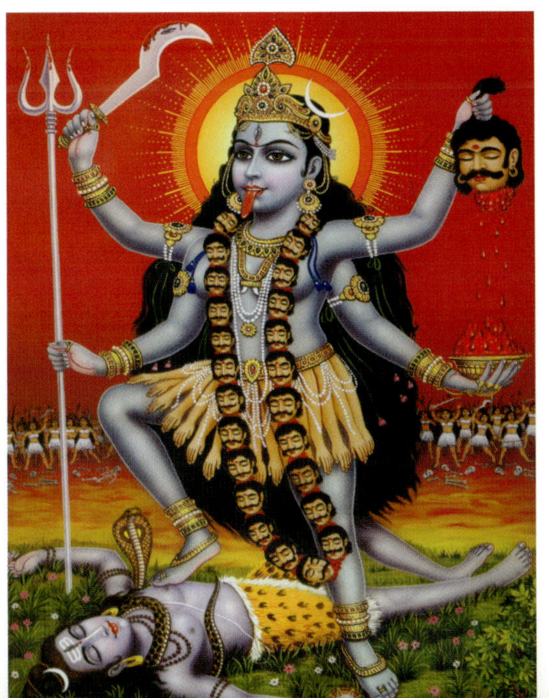

◀ Dark lady

As well as the extra pair of arms and the rather gory wardrobe, Kali also has to be portrayed with dark skin, because Kali means "dark." Blue is often used, as in pictures of Krishna (which also means "dark"), but it should really be black. In fact, very dark skin can take on a bluish hue. Artistically, a pale blue is much easier to work with.

▶ Comic consciousness

Western comics are our modern mythology, our source of heroic deeds. In India, comics are used to recount Indian mythology and cultural history. Amar Chitra Katha is the main publisher of titles covering all the best-loved stories from the Hindu scriptures in an easily digestible format for children, or anyone, looking for an introduction to Indian heritage.

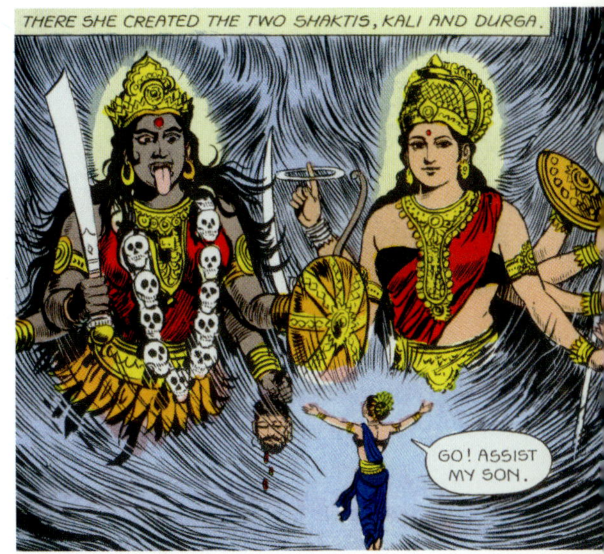

Who is she? Created by the Mother Goddess, Raffaella was given the mission to heal the suffering and afflicted. However, she was not listening properly at the time, being too busy chatting with her friends, so she sometimes gets her objectives muddled.

What does she wear? Even angels need some protection when encountering opposing forces, so body armor is standard issue. It has more style than human armor, but is functional nonetheless. The gossamer-fine skirt is Raffaella's choice, because she wants to retain a feminine appearance, but this is rather annulled by her taste in footwear. **What does she do?** Mostly, she answers the prayers of the faithful, healing them of physical, mental, and emotional afflictions, and restores balance to their gross and subtle bodies. However, because she was not paying attention at the crucial moment, she sometimes afflicts suffering on the unsuspecting. Fortunately, her innate sense of justice restricts this punishment to those who deserve it.

TEEN ANGEL

Illustrations by Chris Patmore

How does she do it? The Mother Goddess gave all her angels a spark of her own omnipotent power that they can use as vibrating energy emanating from their hands. Even though this force can bring light to even the darkest forces, Raffaella prefers the immediacy of the sword when dealing with negative entities.

Making your own character

Once the basic character model has been built in Poser (see pages 60–61), there are several options for achieving a more hand-drawn look: DAZ Studio has a cartoon render option; Poser has a variety of sketch renders; or Photoshop filters or other artistic software like Studio Artist can be applied to the final, exported images.

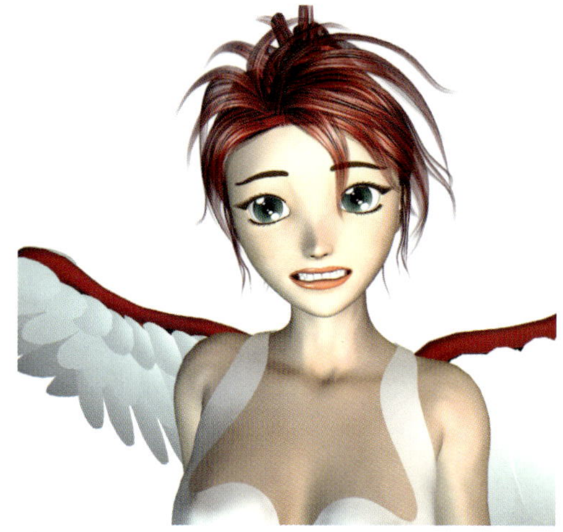

▲ Expressions
Facial expressions can convey a lot about a character's personality. The best places to concentrate are the eyes and mouth. This one conveys the idea of "Oops."

▼ Face lift
Adjusting mouth shapes in Poser and DAZ Studio is done with morphs. These are built into the models and are accessed by selecting the character's head and choosing Parameters in DAZ Studio or Parameter Dials under the Windows menu in Poser. A huge number of options are available (depending on the model) and are adjusted either numerically or by dragging the scroll bar/wheel. It is very much a process of trial and error to get the exact expression you want.

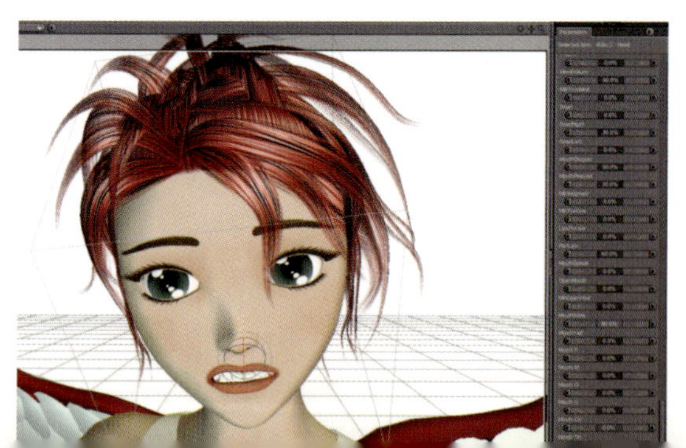

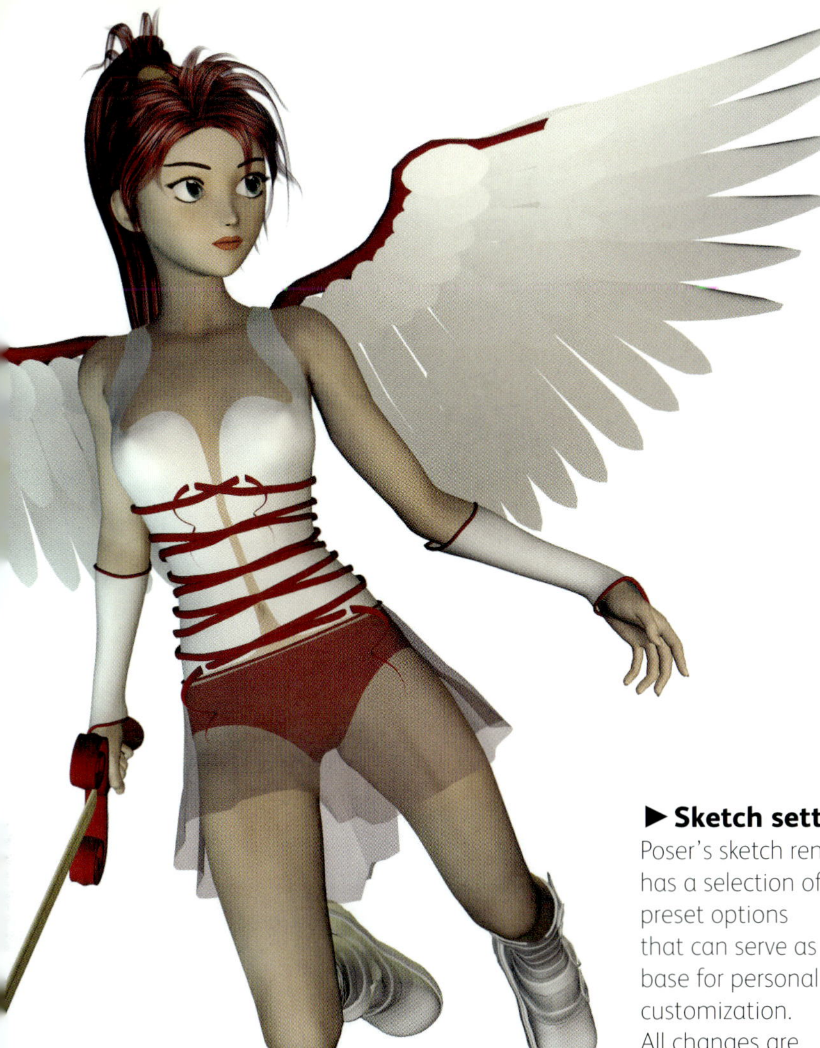

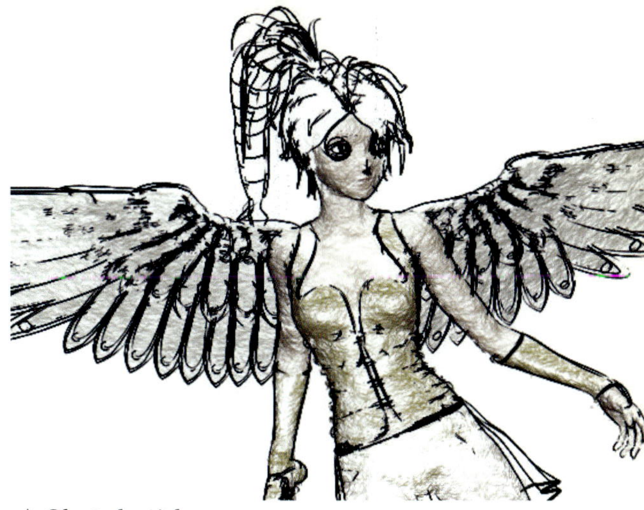

▲ Sketchy ideas

Poser has a sketch render option that produces some interesting effects, but is limited to screen resolution, which may not suit your needs. It also tends to look obviously computer-generated, so it may be better to use a good render and draw over it by hand in Photoshop.

▶ Sketch settings

Poser's sketch render has a selection of preset options that can serve as a base for personal customization. All changes are previewed.

◀ Photoshop toon settings

Photoshop comes with a large selection of filters for altering the appearance of images. Poster Edges, which flattens the colors and adds a black line around the edges, is one of the Artistic filters that closely resembles cel shading.

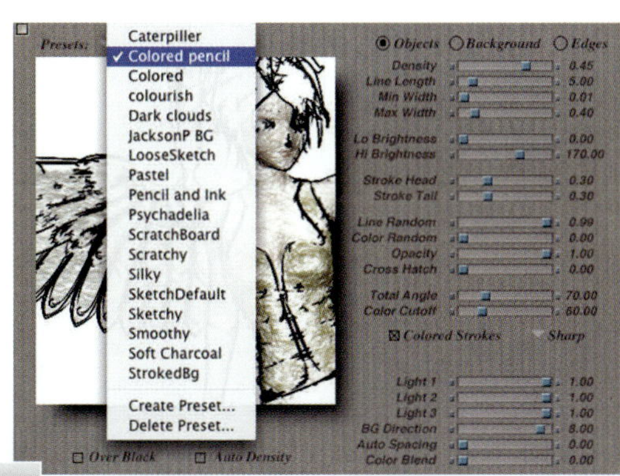

▲ ▶ Toon angel

Some characters, such as manga/anime-style ones, work better with toon shading than others. Try to keep everything simple, with as much flat color as possible. Lighting is also crucial. This image was rendered with DAZ Studio's default cartoon render.

Who is she? This goddess comes in many guises and with many names, but to the Phoenicians she is Astarte, the goddess of fertility, motherhood, and war, and the embodiment of creation, sustenance, and destruction. In India, she is known as Kali (page 40). **What does she wear?** Astarte wears the flowing robes of a goddess. She is sometimes represented with cow horns to reinforce the fertility aspect of her nature. **What does she do?** As mother of the universe, she is the giver of life to everything on Earth. She also rules over the souls in heaven that appear as stars, so another of her names is Astroache, queen of the stars and giver of astral bodies. As a warrior goddess, she revels in the blood of her victims. **How does she do it?** Sometimes she uses traditional weapons, such as an ax and spear, but at other times she uses the subtler weapons of beauty and sexuality to overcome her enemies.

STAR QUEEN

Illustrations by Jesus Barony

Making your own character

Figurative artists are always at the mercy of market trends. The demand for illustrators ebbs and flows, tastes change, and styles go in and out of fashion. To survive, you need to develop not only an original style, but also a variety of techniques and applications. Using traditional techniques and materials, instead of doing everything on computer, will give your work a more unique look.

You will need

- **Canson tinted paper**
- **Pencil and eraser**
- **Pastel colors and conté white pencils**
- **Macintosh or Windows PC**
- **Scanner**
- **Graphics tablet and stylus**
- **Adobe Photoshop**

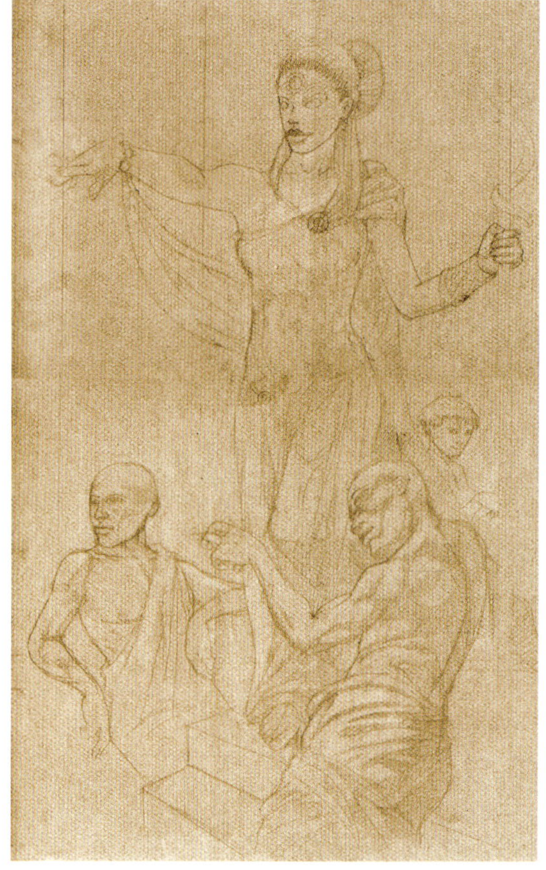

◄ Composition
Starting with a large sheet of Canson tinted paper, the figures and basic composition were sketched using pastel and conté pencils. For the female figure, photographic reference shots were taken to get the correct pose and fall of the cloth. The males were drawn from memory.

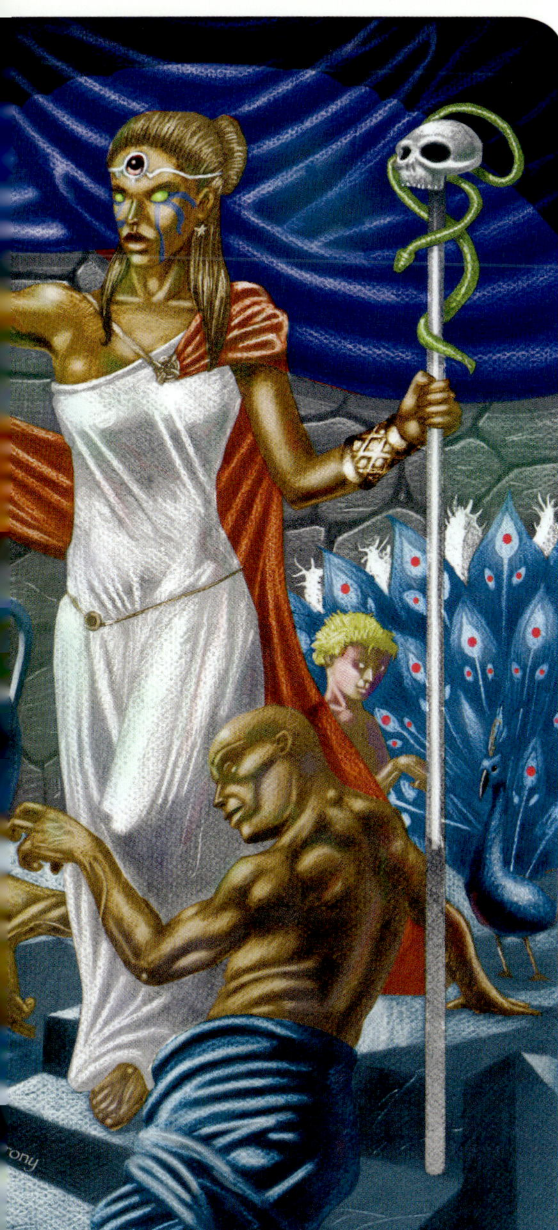

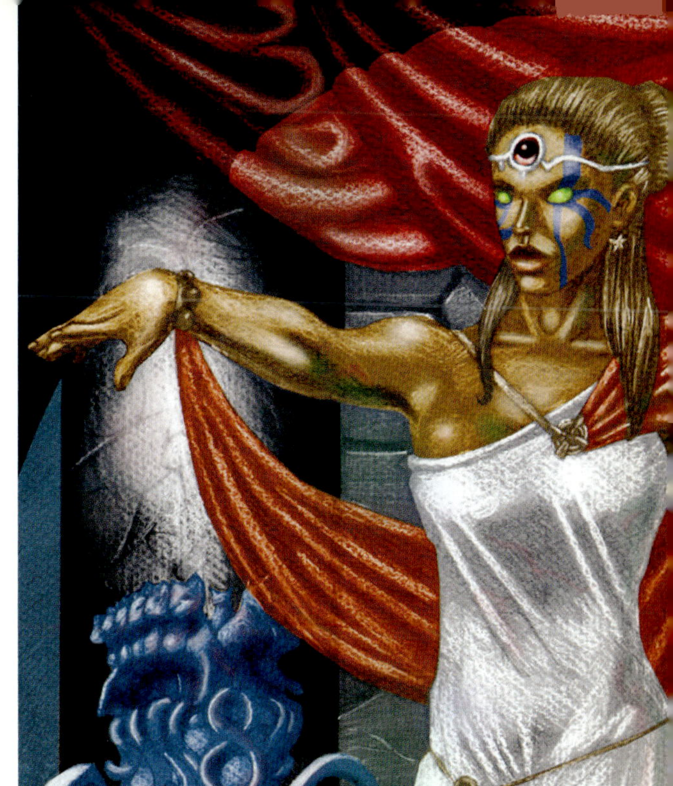

▶ Pastel and digital coloring

Pastels were used to color the image. The paper's texture remains visible under the softness of the pastels, and an eraser was employed to blend and shape highlights. Once the basic color was completed, the image was scanned for refining in Photoshop. Additional effects were applied, such as the green eyes and the glow around Astarte's hand. The color of the drapes was eventually changed from red to blue so that Astarte would stand out from the background.

▼ Digital correction

Because scanning removes some of the vibrancy of the original colors, some adjustments were made to contrast and balance. In addition, pastels are a very soft medium, so with continuous retouching and handling of the paper, the face of the figure on the left became smudged and distorted. To overcome this, a helmet was added to the final image to cover up some of the damage and distract the eye from it. Corrections like this are much easier to do digitally so that further damage to the original can be avoided.

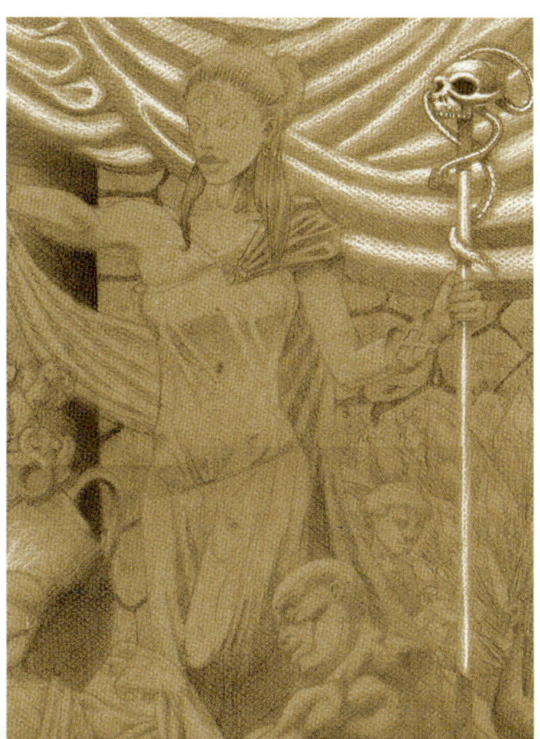

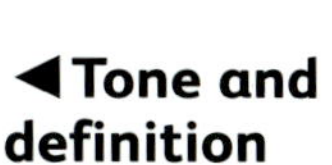

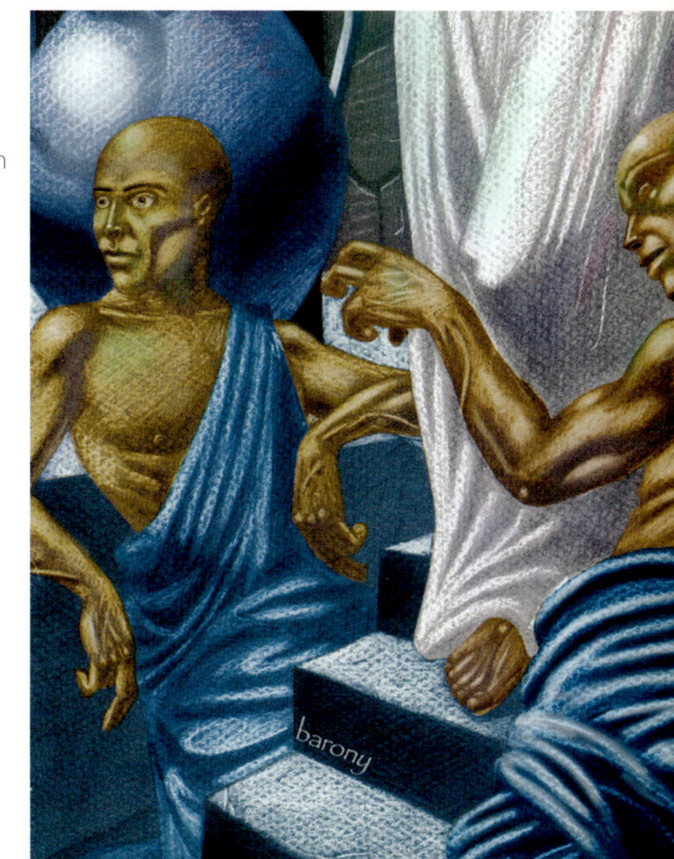

◀ Tone and definition

The tone and shading were built up using white conté pencils for highlights. An eraser was also used to remove areas to help define shapes.

Who is she? As a child surviving in the desolate ruins of a future Chicago in the aftermath of ecological disaster, Keico Loc was taken into the "care" of the delusional, psychotic warlord Black Eye, who trained her as an assassin. **What does she wear?** Black—it has to be black for working, made from the latest tear-resistant, water-repellent, quick-drying synthetic fabric, accessorized with lightweight alloy body armor. **What does she do?** Bounty hunter. After escaping from Black Eye, Keico joined the EBS (Espionage Bounty Specialty) Agency in Chi Nova (the new, safe, domed part of Chicago), working under the name of Ghost Spy. Like most teenagers, she wanted to find out who she really was, but her background made it hard for her to conform to the new society's regulations. **How does she do it?** After years of abuse and training from Black Eye, killing has become second nature to Keico, despite her desire for a more normal life.

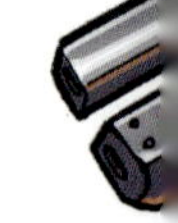

GHOST SPY

Illustrations by Jacob Elijah

Making your own character

Developing a back story for characters helps to establish a reality to them. The simplest way is to use a character profile sheet (see page 19), but building a pictorial record of the character's life will also help greatly in creating the final look of the character.

You will need

- **Bristol board or drawing paper**
- **Pencil and eraser**
- **Black marker pens with various tips**
- **Macintosh or Windows PC**
- **Scanner**
- **Graphics tablet and stylus**
- **Adobe Photoshop**

◄ Innocent Keico

The wide-eyed innocence of the 10-year-old Keico is drawn in a style that resembles chibi anime, with large, round eyes and a minimum of facial features. This is the beginning of her story, immediately after she falls in with Black Eye's gang. Drawn with a 2H pencil, the bold outlines act as a guide for inking.

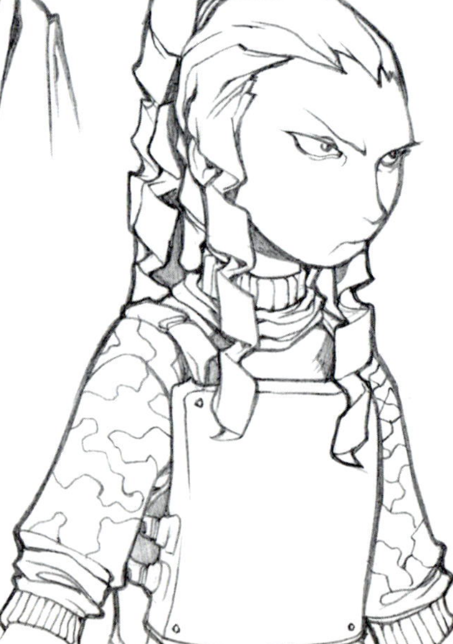

◄ Killer Keico

After years of constant abuse from Black Eye, Keico has become a ruthless assassin. Her wide-eyed innocence has all but disappeared, yet the fierce determination required by her work has kept alive Keico's sense of independence and a hope of freedom when she escapes from her captor.

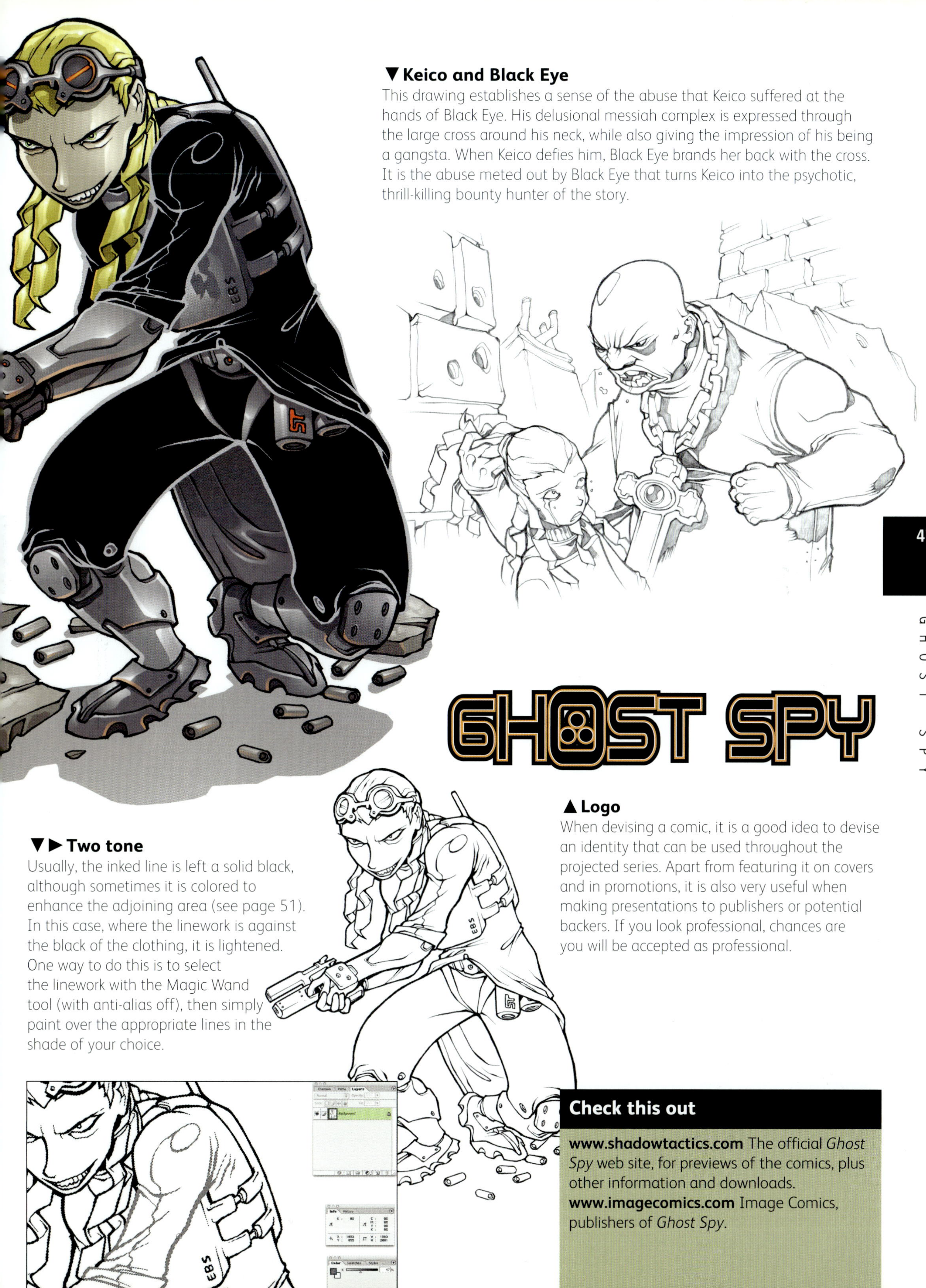

▼ Keico and Black Eye

This drawing establishes a sense of the abuse that Keico suffered at the hands of Black Eye. His delusional messiah complex is expressed through the large cross around his neck, while also giving the impression of his being a gangsta. When Keico defies him, Black Eye brands her back with the cross. It is the abuse meted out by Black Eye that turns Keico into the psychotic, thrill-killing bounty hunter of the story.

▼▶ Two tone

Usually, the inked line is left a solid black, although sometimes it is colored to enhance the adjoining area (see page 51). In this case, where the linework is against the black of the clothing, it is lightened. One way to do this is to select the linework with the Magic Wand tool (with anti-alias off), then simply paint over the appropriate lines in the shade of your choice.

▲ Logo

When devising a comic, it is a good idea to devise an identity that can be used throughout the projected series. Apart from featuring it on covers and in promotions, it is also very useful when making presentations to publishers or potential backers. If you look professional, chances are you will be accepted as professional.

Check this out

www.shadowtactics.com The official *Ghost Spy* web site, for previews of the comics, plus other information and downloads.
www.imagecomics.com Image Comics, publishers of *Ghost Spy*.

Who is she? Bellatrix Orion is the only child of the last generation of occult warriors known simply as Fixers. She is the first female Fixer.

What does she wear? As the first woman Fixer, Bellatrix designed her own costumes. Skintight leather is her favorite, but she also has a PVC outfit that is more flexible and easier to clean after a particularly messy assignment. These clothes also let her pass unnoticed in the places her targets frequent. **What does she do?** With growing public acceptance of the dark side of the occult, uninitiated practitioners have been resurrecting beings that should not have crossed dimensions, resulting in many deaths. Bellatrix's job is to clean up the mess and destroy the malevolent beings.

STAR FIGHTER

How does she do it? Bellatrix has no unarmed combat training, preferring to use guns and swords to complete her missions. Once the beings have taken corporeal form, sword distance is as close as she wants to get to them. She is always accompanied by her panther, Newton, who ensures that she is never taken by surprise.

Illustrations by Chris Patmore

Making your own character

Poser was originally designed to give digital artists a computer version of a wooden mannequin, but it quickly developed into a full-fledged 3D character design and artwork tool that was also capable of animation. As its popularity increased, so did the content available to use in it, making it an ideal starting point for anyone wanting to make realistic 3D character animations. Once you have built and developed your character, getting her to move is relatively easy.

▶ Basic model
Build your basic character model using the steps described on pages 60–61. Bellatrix was based on the Stephanie Petite and Celeste models from DAZ.

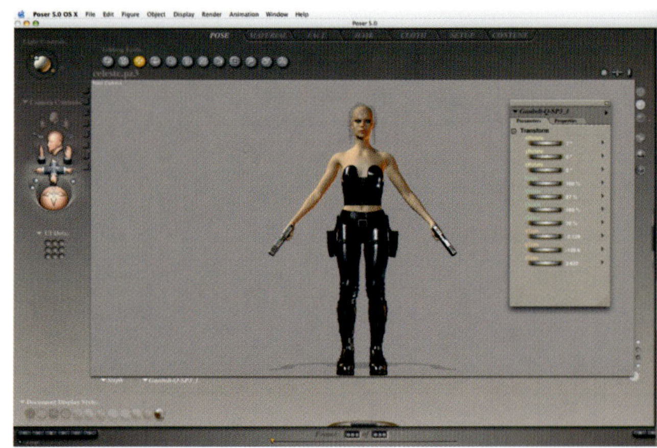

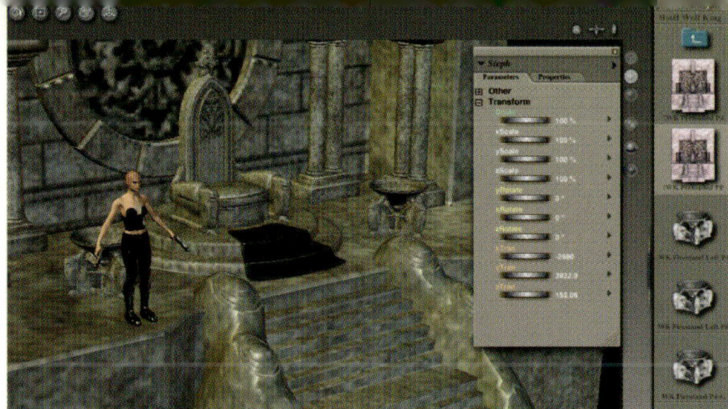

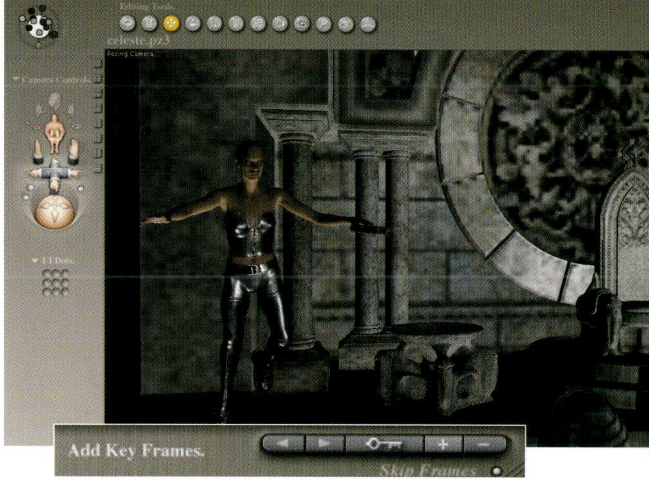

▲ Setting the scene

Place the finished character in a scene. This one is from DAZ's Platinum Club. You can create your own with 3D programs such as Carrara Studio, Vue d'Espirit, or Lightwave, which all work with Poser through plug-ins.

▲ Action

Poser has a built-in walk designer that takes all the hard work out of creating walking and running cycles. Poser animation uses keyframes on a timeline, so you need to set only the extremes of each action. Calculate the time it takes for the action to happen (in frames) and click the + in the bottom right-hand corner of the screen. The number of frames per second (fps) will depend on what you intend to do with the finished animation. If you are going to use a digital editor, such as iMovie, you will need to set it according to your local video standard (30fps for NTSC or 25fps for PAL).

▶ Lighting

Lighting is very important, because it will set the atmosphere for your movie. Lighting in Poser is fairly intuitive, but doing it well requires lots of experimentation and practice. Luckily, there are many preset lighting arrangements available that make the job much easier. You can also study how they are done to help with the learning process.

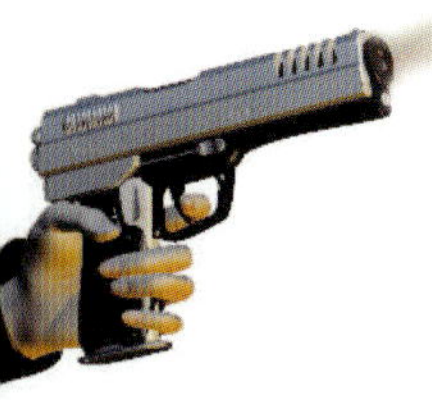

▶ Camera shots

You can "shoot" your animated sequence from various angles using different cameras. These cameras can also be animated using keyframes to get those sweeping tracking shots you see in Hollywood movies.

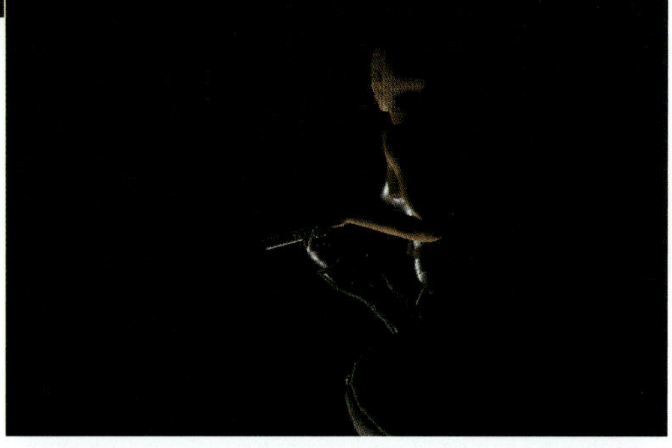

▼ Adding dialogue

It is easy to add lip-synched dialogue to a movie using DAZ Mimic. This software takes a recording (in WAV or AIFF format), creates all the appropriate mouth shapes, and saves them as a sequence that is imported into your animation.

▶ Rendering

Once the animation is complete, you have to render it. The render engine in Poser does a fair job. Save it in a format that will work with your editing software— DV is the most common. Rendering is a long, slow process and is best done when the computer is not performing other tasks. Depending on the length of the scene you have made, it may be best to let it render overnight.

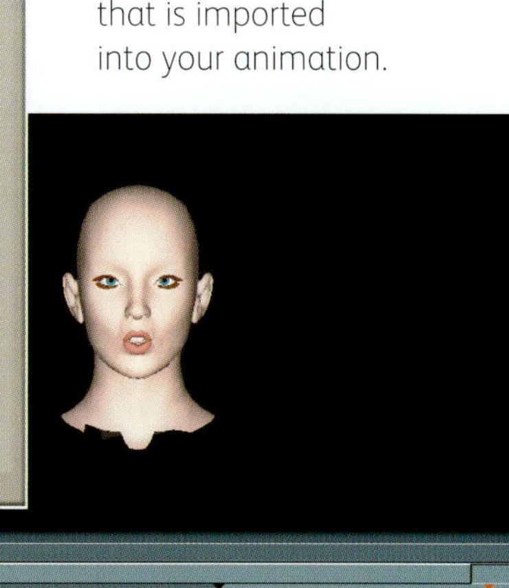

Who is she? By day she is Head Prefect at Madam Fang's School for Splendid Young Ladies; by night she is a daring thief known as the Naughty Red Fox, star pupil of the extracurricular night school. **What does she wear?** Skintight clothes allow her to move easily. A Replicator Satchel (a device that copies the molecular structure of items and re-creates them) is strapped to one leg, and another satchel containing burglary tools to the other. **What does she do?** Although not endowed with the altruism of Robin Hood, she is not as mercenary as some people paint her. All her jobs are carried out according to her own moral code—and her mentor's instructions.

Foxy Lady

Illustrations by Cosmo White

How does she do it? Using her Replicator and tools, she slips soundlessly across the lunar rooftops of Tranquility City accompanied by Gladstone, the Replicator's holographic user-interface dragon.

Making your own character

It is said that "clothes maketh the man," but designing the right costume for your female character will definitely change how she is perceived. Once you have a concept for the character, you have to decide not only how to dress her, but also the drawing style in which she will be represented.

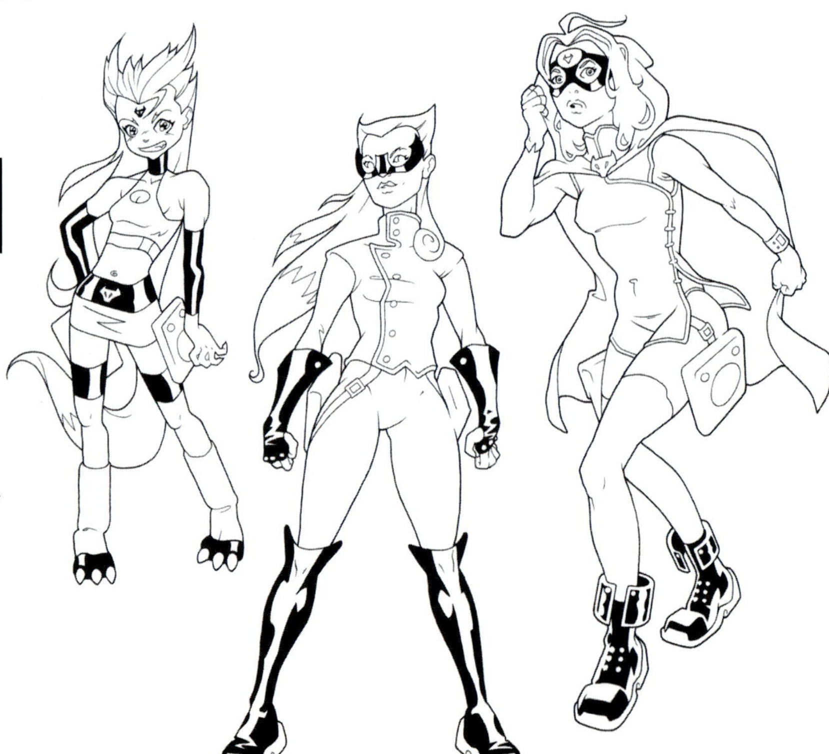

◄ Costume and style

Developing a unique look for a character extends beyond the costume to the overall style of the drawing. A variety of styles from manga to "cartoony" to what could be called a traditional superhero style were all tried. Recurring themes and features are clearly visible.

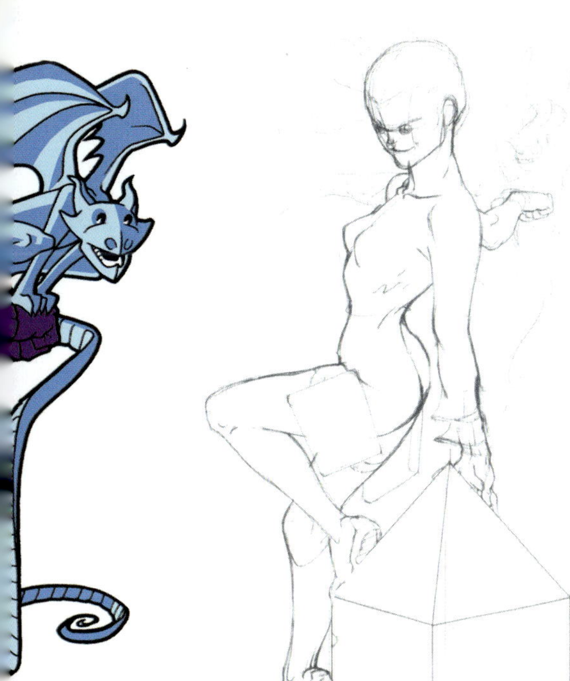

◀ Muscle building

With your initial sketches, it is important to get the underlying anatomy and proportions correct, but without going into too much muscle detail. If you add it at this early stage, you may not want to remove it when you start adding the costume and color. Muscle detail can be alluded to with some well-placed lines that will not detract from the style of the finished drawing.

▶ Fleshing out

Build up the details, over the initial sketch, to get as close as possible to your idea. If you are doing your own inking, you can keep the lines as single pencil-width and embolden them as necessary at the inking stage. If the drawing will be inked by a separate artist, the pencil work will need to be "tight"—that is, it needs to be a finished drawing, perfectly legible, so that the inking artist can see exactly where to put the ink lines.

▲ Double edged

Inking is all about creating the cleanest black lines into which the color can be added. The outside lines are often inked much thicker than the rest, to help bring the drawing out of the background. This is not a hard and fast rule (you may prefer the soft-edged version shown at left, for example) and will be dictated by your overall style.

▶ Soft edges

The final costume and style were chosen and a color scheme decided, using Photoshop's toon shading to add form and depth. In this example, the outlines have been "dropped"—a technique often used in animation—to get an overall softer look. To do this, the black, inked lines are duplicated onto a separate layer in Photoshop and colored with darker versions of the main area color. This can be done using a Brush tool, or by a variety of other techniques, such as adjusting the Hue/Saturation sliders (found under Image>Adjustments or by pressing Cmd-U or Ctrl-U).

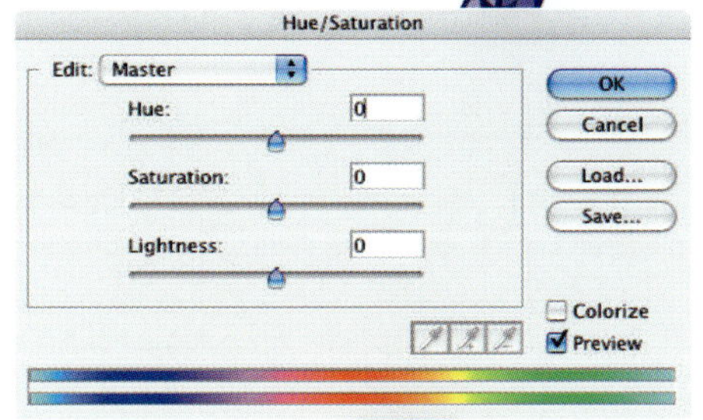

You will need

- Bristol board or drawing paper
- Pencil and eraser
- Black marker pens with various tips
- Macintosh or Windows PC
- Scanner
- Graphics tablet and stylus
- Adobe Photoshop

Who is she? Kaitlin Shepherd is a British agent working for the Special Operations Executive during World War II. She is their highest trained operative and has been assigned to work with the United States' first counterintelligence agent, Jack Hunter. **What does she wear?** Kaitlin wears a supple leather flight suit that she has modified for field usage. In one holster she carries a .455 calibre Webley & Scott automatic pistol, equipped with a silencer, and in the other a sabot club. The club extends to allow her to fend off attackers without bruising her knuckles. Her jacket conceals a Fairbairn-Sykes fighting knife and a single-shot flashlight pistol. Her boots are Royal Marine jungle boots.

SPECIAL AGENT

Illustrations by Matt Haley

What does she do? Together with Jack Hunter, Kaitlin is investigating a secret Nazi plot to build a fleet of "wonder weapons" in a hidden Antarctic fortress that could give the Axis control of the free world forever. **How does she do it?** With grace, style, panache, and a bit of wry wit.

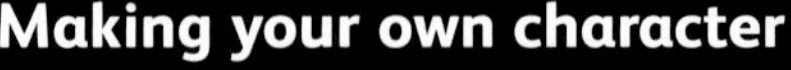

Making your own character

When it comes to sexy British female agents, the names Modesty Blaise and Lara Croft are always going to spring to mind, so creating a new contender requires a great story written with snappy dialogue, sympathetic lead characters, and really evil bad guys. The heroine also has to look the part. Writer Andrew Cosby and artist Matt Haley got the right formula for their graphic novel *Jack Hunter: G.I. SPY*.

◄ 1950s heroine

Drawn in a style reminiscent of 1950s adventure and romance comics, this early sketch of the character has many of the final attributes well established, in particular the weapons and basic uniform, which is more modest than the eventual style. The face and hair were changed, as were other aspects that defined the final personality. Experimenting with these subtle changes will help your character grow. If you are working with a writer, it is important to get his or her feedback and input.

▼ Soft tone

Generally, tonal shading with pencil is not used, but in this case it was retained to give a softer, textured look, especially to the clothing. To achieve this you have to set the pencil layer to Multiply. You may also want to experiment with the contrast settings, depending on the drawing and the overall effect you want to achieve.

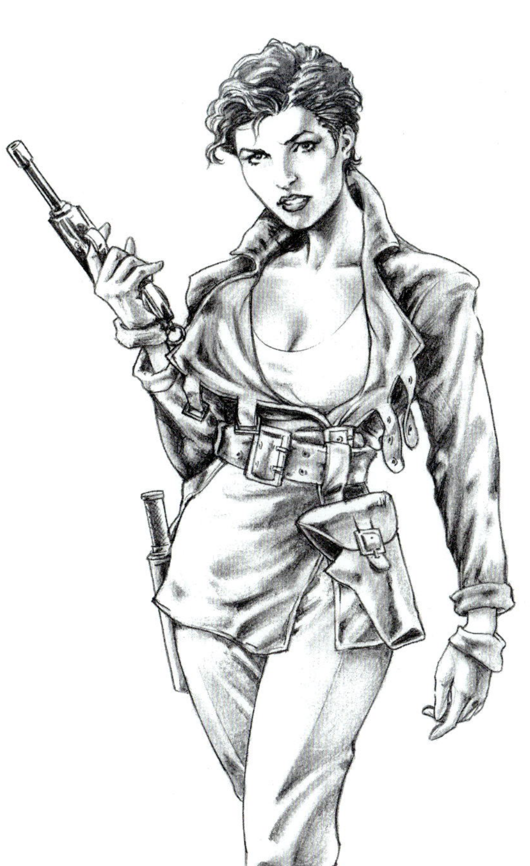

► Nighttime nuances

Developing characters is all about making them believable, even if they are doing unbelievable things. Images like this can reveal a lot about a character's personality. The choice of nightwear, the eyeshade, sleeping with a pistol—these are all aspects that have to be decided by the artist and the writer to add nuances to the character and help the story unfold.

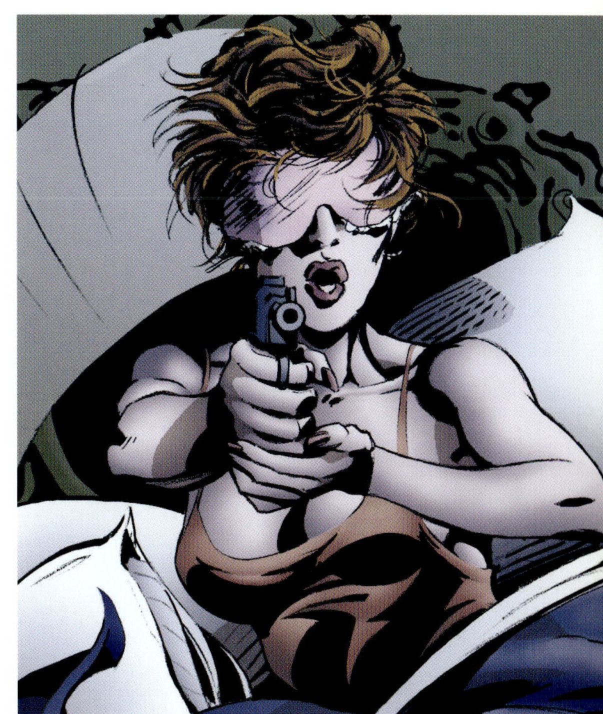

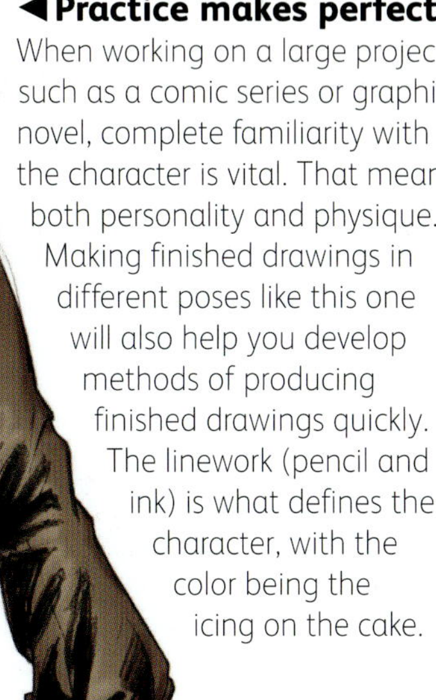

◄ Practice makes perfect

When working on a large project, such as a comic series or graphic novel, complete familiarity with the character is vital. That means both personality and physique. Making finished drawings in different poses like this one will also help you develop methods of producing finished drawings quickly. The linework (pencil and ink) is what defines the character, with the color being the icing on the cake.

You will need

- Bristol board or drawing paper
- Pencil and eraser
- Black marker pens with various tips
- Macintosh or Windows PC
- Scanner
- Graphics tablet and stylus
- Adobe Photoshop

Who is she? Lady Astra Luisa Aurelia is head of the elite bodyguard to Emperor Adham I. She originates from Tagarna, in the north-west of Karkistan, which was one of the first areas to be liberated by the Phantom Noir under Adham's leadership. **What does she wear?** The imperial uniform of the Daughters of the Rose regiment. The uniform is designed to be practical, to cope with Karkistan's extremes of weather, while still allowing freedom of movement. The black uniforms are decorated with designs to ward off evil. **What does she do?** As one of the leading Daughters of the Rose, Astra protects Emperor Adham I, ready to lay down her life for his.

BODYGUARD

How does she do it? Highly trained in advanced sword and firearm skills, coupled with cunning stealth and fearless ferocity, Astra and her compadres have been known to cause men to surrender without having to strike a blow.

Illustrations by
Nic Brennan

Making your own character

Although most artists prefer the paper>pencil>ink>Photoshop route to creating images, it is by no means the only one available. Adobe Illustrator and other vector-based illustration software offer the artist the chance to develop a style quite different from the more established pixel-based method. The illustrations shown here were drawn and colored directly in Illustrator using a graphics tablet and stylus.

You will need

- **Macintosh or Windows PC**
- **Graphics tablet and stylus**
- **Adobe Illustrator**

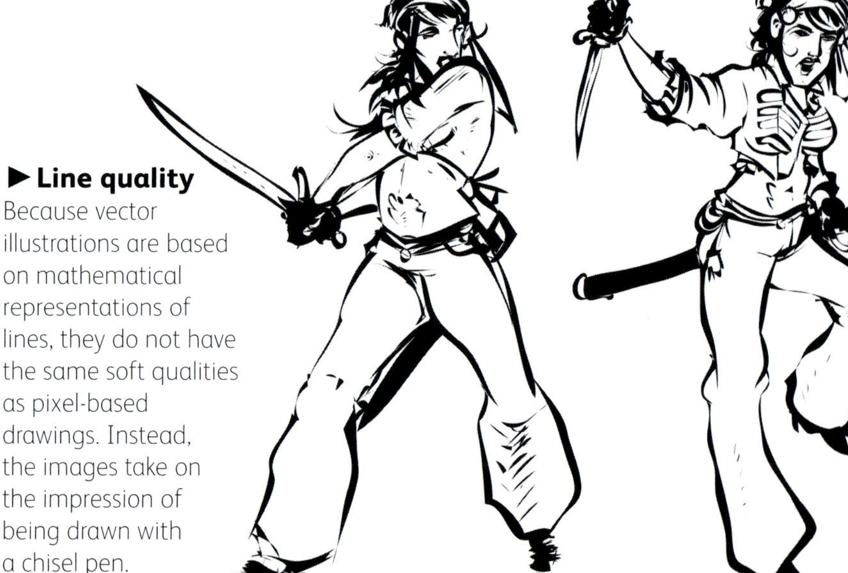

► Line quality
Because vector illustrations are based on mathematical representations of lines, they do not have the same soft qualities as pixel-based drawings. Instead, the images take on the impression of being drawn with a chisel pen.

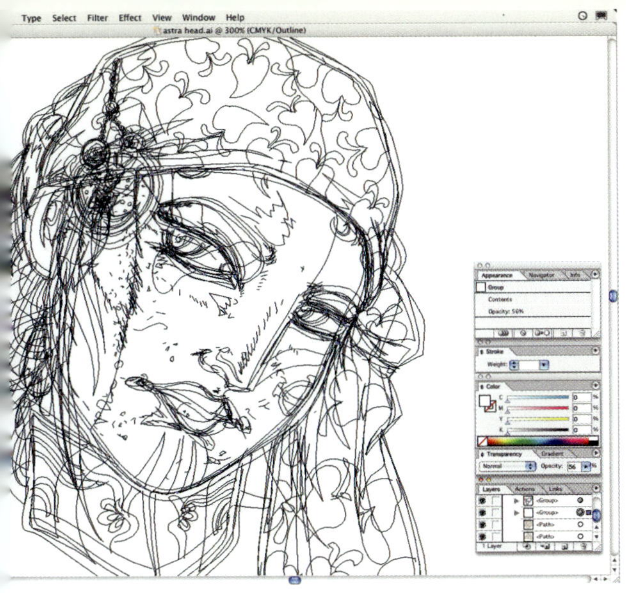

◄ Outlines

This portrait was drawn using the Pencil tool in Illustrator, and built up layer by layer as each color and detail was added. When viewed in Outline mode, you can see all the lines that make up the finished drawing. These lines create shapes that can be filled with color, and even the black edges are not a single line but a shape filled with black.

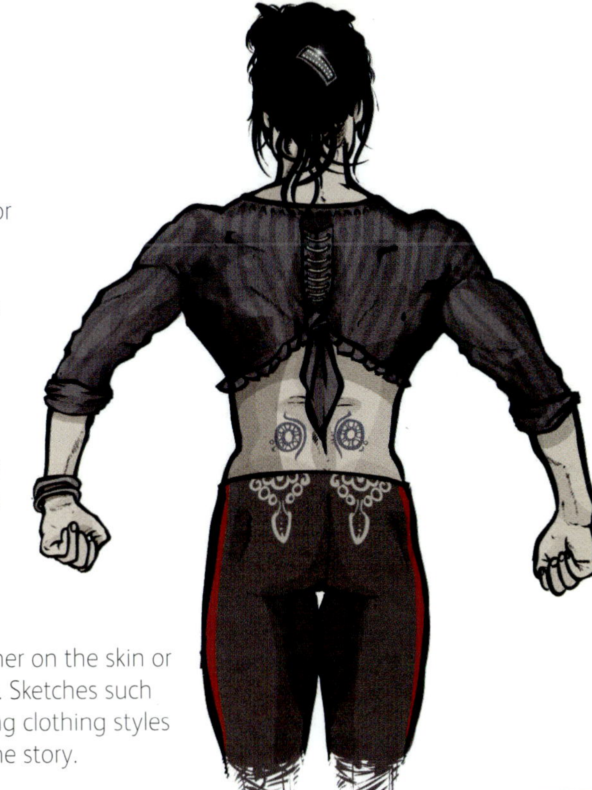

▼ Shading and highlights

To achieve a sense of depth, shading and highlights were added to the main drawing. These were created using the same type of color-filled shapes used for solid color areas, but are fills of black or white with varying degrees of Transparency applied.

► Decorative detail

All the decorations, whether on the skin or clothes, have significance. Sketches such as this one help in creating clothing styles for similar characters in the story.

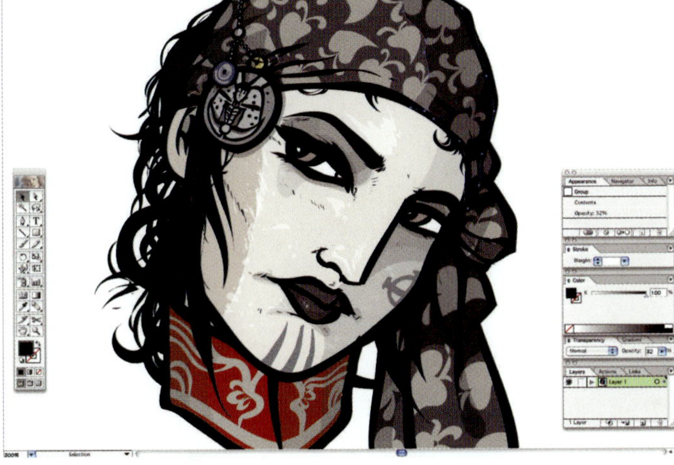

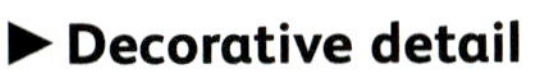

► Editing lines

One of the advantages of vector illustrations is that every line remains fully editable, so its shape or color can be changed without affecting any of the lines around it. Although a rough, hand-drawn look is what has been designed here, the lines can easily be smoothed or made more angular. Although these images have been drawn with the Pencil tool to create a unique style, Illustrator has a comprehensive range of pressure-sensitive brushstrokes that can enhance single lines.

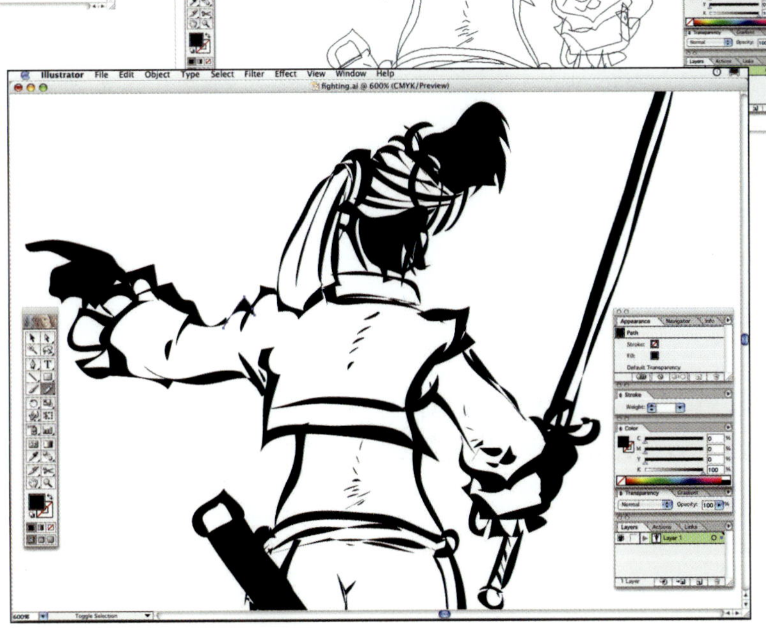

Who is she? In the bizarre world of 12-volt slot-car racing, there are teams that are overseen by toys. Dark Sister was originally a sculpture from a comic store and the star of her own "Parental Advisory" comic series. **What does she wear?** Her preference is leather, although she is also partial to an occasional item of carefully constructed latex. Whatever material she wears, thigh-high stiletto boots are de rigueur. Her favorite accessories include a long leather whip and a pair of handcuffs. **What does she do?** Every slot car has a human driver, but they usually need lots of encouragement to win their races. It's not the competitive edge they lack, but the ruthlessness to win at any cost. Dark Sister knows some very underhanded methods of sabotaging the opposition, and uses them whenever the chance arises.

DOMINATRIX

How does she do it? Dark Sister whips her team into shape with physical and verbal abuse, and cajoles them with salacious promises. Once she has captured the driver's attention, he (and it usually is a he) is invariably a winner, but at a price. Although she is more an antihero, she always leads her driver to the final goal.

Making your own character

Computer games have for years been the home of many strong and beautiful women, from the iconic Lara Croft to *Final Fantasy*'s bevy of anime heroines. Although they all finish up as 3D computer-generated models, they begin life as 2D pencil concepts. The main reason for this is speed, because drawings are much quicker to create and amend than constructing a 3D character. Pencils also allow for better stylization that can be later transferred to CGI. Despite huge advances in rendering for games, when designing characters for this medium it is better to err on the side of simplicity, especially with costumes—skintight clothes rather than flowing robes, for example.

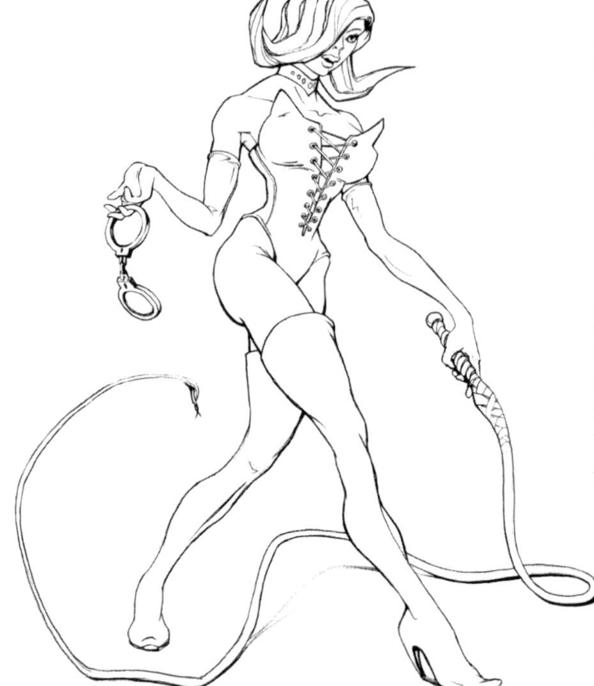

Illustrations by Mason Doran

◄ First step

Starting as a pencil sketch, the drawing was cleaned up with a soft (2B) pencil and scanned without inking. The contrast was adjusted to make the lines blacker.

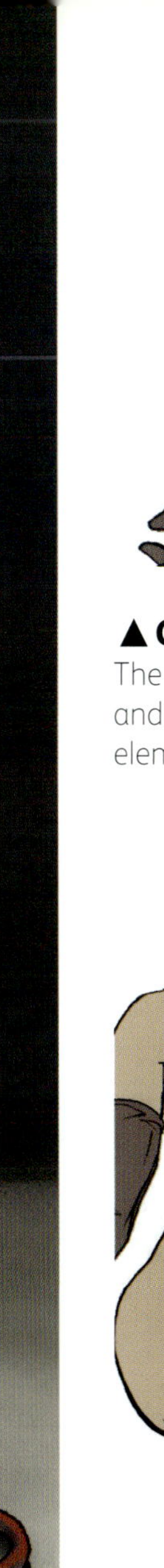

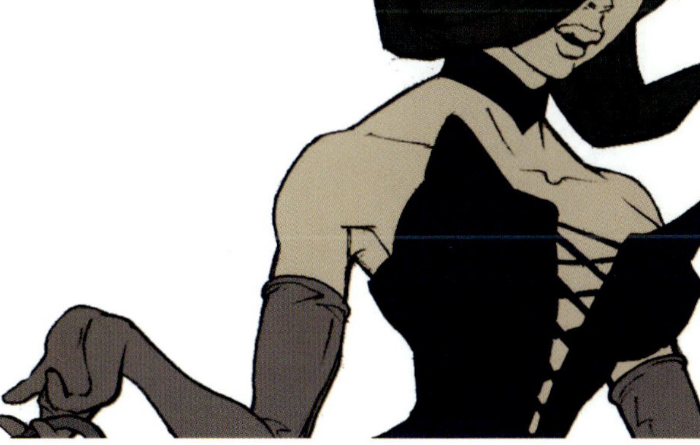

▲ Coloring

The scanned image was placed in Corel Painter, and flat, base-color fills were applied to the different elements, with each color on a separate layer.

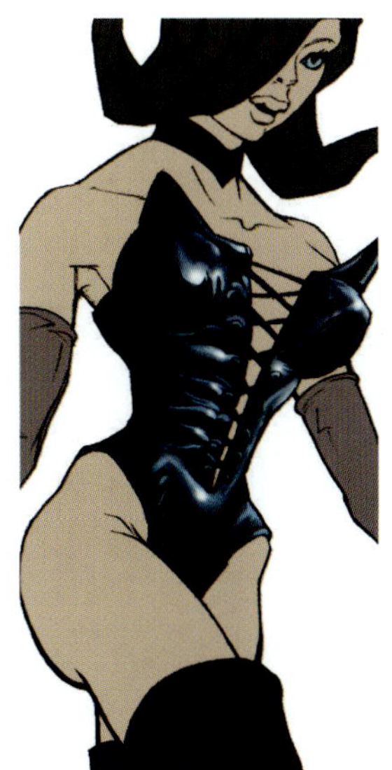

◄ Form and texture

Highlights and shadows were painted onto the clothing to give them form and texture. Painter's natural media emulation and a graphics tablet make color blending easy.

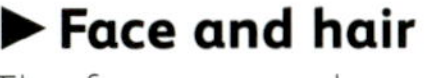

► Face and hair

The face was redone in Photoshop to make it look less cartoony, and the skin given more color and sheen before highlights were added to the hair.

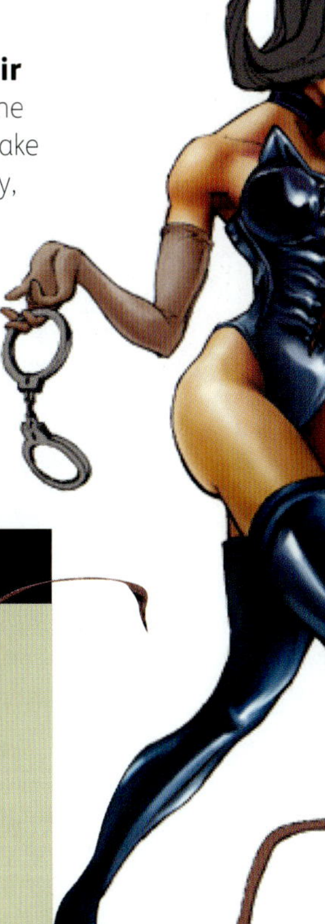

▼ Second skin

Skin tones were added and built up using Painter's easy-to-customize brushes. Correct textures can be achieved by mixing different media together in a way that is not usually possible, such as pastels and watercolors.

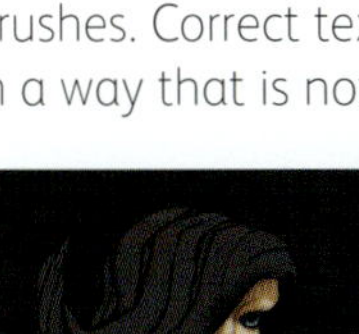

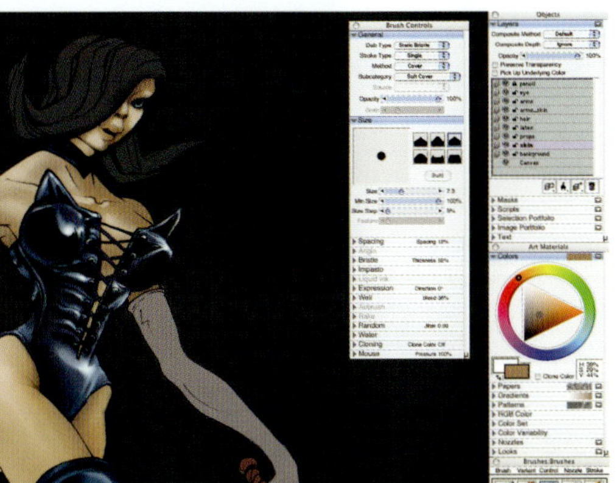

You will need

- Bristol board or drawing paper
- Pencil and eraser
- Macintosh or Windows PC
- Scanner
- Graphics tablet and stylus
- Corel Painter
- Adobe Photoshop

Who is she? Caitlan Maddox was a revolutionary, using words and pictures to undermine the political system, but never planned to be a fighter until her arm was crushed during a raid on the free press headquarters. **Where does she live?** A 21st-century metropolis that is rife with corruption. The whole infrastructure was decaying after fierce rioting, and before long, barricades surrounded the city's extremities. **What does she do?** Caitlan joins the periphery guard after losing her arm. Because the robotic arm that replaced her crushed one is no good for creative pursuits, she decides to put its strength to use in protecting the city's pacifists.

PEACEKEEPER

How does she do it? The strength of her arm and the firepower of her weapon, a mind-controlled Smart Gun that has ammunition that will target only those designated, are more than enough to stop anybody.

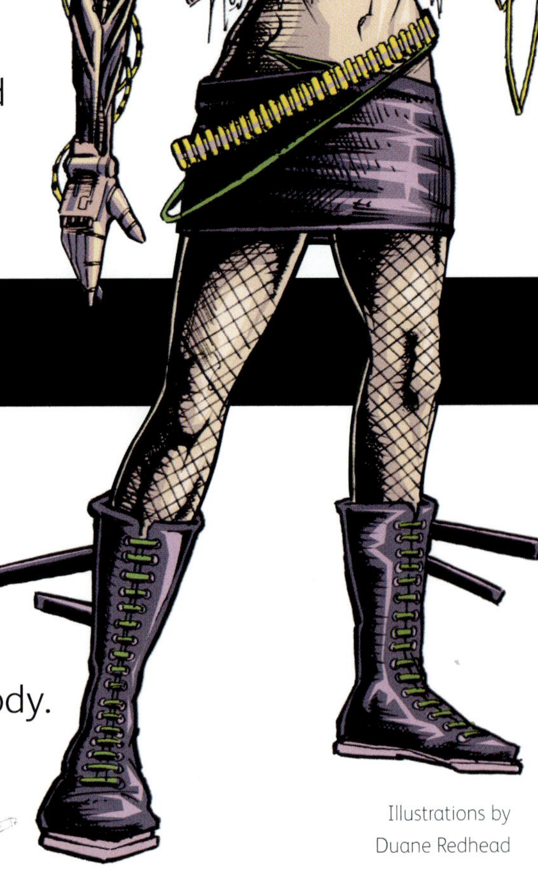
Illustrations by
Duane Redhead

Making your own character

Typically, the two most difficult elements to draw convincingly are hands and cloth. One of the quickest ways for a commissioning editor to judge an artist's ability is to look at how they draw these elements, particularly hands.

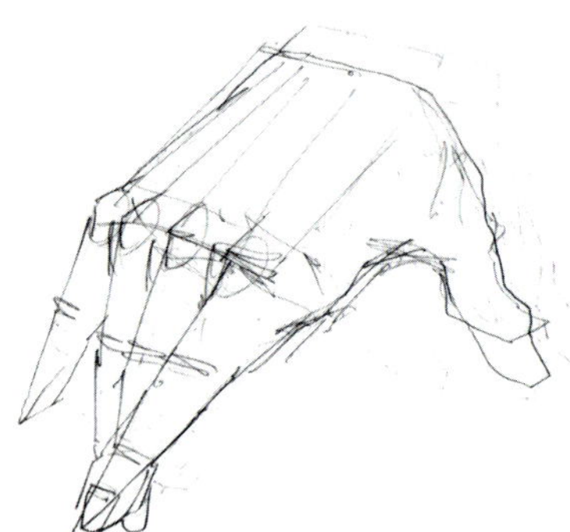

◄ Hand sketch
Start with a simplified sketch of a hand, with some anatomical guides for joints and other bones. Study anatomy books to understand how these work. Start adding details and shading.

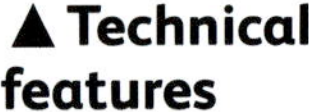

▲ Technical features
Add gears, hinges, and other engineering devices. Working from technical reference material will help you create something that looks functional.

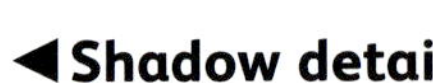

◄ Shadow detail
Finally, tidy up the drawing in ink and add the shadow detail, ready for coloring, or simply leave it as a monotone study for reference.

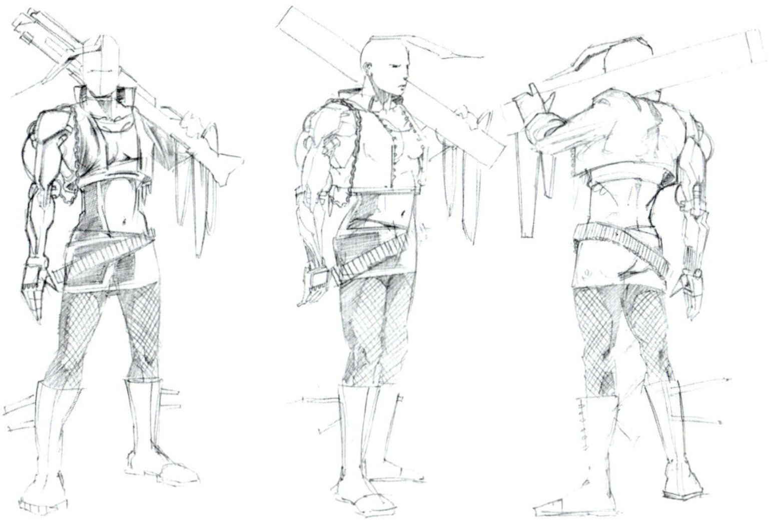

▶ Different views
These initial sketches establish anatomical proportions and a simplified, general design for the character. The final concept is clearly evident and ready for more detail to be added.

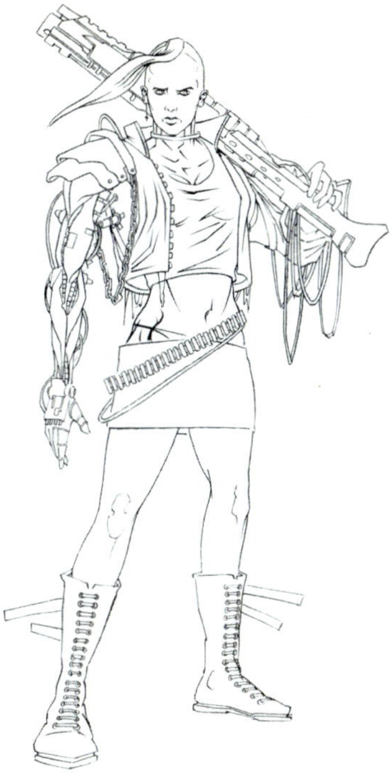

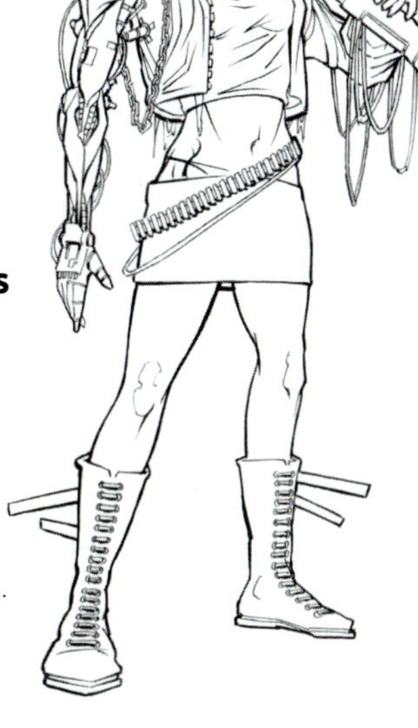

◀ Finished pencil drawing
The finished pencil drawing still shows some of the previous sketch work, but has all the details and shading in place, ready to be inked.

▶ Finishing the ink outlines
With a wider pen, go over the outer extremities and any other edges, such as the jacket, that will benefit from enhancement.

▲ Initial ink outlines
At the first stage of inking, trace over the pencil lines with a fine pen. Use steady, single strokes without pausing on a line. At this point, just concentrate on the outlines, leaving the shading until last.

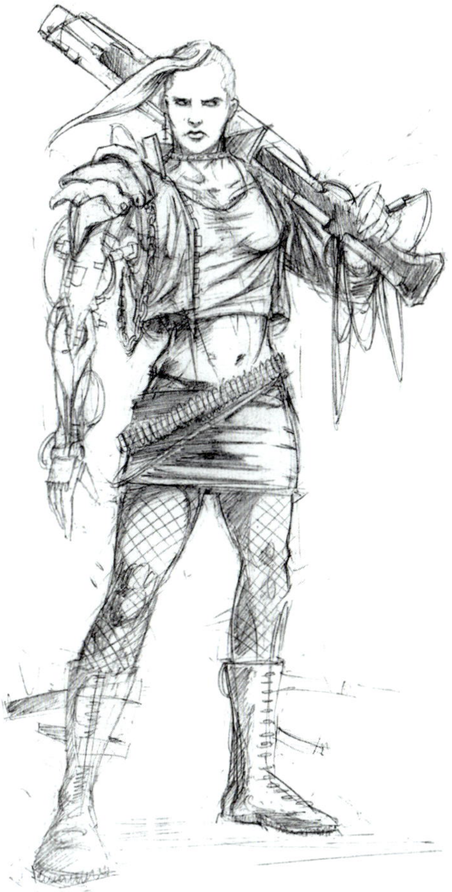

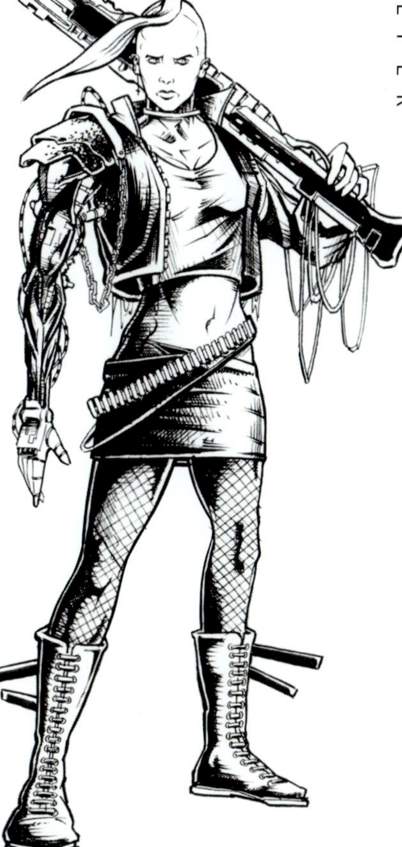

▶ Depth and texture
Once the ink outline is finished, you can start adding depth and texture with shading, to match the original pencil drawing. Try to keep the solid shadows as black as possible. Any minor tonal differences will disappear when the image is scanned for coloring, but it is still good practice to keep the blacks black. Hatching and stippling are good ways to add halftones. Ideally, the final inked image should be effective as it is, before any color is applied to the drawing in Photoshop.

You will need

- Bristol board or drawing paper
- Pencil and eraser
- Black marker pens with various tips
- Macintosh or Windows PC
- Scanner
- Graphics tablet and stylus
- Adobe Photoshop

Who is she? Vira is an enigma. She has erased her personal history so that she can move undetected through the world. She is an impeccable warrior who knows death may touch her at any moment, leaving her no time for fears or regrets. **What does she wear?** With the huge climatic changes brought about by the petro-chemical wars, she does not need many clothes. What little she does wear is mostly made from leather, for its durability. The clothes also have to give protection. The markings on her skin are from an encounter with an unknown entity that also left her with heightened awareness. **What does she do?** Vira battles against forces both manifest and unmanifest. Her goal is the liberation that comes from overcoming the unknown and the unknowable. She usually travels alone, although she belongs to a party of warriors under the watchful eye of their mentor, Nagual. She has also been delegated the task of forming her own warrior group to share the knowledge of liberation.

FREEDOM FIGHTER

Illustrations by Chris Patmore

How does she do it? There are no rules. Every situation requires a different solution. Spontaneity and experience are her weapons. The Pravana Gun she carries can be used to neutralize malevolent forces, but she prefers to avoid them altogether.

Making your own character

Creating an image using Poser is much the same as doing it photographically, but without the glamour or expense of traveling to an exotic location. It still requires finding the right model, getting some clothes, applying makeup and hairstyling, choosing props, and setting the location and lighting.

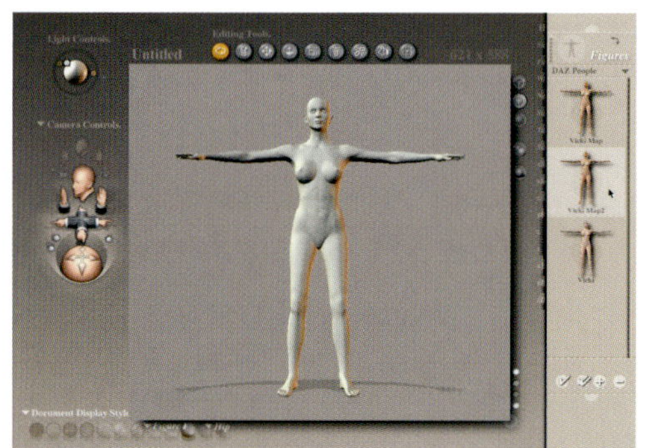

◄ Choosing a model
Begin by replacing the default Poser character with your female model from the Figures palette (in this example, Victoria 1). Click on the single tick to substitute the new figure for the old one.

You will need

- **Macintosh or Windows PC**
- **Curious Labs Poser**
- **DAZ's Victoria**
- **Clothes, props, backgrounds, etc.**

► Wardrobe
Select an item of clothing (usually found in a submenu of the Figures palette) and click on the double tick to bring it in as a separate model. Select Conform To from the Figure menu to attach the item to the figure so that they move together.

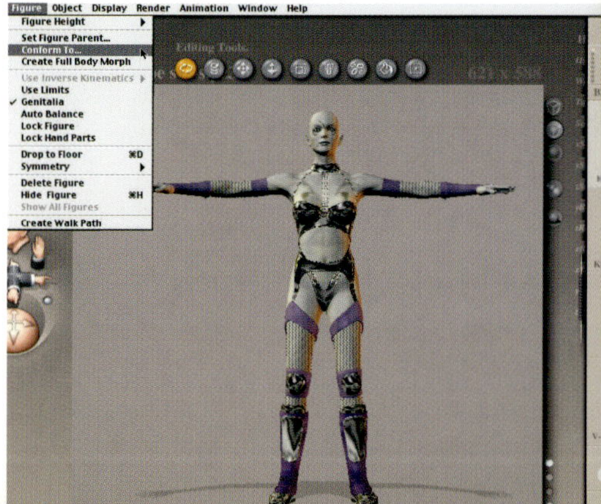

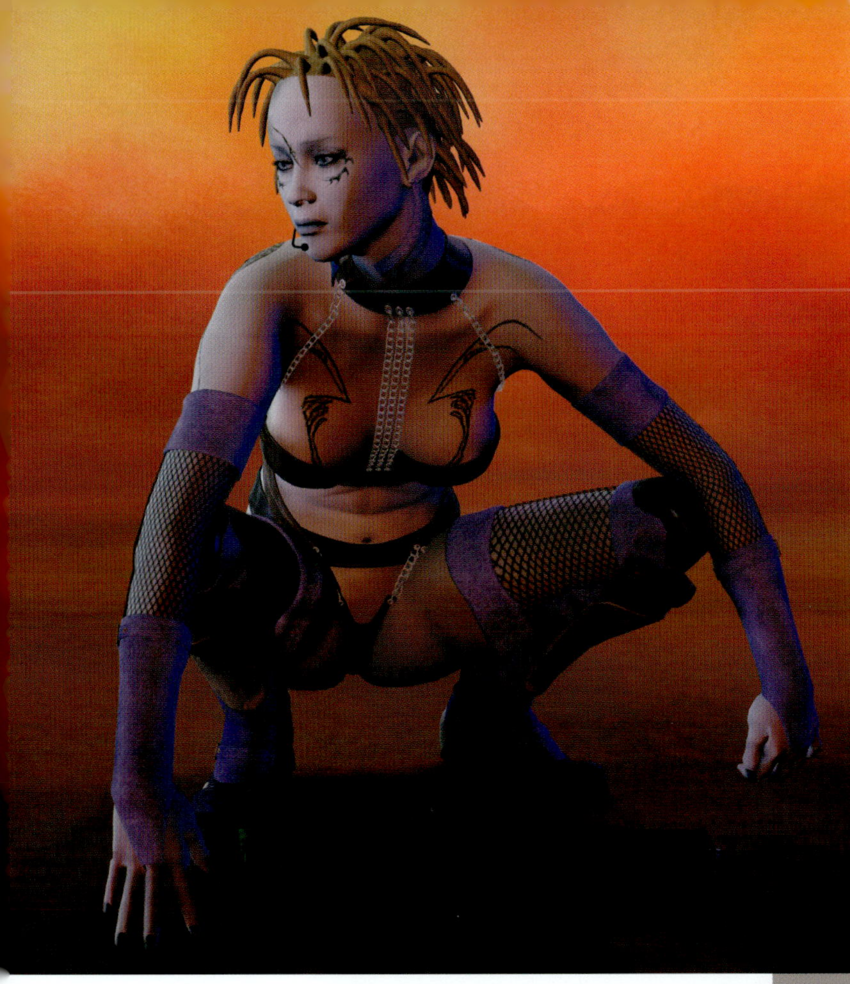

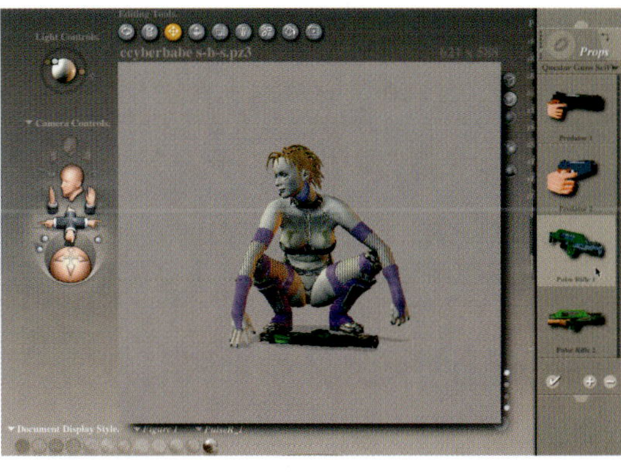

▲ Adding props

Props, such as the gun, are independent items that can be placed and manipulated within the scene.

▶ Hair and pose

Hair is added from the Hair palette and a pose is chosen from the Poses palette. Using a prepared pose will make your initial work much quicker, not to mention anatomically correct.

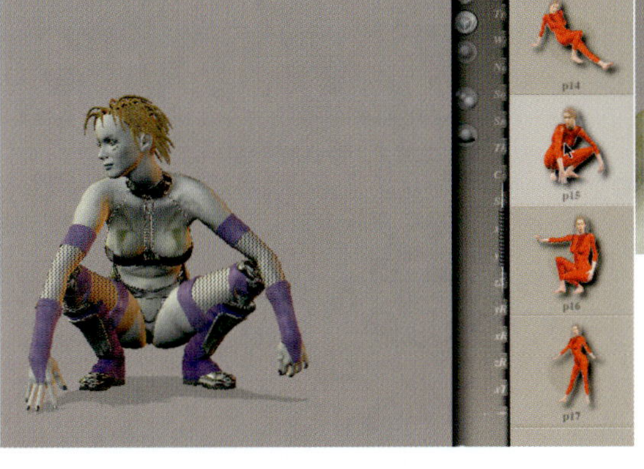

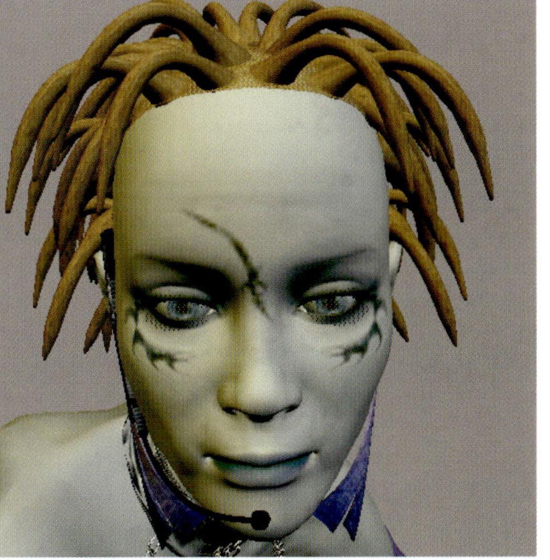

▲ Perfecting the face

One of the most important parts of the character is her face. Poser gives incredible control to change everything from ethnicity to expression.

◀ Backgrounds

Backgrounds can be added as either figures or props, depending on how they are created, and can range from full 3D objects to photographs.

▼ Lighting and camera angles

Preset lighting is used for this picture. Experimenting with your own lighting effects is time-consuming, but can produce interesting results. Experimenting with camera angles and composition is the final step before rendering the image.

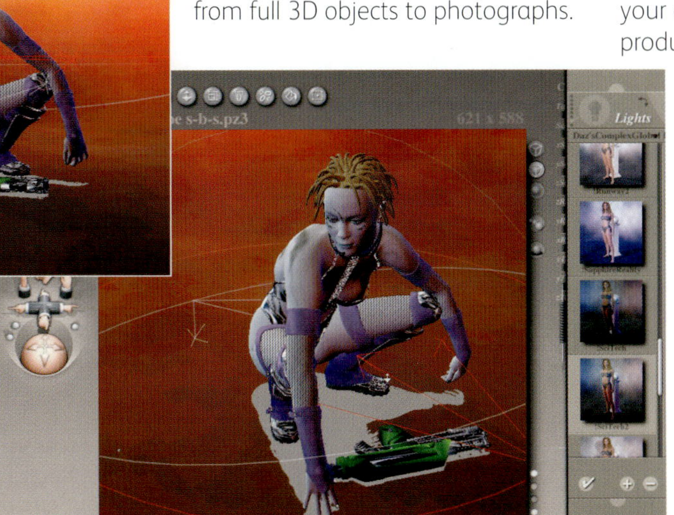

Check this out

www.daz3d.com Home of Victoria, the world's most popular female Poser figure.
www.renderosity.com Huge selection of Poser models for sale and for free, with an excellent gallery.

Who is she? Octavia is the code name for Agent 8, a member of the government's cloned assassin program. Agents are linked to HQ through remote telepathic viewers that wipe the agents' memories after a mission and activate a self-destruct command, causing the agents to be recloned. However, Octavia's self-destruct command failed, leaving her without memories and on the run. **What does she wear?** A standard-issue uniform consisting of a Smart Jacket and Impact Boots—not the most discreet outfit for a covert operation, but practical. **What does she do?** Agent 8 was created as a one-hit killer and assassin. Since the self-destruct program failed, she has been on the run from the authorities.

KILLER CLONE

How does she do it? Octavia, like the other assassins, is powered by an alien macro-virus, enabling her to create weapons from nanite-clusters exuded through the skin.

Making your own character

If you are writing a story for a comic book series, you need to prepare all the possible aspects of the character, from personality traits and history to different props and costumes. Some things, like history, can be written, but costumes and color schemes need to be explored visually.

You will need

- Bristol board or drawing paper
- Pencil and eraser
- Black marker pens with various tips
- Macintosh or Windows PC
- Scanner
- Graphics tablet and stylus
- Adobe Photoshop

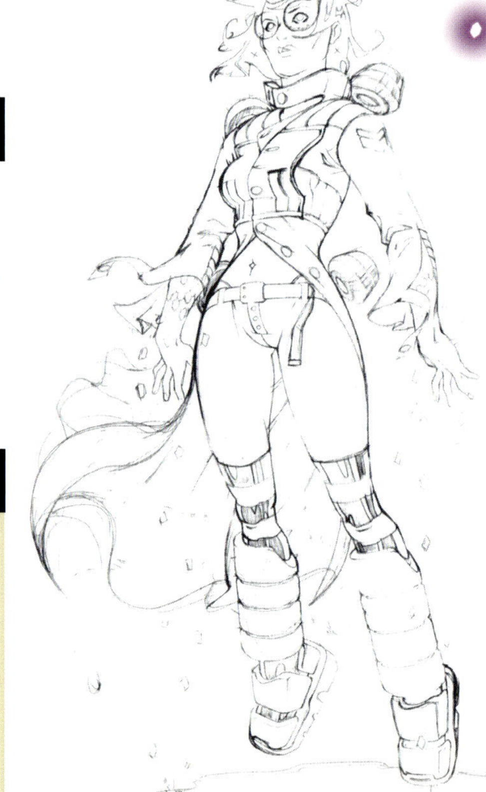

Illustrations by Cosmo White

◄ Pencil drawings
Producing detailed pencil drawings is very important for comic book artists. If you intend to do your own inking, you can use single-width pencil lines and add varying line weight as you ink. It is a good idea to develop good working practices as soon as possible, and a full range of skills, to increase your chances of getting professional work.

▼ Costumes

Designing functional costumes for your characters requires you to know all about their personalities, histories, and the actions they have to perform.

► Helmet

The helmet is used as protection from gas and viral attacks. It also doubles as a crash helmet in combat situations, or in case there is ever a problem with the Impact Boots.

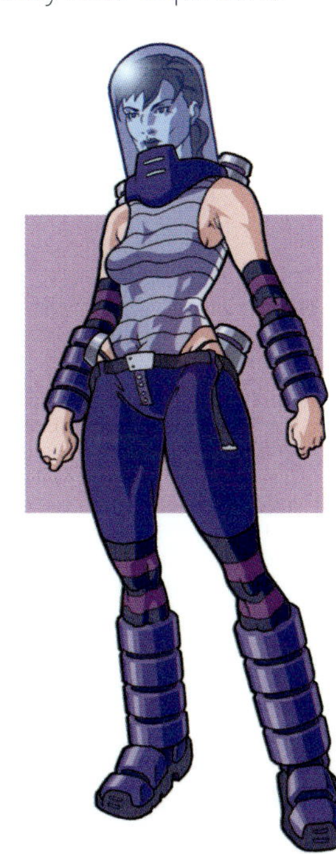

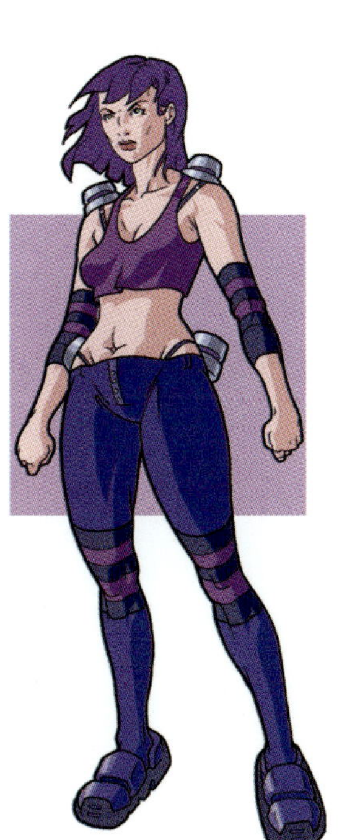

▲ Leggings

The striped leggings are not strictly uniform, but she likes to wear them because they remind her of a childhood she may have had in a recent life, before being cloned.

► Jacket

The Smart Jacket is made of a fabric impregnated with nanites, allowing it to shorten or lengthen itself as the situation requires.

▲ Boots

The military-issue Impact Boots are designed to absorb kinetic energy, allowing her to fall or jump from great heights and land safely.

► Ink drawings

Good inking is the secret to good finished art. Depending on the style of coloring to be employed, keeping areas of solid black to a minimum is advisable. When scanning your ink drawing, do so at a resolution of at least 600 dpi, then convert it to your preferred color mode (RGB or CMYK).

▼ Battery cells

The battery cells on her shoulders and hips are for recharging the nanites.

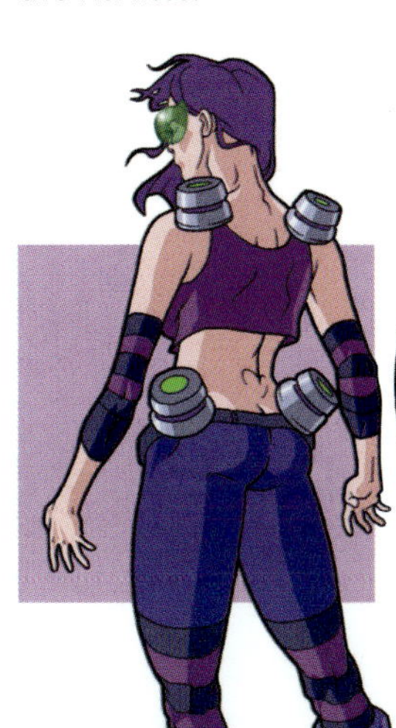

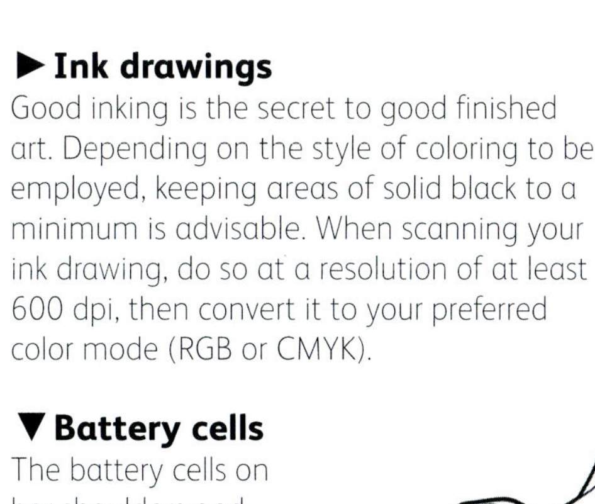

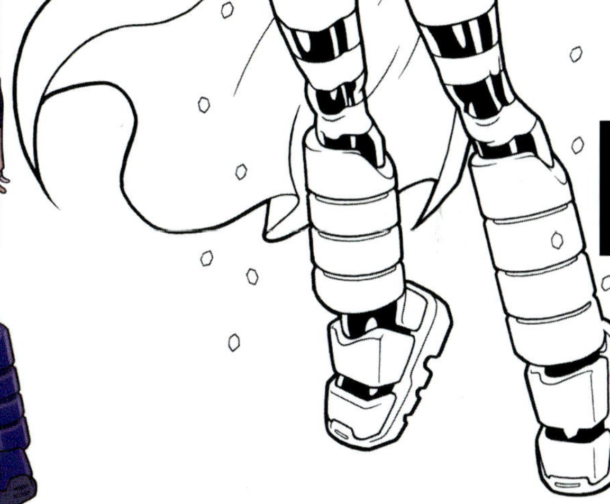

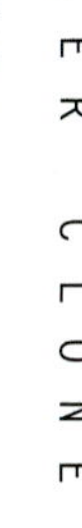

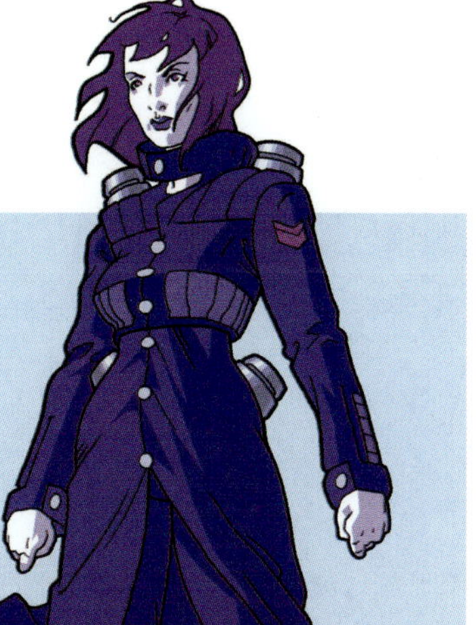

Who is she? Ayindree Callista lives in a future world of two disparate societies: the affluent and the poor. Ayin lived in the cloistered world of the affluent, with a doting husband who loved her for her old-fashioned feminine values. All law-abiding citizens have ID microchips implanted under their skin, supposedly for their protection, but also to identify potential candidates for a secret law enforcement task force. Ayindree was a perfect match. She was kidnapped and trained, and her records were deleted. **What does she wear?** Ayin's uniform is a high-mobility, sound-absorbing, heat-isolating, and light-responsive suit that also features a high-pressure air system to absorb the impact of jumps from buildings or drop-ships. Other features include night-vision goggles and sensors that extend peripheral vision to 360 degrees.

Rebel Assassin

What does she do? Once the training/indoctrination was completed, Ayin became a field operative who believed it was her moral right to kill insurgents or anyone who questioned the government's social policies, even if they were children. Despite her programming, she started having doubts about what she was doing, which reached crisis point when she fell in love with the man marked as her next target.

How does she do it? Her high-tech suit has miniature speakers that emit negative soundwaves that are calculated to balance any noise made by an agent's movements. Quick-assembly weapons and communications devices are also integrated into the suit.

Making your own character

When creating science-fiction characters, it is important to pay attention to the science part as much as the fiction. Whether it is physics, chemistry, or biology, your creations have to abide by the rules of nature. Even if you throw in chaos theories, everything in your story has to have a certain scientific logic to it. Thanks to the Internet, you can easily access research information on anything from mind control to weapons construction to acoustics. Use this to help give your stories authenticity.

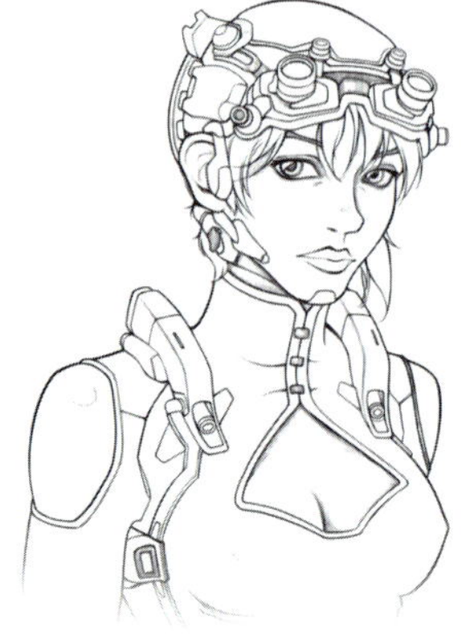

◀ Fluctuating weight

Different inking tools produce different results. Technical pens are ideal for creating consistently even lines of a specific weight, but if you want something more variable, ink and a fine brush are your best choice. Varying the pressure on the brush during a stroke will produce lines that can start thin, thicken where emphasis is needed, and become thin again. Working with brushes requires a lot of practice to avoid inconsistent linework, smudges, and over- or under-inking, but it is well worth the effort.

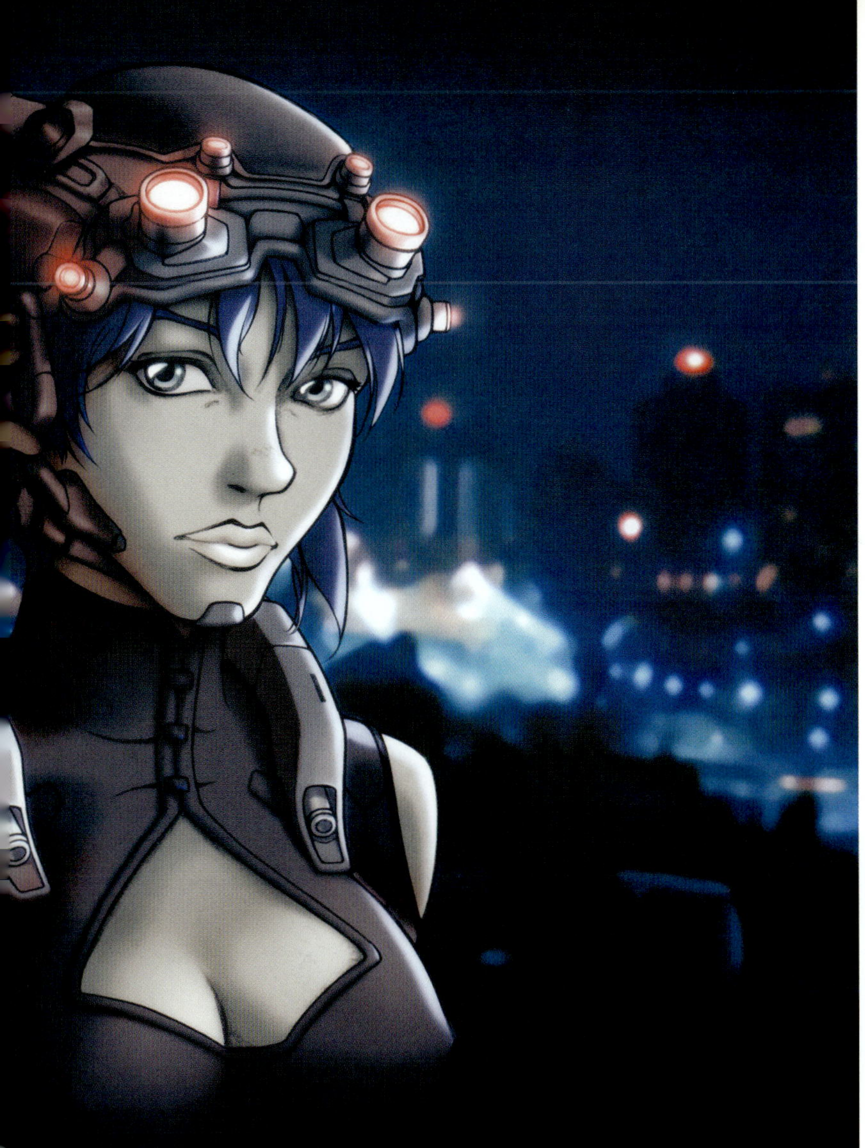

Illustrations by Simon Valderrama

REBEL ASSASSIN

▶ Rough around the edges

It is important to achieve an outline you are happy with, but this can result in thick, overdrawn pencil lines. However, the inking process will resolve any discrepancies.

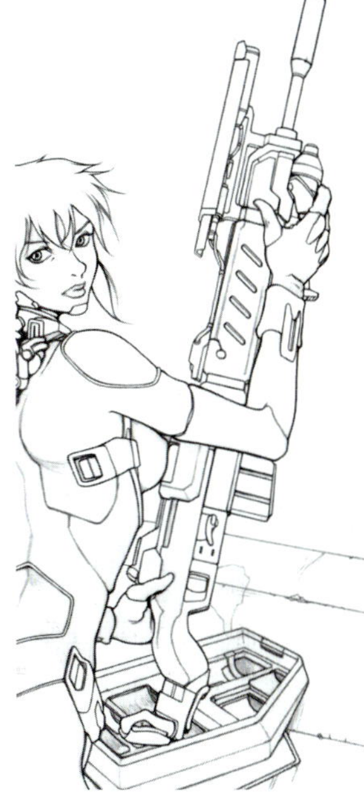

◀ Clean lines

Ink lines give the drawing its defined form for scanning and final coloring. Some of the lines can be left as pencil to give softer areas of tone and shade when the image is colored.

▼ Rubber and bullets

To achieve the sheen on the costume and equipment, areas were masked off and colored using blending and airbrush tools along with texture and blur filters in Photoshop. An understanding of how light works on various surfaces will add that important touch of realism. Poser or DAZ Studio are very useful for references.

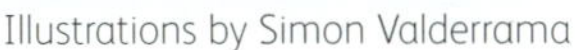

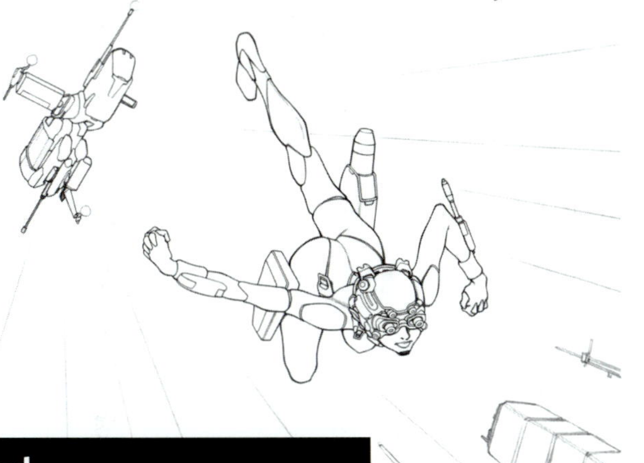

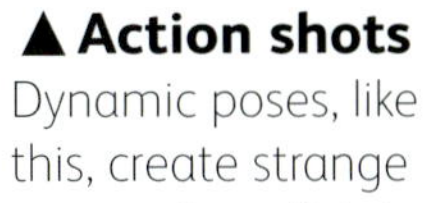

You will need

- Bristol board or drawing paper
- Pencil and eraser
- Rapidograph or similar technical pen
- Brush and ink
- Macintosh or Windows PC
- Scanner
- Graphics tablet and stylus
- Adobe Photoshop
- Curious Labs Poser or DAZ Studio for reference

▲ Action shots

Dynamic poses, like this, create strange perspectives. It is in situations like this that Poser becomes a valuable tool, and much easier to control than live references.

Who is she? Synchronicity lives in a London of the not-too-distant future. As was not uncommon for teenage girls of that time, she disappeared, believed runaway. Unusually, she returned after five years, unaged and with no recollection of where she had been. **What does she wear?** T-shirts, combat trousers, and boots are her favorites—those five missing years did nothing for her fashion sense. When it comes to clothes, her priorities are comfort and practicality—things she is not concerned with when it comes to hairstyles. **What does she do?** Synch feels like she is on a mission, but does not know what it is or whom it is for. Since her return, her life has been filled with coincidences and apparent distortions of time, which she feels impelled to follow.

KILLING TIME

How does she do it? Some people explain her "luck" by believing that she has control over time, but Synch feels that she is at the mercy of a much greater power that is controlling her destiny.

Illustrations by
Liz Powell

Making your own character

Not everybody uses Adobe Photoshop and, if you are short of cash, there is no reason why you should. There are plenty of shareware and low-cost applications more than capable of producing great artwork without putting a strain on your computer or your pocket. One of these is a program from Japan called openCanvas. It has its own quirks and idiosyncrasies that regular users of Photoshop might have difficulty adjusting to, but the results speak for themselves.

You will need

- **Windows PC**
- **Graphics tablet and stylus**
- **openCanvas3**

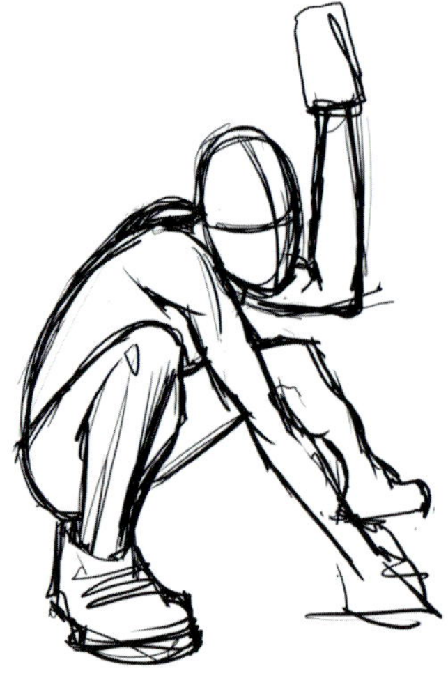

▲ Initial sketch

A basic pose with minimal detail was drawn directly into openCanvas. Using a graphics tablet and stylus is similar to using paper and pencil, but different enough to render a different style to your drawing.

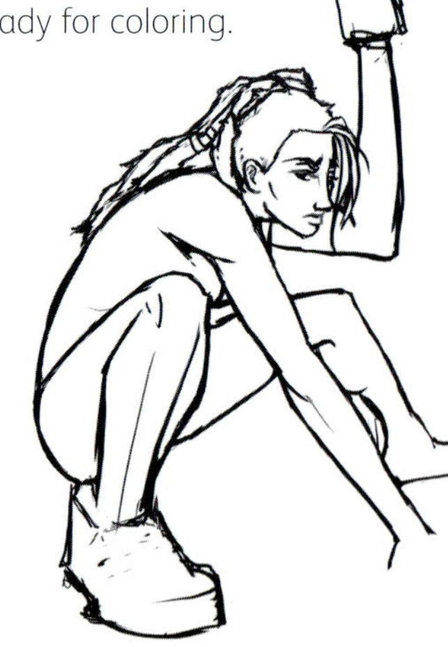

▼▶ Cleaning up

Working over the original outline, lines were added and removed until the desired character was ready for coloring.

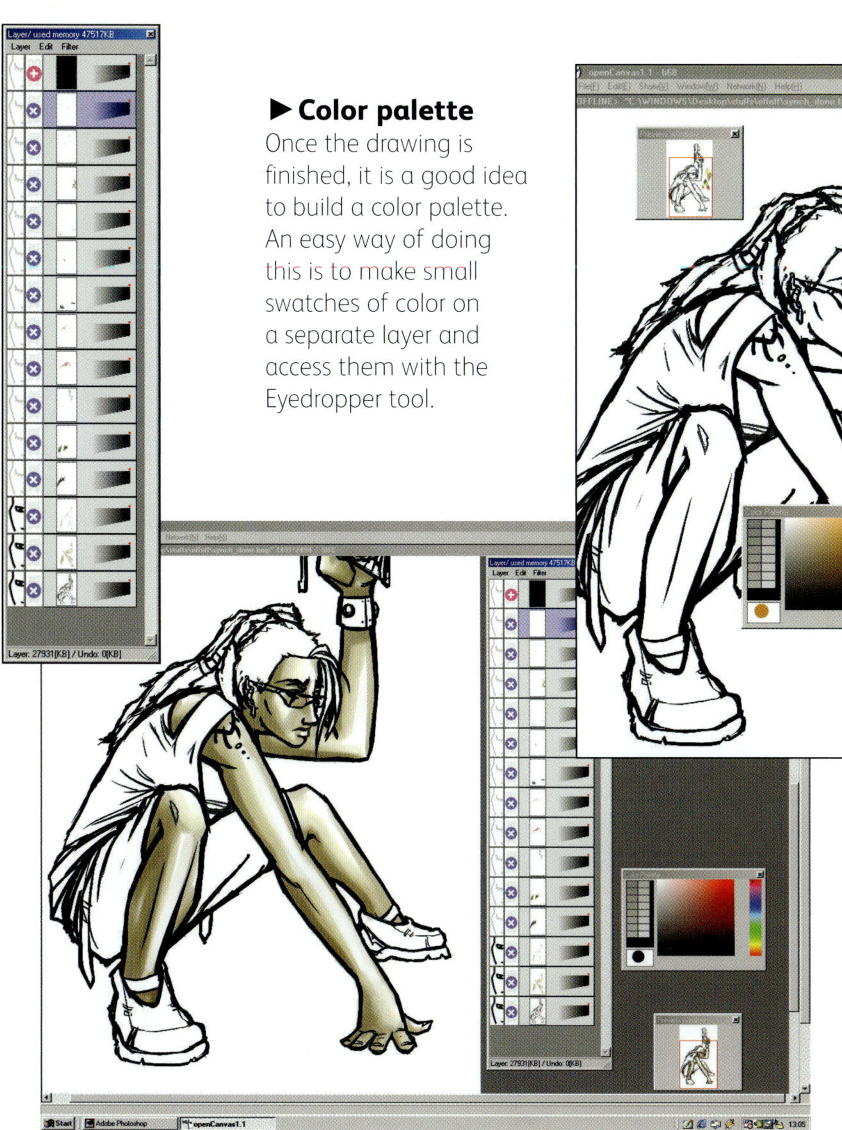

► Color palette

Once the drawing is finished, it is a good idea to build a color palette. An easy way of doing this is to make small swatches of color on a separate layer and access them with the Eyedropper tool.

◄ Laying down some skin

All of the coloring for this character was done with the Watercolor brush, with the transparency option switched on. As with real watercolor, layers of color were added to achieve subtle shading. A digital brush is a lot easier to control than a real one and has the advantage of Undo.

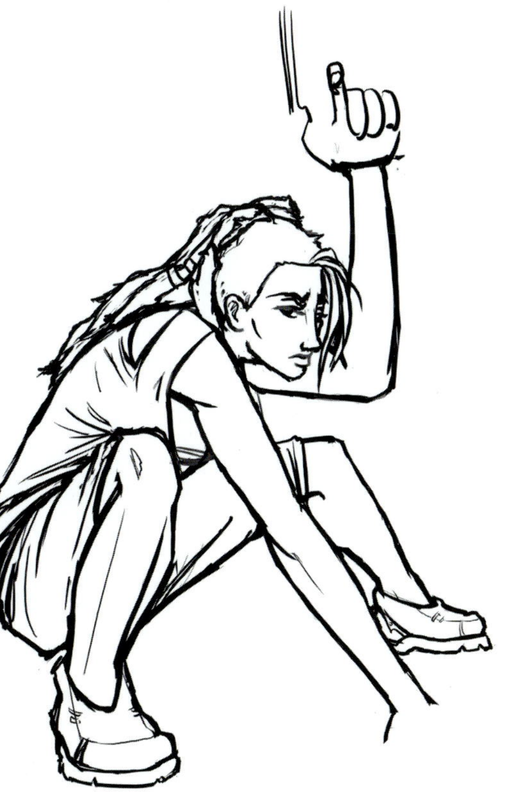

▼ Adding shades

Layers and transparency are particularly useful when it comes to coloring items such as the lenses of Synch's glasses.

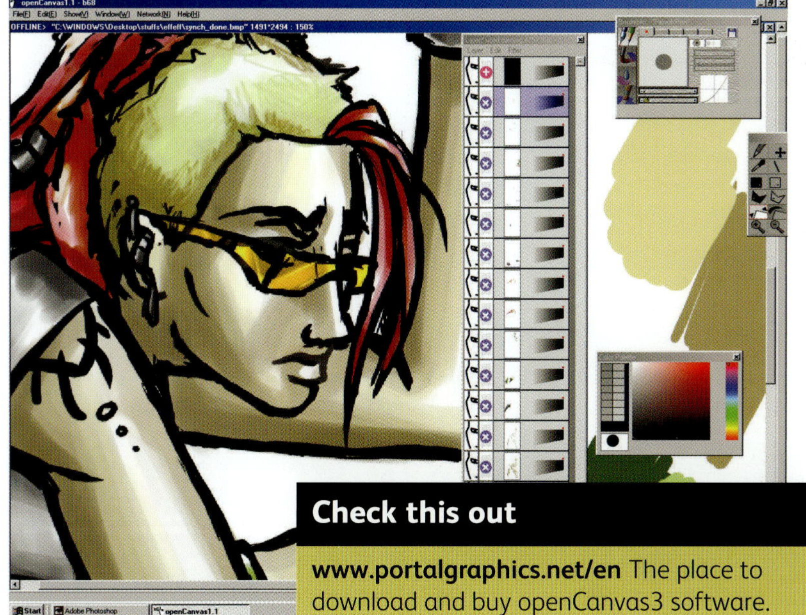

Who is she? Zahara is a member of ChronoCorps, the time-traveling police of Chronostratum, the four-dimensional stream of time. **What does she wear?** The uniform of the ChronoCorps, which is designed to enhance her powers of attraction. **What does she do?** Answering a distress beacon, Zahara uses a time portal to get to the Eden-like, prehistoric island of Mu. Here, she discovers that galactic merchants, called Skylords, have brought death and destruction to the island paradise. Having enslaved the local population (see page 74), the Skylords set about stripping the world of its natural resources. Zahara knows that the survival of the natives of Mu must be safeguarded, because they will evolve into the first human tribe. **How does she do it?** Zahara uses her powers of *l'amour* to forge alliances between the rebel factions of Mu, in order to restore power to its natives and re-establish the correct chronology that will ensure the evolution of humans.

VENUS OF TIME

Illustrations by Alessandro Scacchia, story by Ka Gunstone

Making your own character

The story of Zahara is exotic and psychedelic, filled with bright colors, strange creatures, and humor, all of which are reflected in the drawings. If you want to create your own fantasy/science-fiction characters and stories, use exaggerated palettes to add vibrancy to the art and sexy, impractical clothing to enhance the fun.

▶ Strike a pose

The ability to produce a properly proportioned sketch, using few lines and without any underlying structural guide, comes with lots of practice. Copying or tracing reference material, such as fashion magazines, will build up your confidence.

You will need

- Bristol board or drawing paper
- Pencil and eraser
- Black marker pens with various tips
- Macintosh or Windows PC
- Scanner
- Graphics tablet and stylus
- Adobe Photoshop

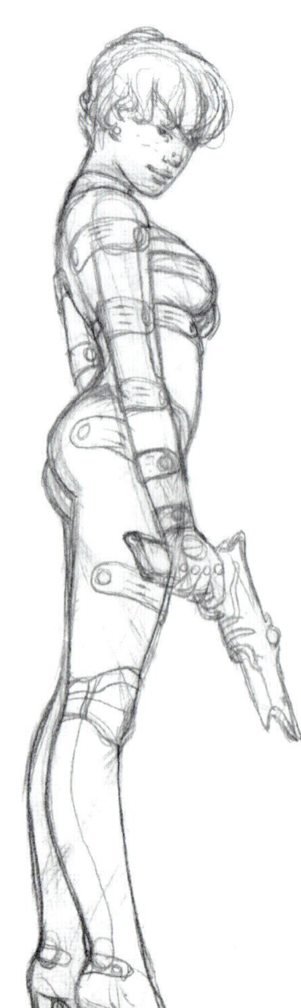

▶ Clean, consistent inking

Developing confident strokes during the pencil stage will reap benefits when it comes to inking. Single, flowing movements are needed to create clean, consistent lines. Although mistakes can be corrected with Wite-Out or similar products, the old adage of prevention is better than cure holds true in art as well.

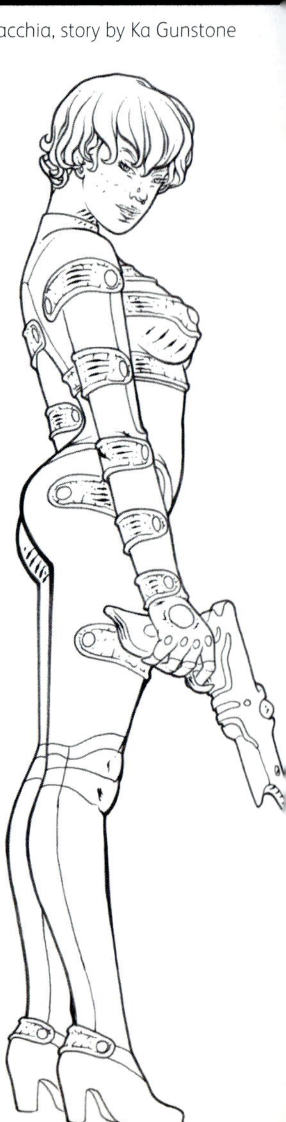

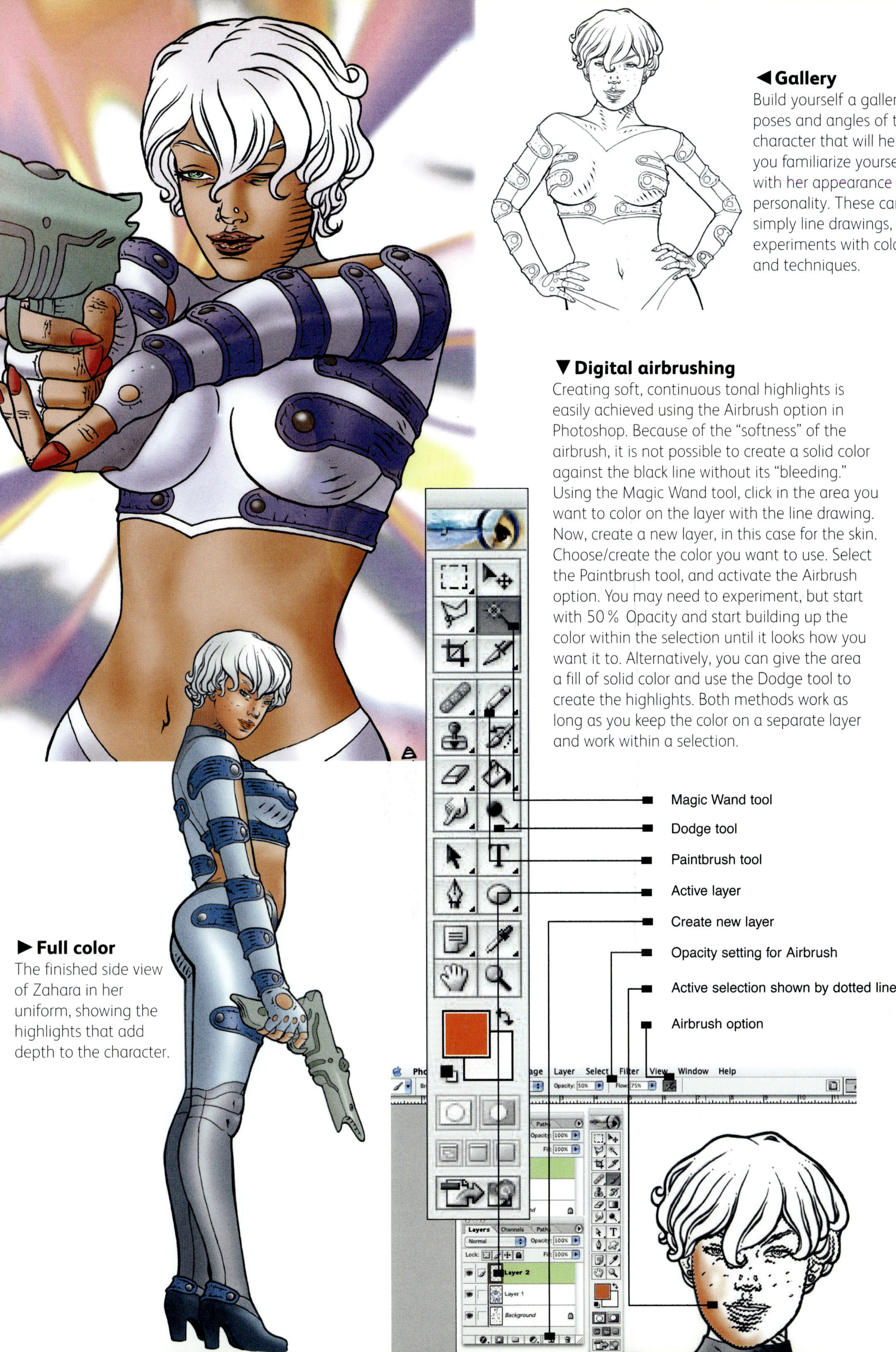

◀ Gallery

Build yourself a gallery of poses and angles of the character that will help you familiarize yourself with her appearance and personality. These can be simply line drawings, or experiments with colors and techniques.

▼ Digital airbrushing

Creating soft, continuous tonal highlights is easily achieved using the Airbrush option in Photoshop. Because of the "softness" of the airbrush, it is not possible to create a solid color against the black line without its "bleeding." Using the Magic Wand tool, click in the area you want to color on the layer with the line drawing. Now, create a new layer, in this case for the skin. Choose/create the color you want to use. Select the Paintbrush tool, and activate the Airbrush option. You may need to experiment, but start with 50 % Opacity and start building up the color within the selection until it looks how you want it to. Alternatively, you can give the area a fill of solid color and use the Dodge tool to create the highlights. Both methods work as long as you keep the color on a separate layer and work within a selection.

▶ Full color

The finished side view of Zahara in her uniform, showing the highlights that add depth to the character.

Who is she? Arundina was named by the human observers whose robotic probes made contact with her species. **What does she wear?** Clothing is not a concept these creatures are familiar with. In fact, the survival of the species relies on unfettered access to the hivelike structure attached to the torso, from which the females spawn up to a few hundred mothlike male offspring at a time. **What does she do?** Arundina was assigned to a team studying the probes sent by the human race. She developed the osmotic computer that translates human communication signals. This device can be seen as the metallic construction attached to her lower torso. **How does she do it?** Doing anything is a very difficult process. The females of her species have no eyes, so they depend on the males to relay visual information to them. This is a slow process, so they rely on their other senses of smell, touch, and hearing for survival.

ALIEN LIFEFORM

Illustrations by Ruben de Vela

Making your own character

There is a long tradition in science fiction, movies in particular, of making aliens humanoid. This is mostly because of the limitations of the costume departments, and not necessarily the writer's imagination. Very few people have had any encounters (real or imagined) with aliens, so there is not a lot of information available on their biology. Of the myriad creatures on our own planet, there are many weird and wonderful ones that could serve as a starting point for aliens, and they come complete with an existing ecological and biological system. Creating a believable biology is very important.

► Concept
This early version of Arundina is very similar in shape to the final one, although the "limbs" are less defined. The original male version (below right) was changed considerably for the final design (below left).

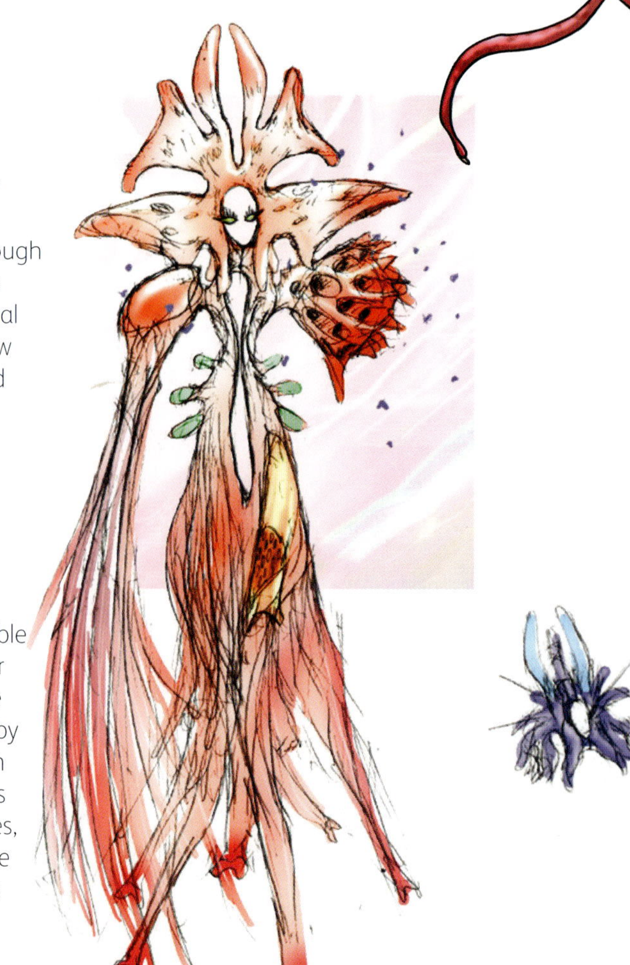

◄ Male
Having no discernible intelligence of their own, the males are directly controlled by the female through biochemical means to serve the females, in a relationship like that of worker ants and their queen.

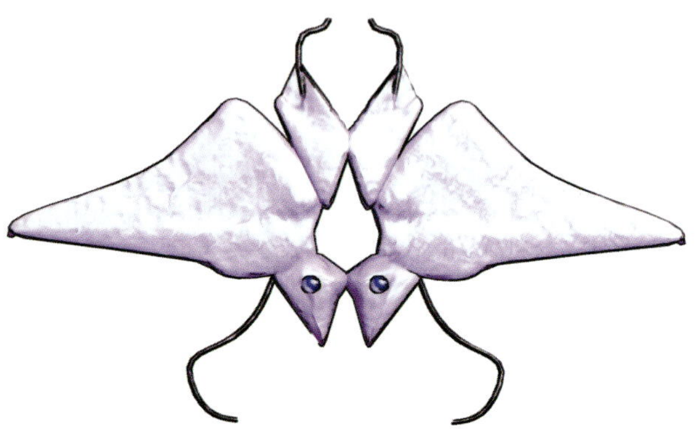

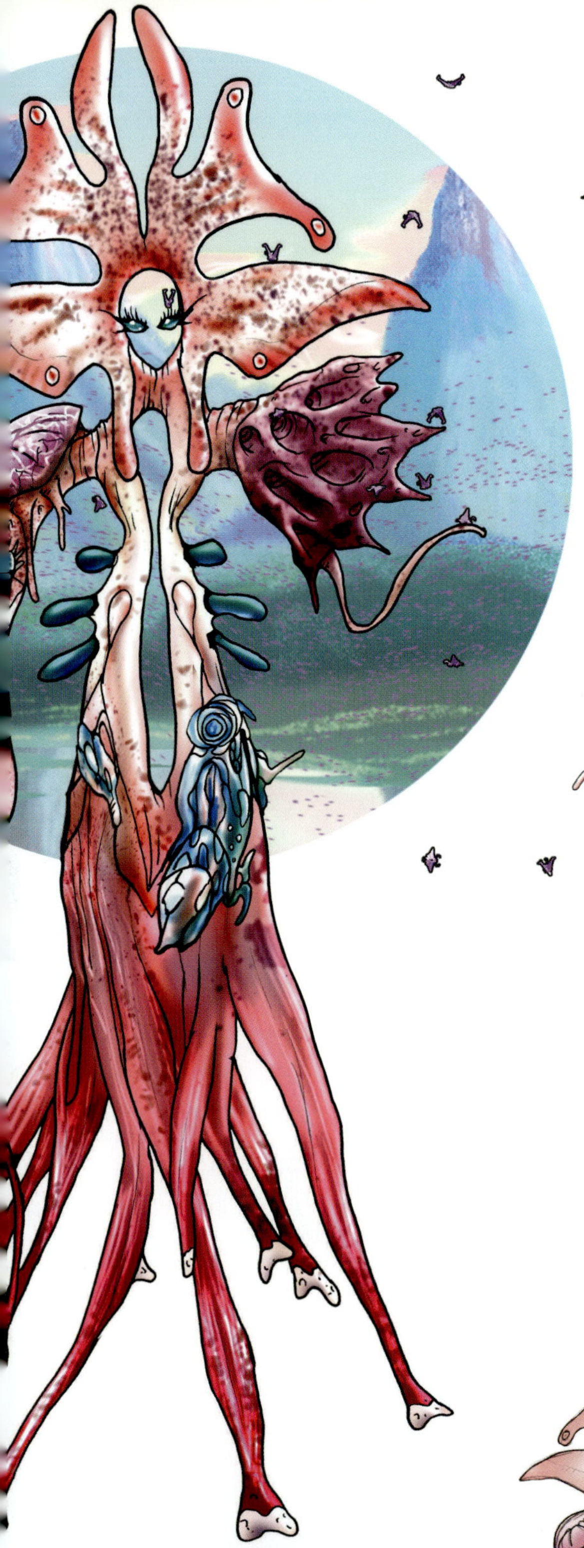

► Brain
A close-up detail of Arundina's brain. Although most of the species' energies are put into survival and procreation, they have phenomenal intelligence and inventiveness that belies their ungainly appearance. It was this intelligence that led Arundina to help develop the osmotic computers used to translate human speech.

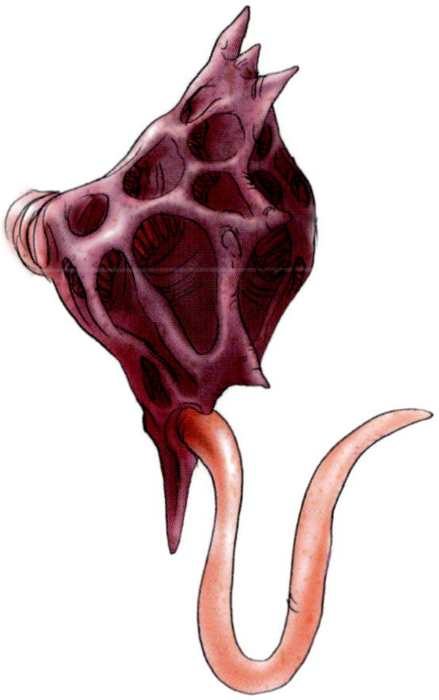

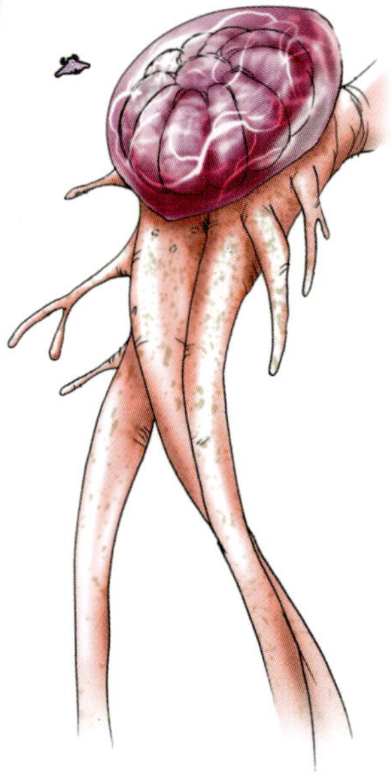

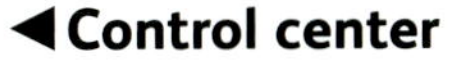

◄ Control center
This hivelike structure attached to the torso is where her species continually spawn up to a few hundred male offspring at a time. The females communicate with each other through the males, and can accept up to a dozen of each other's males in one go, which then take up residence in the hive structure. All the mobile male forms are controlled by the biochemical secretions from this "gland."

▼ Turnaround
The three different views of the plantlike creature give a clear look at her structure, with the narrow central picture being the front. These turnaround views are used by animators to establish physical characteristics that can be easily referenced. The eyelike structures in the central gap of the "head" are actually ears.

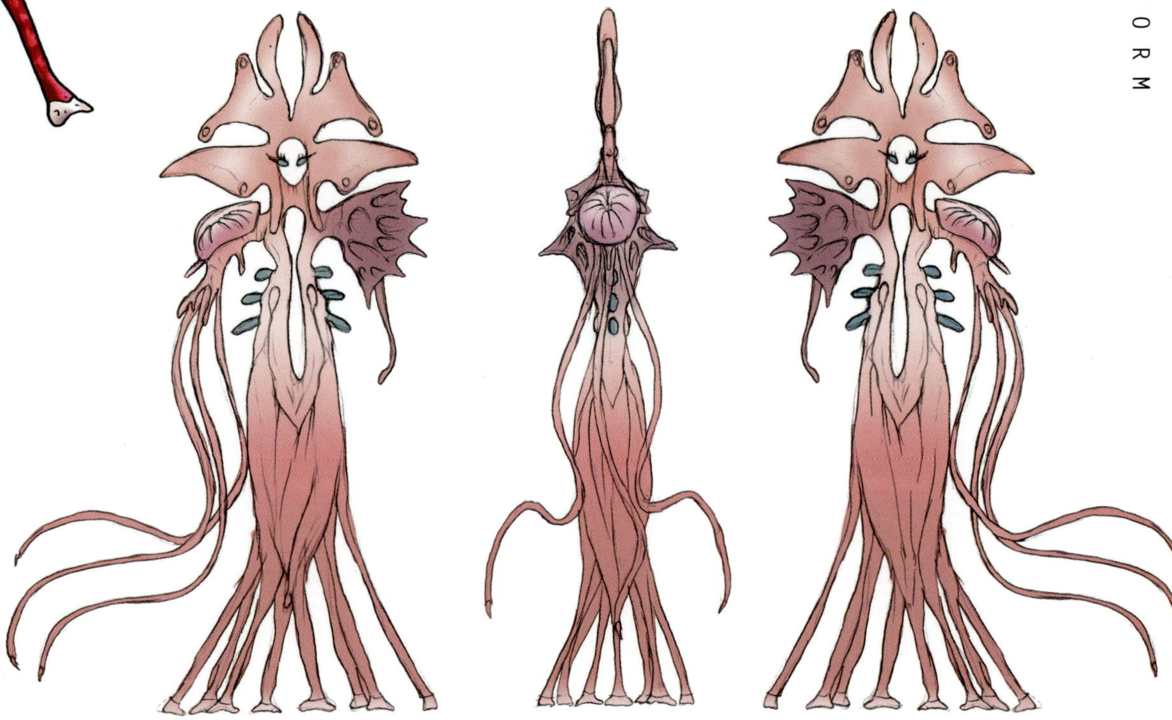

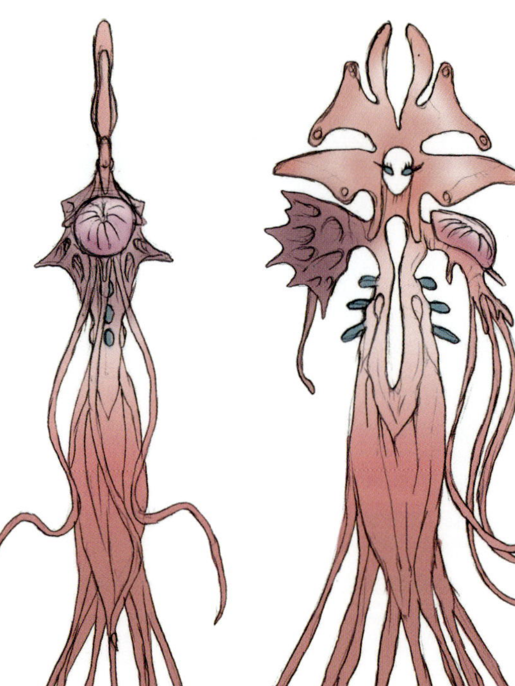

You will need

- Bristol board or drawing paper
- Pencil and eraser
- Black marker pens with various tips
- Macintosh or Windows PC
- Scanner
- Graphics tablet and stylus
- Adobe Photoshop

Who is she? Valentina was a member of the all-female Soviet cosmonaut squad, training with her namesake Valentina Tereshkova, the first woman in space. **What does she wear?** She wears an updated version of the Soviet standard-issue space suit and carries a pair of experimental Scalar pistols. **What happens to her?** She was launched in a sister Vostok craft, to attempt the first joint space walk with Tereshkova. Before the two spaceships could join up, Valentina's was sucked into the hyperspace eddy of a passing alien craft and she was transported to an uncharted corner of the universe. All knowledge of her existence and mission was denied by the Soviets.

COSMONAUT

Illustrations by Thor Goodall

What does she do? To survive in the hostile alien environment, Valentina's hair has mutated into thick strands that can absorb from the cosmos all the vital elements her body needs to survive. This new diet has created a lithe body that does not age. Her only protection are the Scalar pistols.

Making your own character

Science fiction is fiction with a scientific basis. For it to work, it has to have a certain amount of verifiable factual information. In this story outline, some of the facts are historically correct, such as keeping the names of the women in Tereshkova's training squad a secret. The Soviets allegedly also did research into the possibilities of scalar weapons. And as for the existence of aliens…

▶ Foundation sketches

Clear ideas and lots of practice will help you create sketches that can be adapted for the finished images. A very quick foundation can be laid down with a few faint lines, with the rest of the sketch being done with a soft (B) lead pencil.

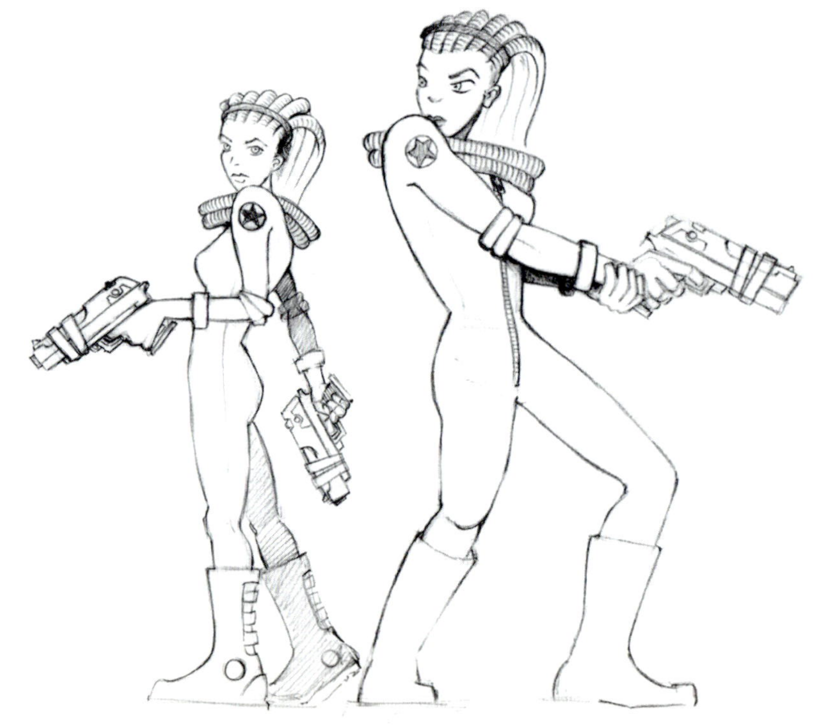

► Quick turnover

For animations, simple drawings like this work well. The bold, flat colors, minimal detail, and strong black outlines are easy to reproduce in the volume needed for cartoons. Some tonal work can be added for shading, using Photoshop's Airbrush tool.

▼ Strong lines

Strong black lines such as these are easy to achieve in Photoshop using the Pencil tool. Create separate layers for the sketch, for inking, and for the color. If your drawing has closed paths, you can use the Paint Bucket tool to fill an area with a chosen color. The open paths shown here, where the black lines do not meet, require either making a selection with the Lasso or Pen tool and filling that area, or carefully using the Brush tool, which will slow down the process.

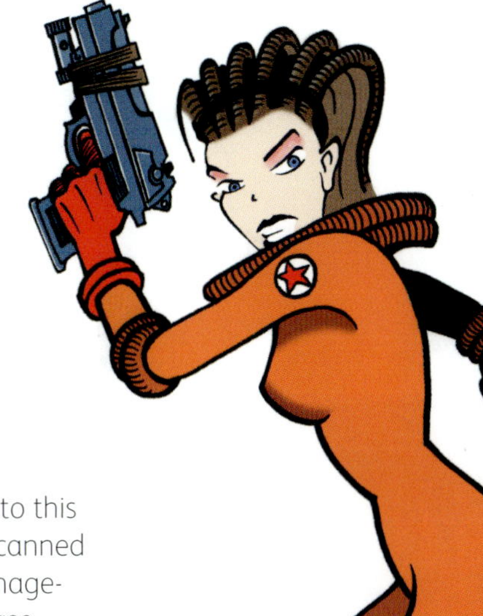

◄ Scanning

When a sketch is finished to this degree, it can simply be scanned and imported into your image-editing software, in this case Photoshop, for inking and coloring.

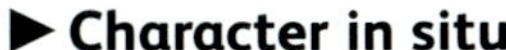

► Character in situ

In situ pictures like this can be used for publicizing your comic or animation. It should tell the viewer the subject and the style of the finished project.

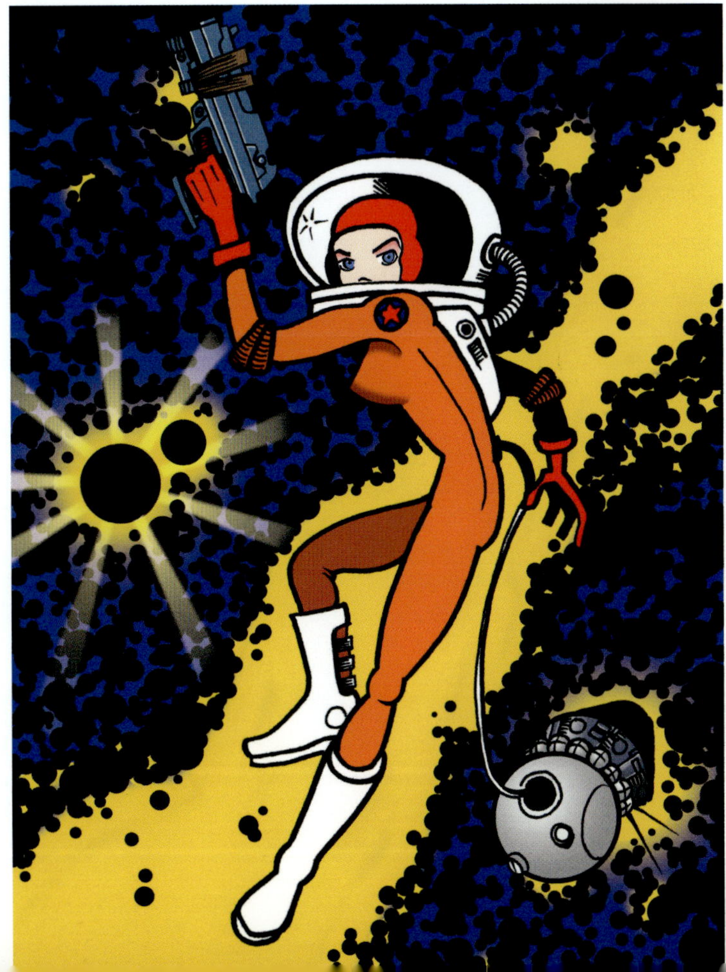

You will need

- Bristol board or drawing paper
- Pencil and eraser
- Black marker pens with various tips
- Macintosh or Windows PC
- Scanner
- Graphics tablet and stylus
- Adobe Photoshop

Who is she? Jaguarwoman is one of the indigenous inhabitants of Mu, an Eden-like, prehistoric island from another time dimension. The island has been invaded by galactic merchants called Skylords, who have enslaved the local population and taken their monarch hostage. **What does she wear?** Being feral in nature, Jaguarwoman's need for clothing is minimal. With the arrival of the Skylords, the females of her tribe began to wear leather pants, not only to protect their modesty but also to prevent the merchant invaders from forcing cross-species breeding on them. **What does she do?** Having evaded capture at the hands of the Skylords, Jaguarwoman tries to unite the island's remaining free inhabitants in rebellion against the invaders. However, this proves to be a difficult task because of past differences.

Wild Thing

How does she do it? She sends out a distress beacon, which is traced by Zahara, a member of the ChronoCorps time-traveling police (see page 68). Teaming up with Zahara, whose powers of *l'amour* are able to unify the rebel factions, Jaguarwoman is able to help restore natural order to Mu.

Illustrations by
Alessandro Scacchia,
story by Ka Gunstone

Making your own character

Creating alien and/or, in this case, cross-species characters requires research into biology, not only into physical appearances but also behavior. Which physical attributes do you include and how should they be integrated? Should the behavior be more animal or more human? Apart from studying biology, also look at existing mythological beasts—for example, centaurs (horse/human), mermaids (human/fish), Pan (human/goat), Narashima (human/lion)—for further inspiration.

▼ Human to animal

Study reference material of existing cross-species creatures such as centaurs to see how other artists have approached this type of character, then try your own experiments in coss-breeding.

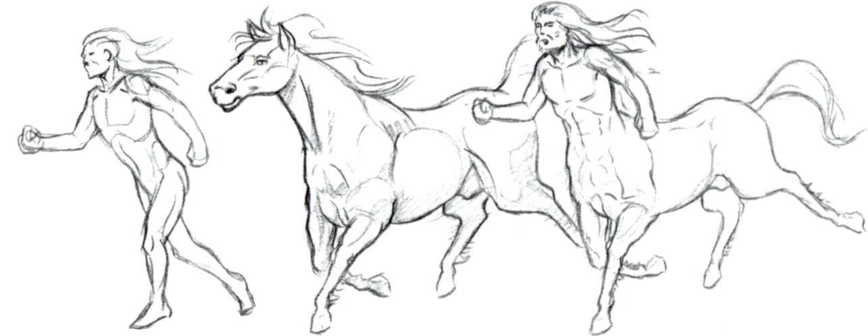

▶ Establishing the concept

The concept is clearly established at the pencil stage. The low angle of view makes the character appear more dominating, although with no comparable reference points it is not possible to gauge the character's actual size.

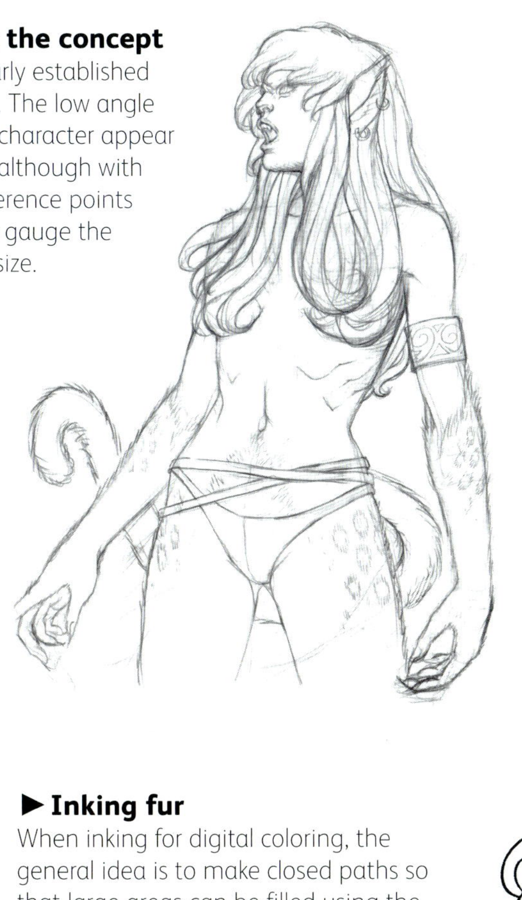

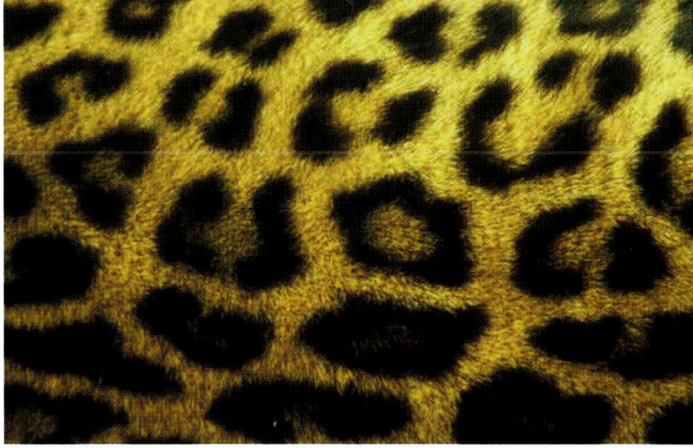

▲ Collecting reference

Reference photos of animal skins and fur will help you get the right markings, in this case those of a jaguar. A visit to the zoo with a camera could supply a good source of material.

▶ Inking fur

When inking for digital coloring, the general idea is to make closed paths so that large areas can be filled using the Paint Bucket tool, without the color filling adjacent areas. To achieve a believable look for the fur, a ragged edge has to be created that will require careful coloring.

▶ Coloring fur

To create the fur effect in Photoshop, a very simple technique is used. First, a base of a solid pale color is laid down, followed by a darker shade using a brushstroke called Dune Grass. This is found under the Brushes preset tab and, at a distance, will look like hairs.

You will need

- Bristol board or drawing paper
- Pencil and eraser
- Black pen
- Macintosh or Windows PC
- Scanner
- Graphics tablet and stylus
- Adobe Photoshop

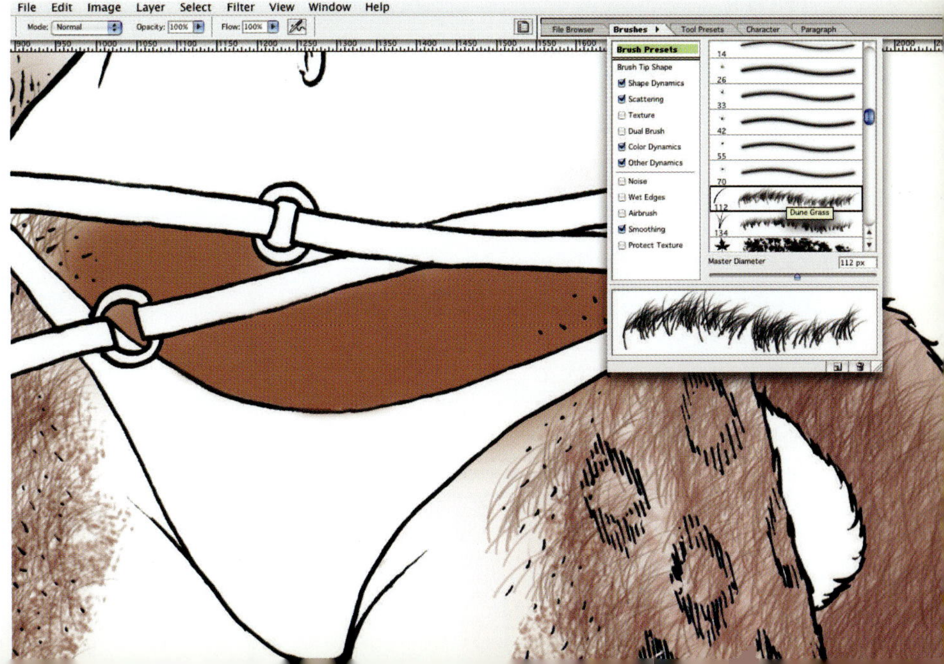

Who is she? Jessica Drake (if that is her name) is a paranormal investigator, the latest in a long line of Nobodies, whose origins are as mysterious as their activities. **What does she wear?** When alone, she favors simple, casual clothes, but dresses according to the assignment, in everything from a catsuit to a police uniform. **What does she do?** As a Nobody, she has given up a normal life (if she ever had one) to safeguard society from the disruptive forces of the supernatural. **How does she do it?** Apart from her training in martial arts, firearms, and acrobatics, she can change her appearance at will, making her the ideal covert operative.

INVESTIGATOR

Making your own character

The *Nobody* comic series was created in a stark, monochromatic style to convey the story's dark, moody atmosphere. When working in black and white, you have to decide on the look you want and the best technique to achieve it. Apart from the high-contrast mode used for *Nobody*, other styles include simple outline drawings or ones that use tone, which can be achieved with either cross-hatching, stippling, or by using screens. Apart from the creative possibilities of black and white, low printing costs are always an incentive to working in monochrome.

▼ Balance

Illusion and perception are the two principal methods of getting this style of drawing to work. The world is so familiar to us that even symbols can convey the idea of a face. E-mails are full of such examples, created from keyboard characters—for example, ^_^ is instantly recognizable as a face. The images shown here are all drawn with correct perspective and anatomical proportions, but there is very little structural detail. Because of the strength of the shadows, it is important that they be correct in relation to the perceived light source.

Illustrations by Charlie Adlard, story by Sharon Cho and Alex Amado

You will need

- Bristol board or CS10 board
- Pencil and eraser
- Black marker pens with various tips
- Scraperboard and scalpel, or Adobe Photoshop or Corel Painter

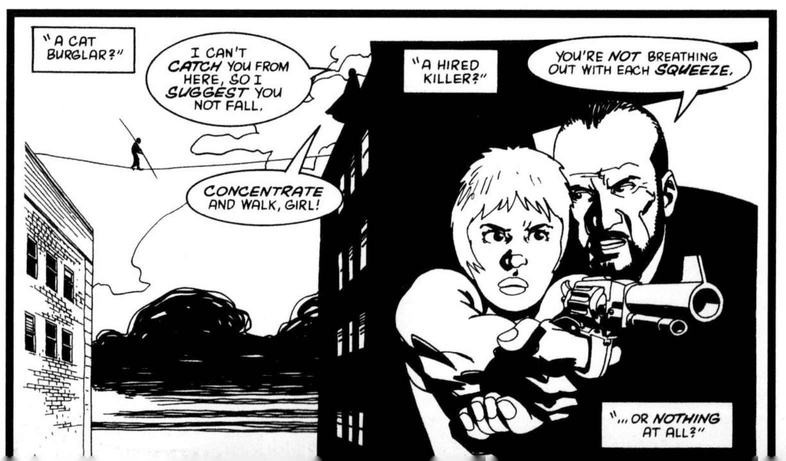

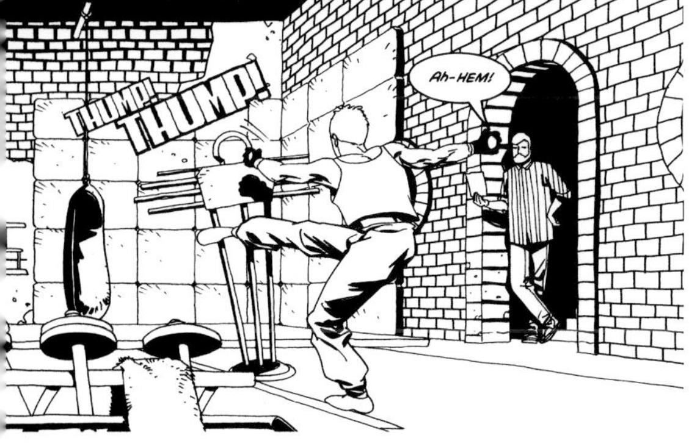

◀ Angles

Whether using color or black and white, try to add variety to your panels, from establishing shots to close-ups.

▼ Minimal detail

Using black and white to convey the mood of the story is very important, but it goes even beyond this: keeping the visuals simple stops them from overpowering the story. Although many facets of the story can be conveyed through the pictures, too much detail can distract from the pacing and rhythm of the tale.

▼ Black as night

This high-contrast style works very well for nighttime pictures like this one, where high-contrast shadows are more natural. A crime scene would have a very bright single light source, which adds to the realism of the image. The fine vertical lines are very effective in conveying the sense of torrential rain, which is enhanced by the use of white lines against the black. Provided you have done your drawing on smooth-surfaced board, such as Bristol or CS10, you can scratch the black ink away using a sharp instrument, such as a scalpel or compass point. If you like working in black and white, you could try using scraperboard, a specially manufactured board with a base of hard white china clay coated with india ink. In a technique not dissimilar to engraving, the surface is scratched away, using special cutter tools, to reveal the underlying white. It can easily be done digitally using Photoshop, drawing white onto a black background. Corel Painter comes with simulated scraperboard tools.

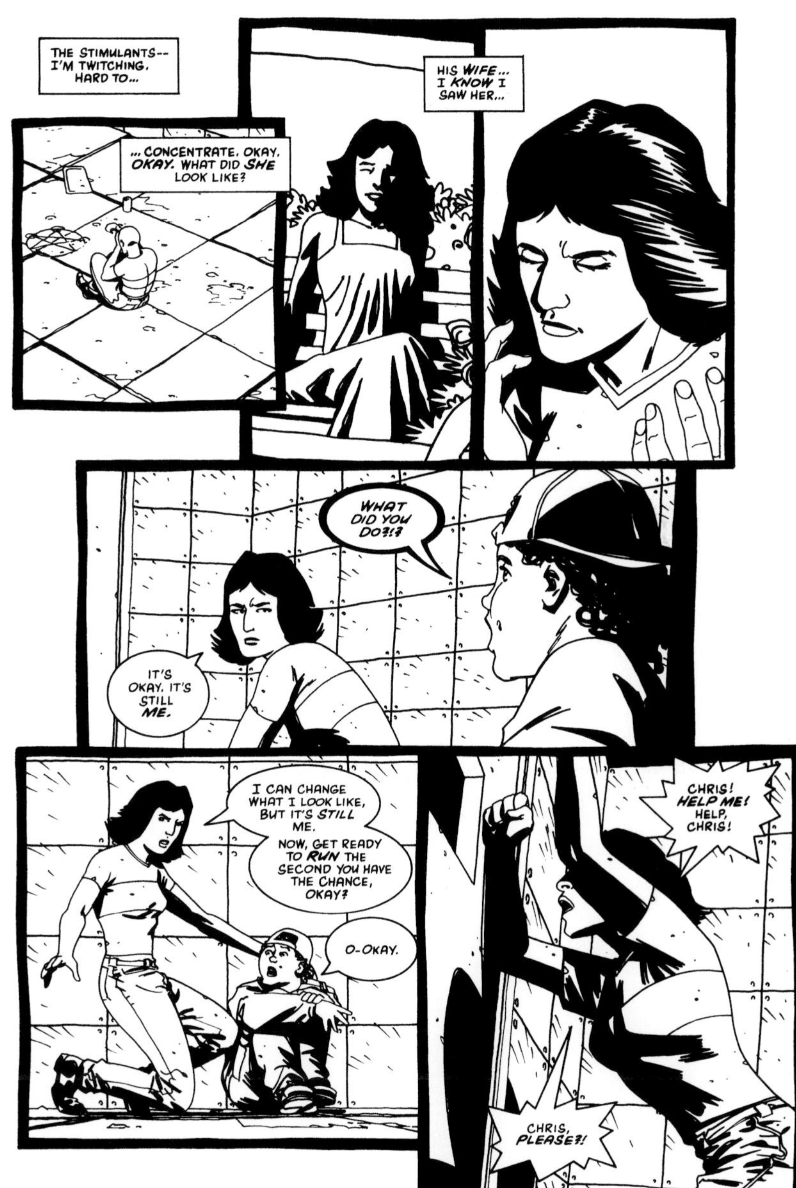

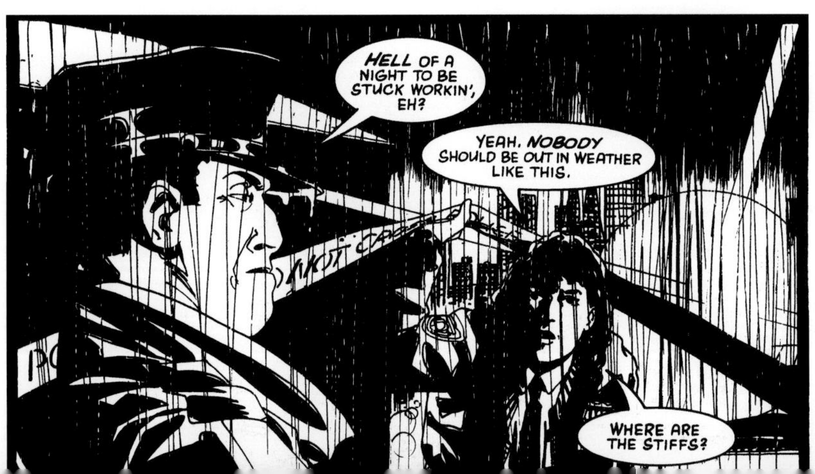

Check this out

Nobody (published by AiT/Planet Lar)
Kabuki—Masks of the Noh by David Mack (Image Comics) for excellent examples of black-and-white female characters.
Sin City by Frank Miller (Titan Books) for interesting ways of drawing women in black and white.

Who is she? Oni was tricked into marrying Tengu, a shape-shifting demon, when he killed and assumed the form of her betrothed, a samurai warrior, on their wedding day. For 500 years she is his slave and concubine. **What does she wear?** Fashions change a lot over 500 years, so she wears everything from traditional kimonos to skin-hugging gym wear to the tawdry dress of a streetwalker. **What does she do?** She is forced by the demon to act as an assassin in his plans to gain power in both the criminal and demon underworlds. After killing a child, she realizes that she has lost her humanity, becoming no better than her demon captor, and decides to take revenge. **How does she do it?** Her skills in the ways of the samurai and other martial arts have become finely tuned over the centuries. Combined with her beauty, she is a deadly assassin, killing with ease those who hinder her "husband's" plans.

DEMON'S WIFE

Illustrations by Al Davison

Making your own character

In the creation of the character, Japanese history and mythology were researched. The study of traditional clothes was mixed with an investigation into contemporary Japanese culture and fashion. By having a futuristic setting, there is also plenty of scope for whimsical clothing designs and makeup. To retain a semblance of authenticity, the pencil drawings were inked using traditional Japanese brushes. The inked drawings were scanned and colored using the standard, modern tool: Photoshop.

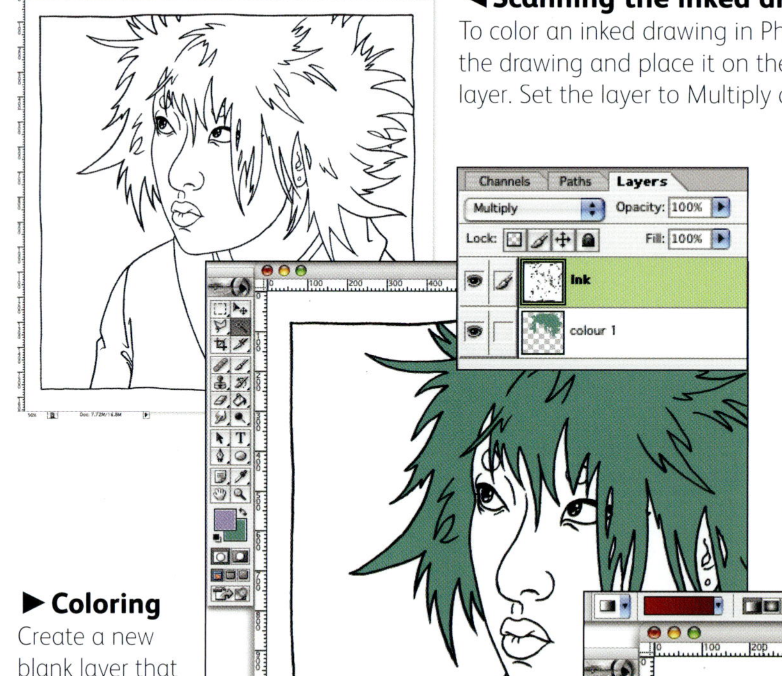

◀ Scanning the inked drawing

To color an inked drawing in Photoshop, scan the drawing and place it on the topmost layer. Set the layer to Multiply and lock it.

▶ Coloring

Create a new blank layer that sits below the line art layer. Using the Magic Wand tool (with anti-alias off), click in the area you want to color. Hold down the shift key to select multiple areas that need the same color. Click on the new layer you created and use the Paint Bucket (Fill) tool to add the color.

▼ Blend into the background

To make the graduated background, use the Magic Wand to color it, as before. Select the Gradient tool, which is in the same place as the Paint Bucket, then set the two foreground and background colors in the Tools palette, and drag the Gradient tool until the desired effect is achieved.

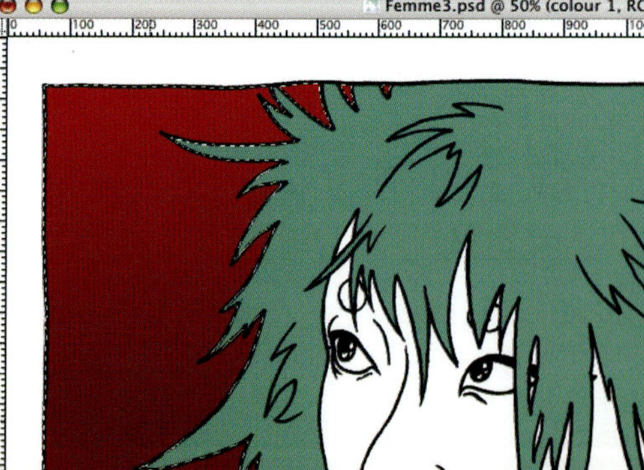

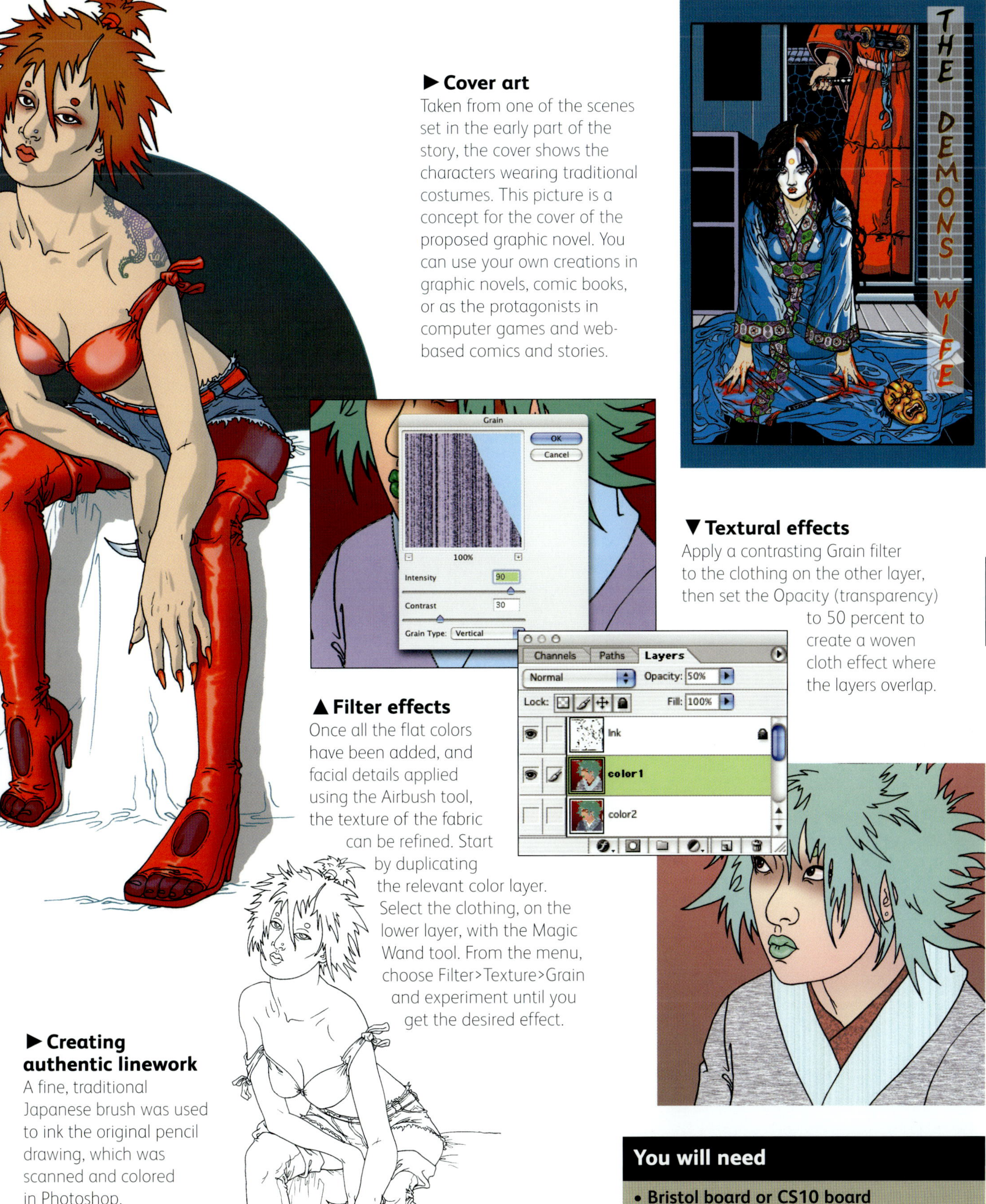

▶ Cover art

Taken from one of the scenes set in the early part of the story, the cover shows the characters wearing traditional costumes. This picture is a concept for the cover of the proposed graphic novel. You can use your own creations in graphic novels, comic books, or as the protagonists in computer games and web-based comics and stories.

▼ Textural effects

Apply a contrasting Grain filter to the clothing on the other layer, then set the Opacity (transparency) to 50 percent to create a woven cloth effect where the layers overlap.

▲ Filter effects

Once all the flat colors have been added, and facial details applied using the Airbush tool, the texture of the fabric can be refined. Start by duplicating the relevant color layer. Select the clothing, on the lower layer, with the Magic Wand tool. From the menu, choose Filter>Texture>Grain and experiment until you get the desired effect.

▶ Creating authentic linework

A fine, traditional Japanese brush was used to ink the original pencil drawing, which was scanned and colored in Photoshop.

You will need

- **Bristol board or CS10 board**
- **Pencils and eraser**
- **India ink**
- **Japanese brushes**
- **Macintosh or Windows PC**
- **Scanner**
- **Graphics tablet and stylus**
- **Adobe Photoshop**

Who is she? The youngest daughter of Squire Daley Darling, a sometimes cruel landowner in the early 18th century, Rose was born with a rebellious streak. **What does she wear?** At home, she wears the demure female clothing of the 18th century. For her forays into the world of outlaws, she dresses in riding clothes that her brothers discarded and she secretly altered to fit her slender body. She wears masks to hide her identity. **What does she do?** Rose started the life of a highway robber as a way to escape from the tedium of her life, but she soon realized that she could relieve the suffering caused by landowners by stealing from them and distributing the cash to the tenant-farmers.

SECRET OUTLAW

How does she do it? As the youngest daughter, Rose is often ignored by the household, giving her the freedom to do what she wants, which includes taking one of her father's horses and holding up the gentry. To avoid the risk of implicating herself, she gives cash only to the poor and passes any treasures on to other highwaymen. Unlike most of the other highwaymen, she never uses a name, not even an alias, which adds to her mystery.

Illustrations by Kate Brown

Making your own character

When dealing with historical periods, be as accurate as you can with details such as costumes. Sources of reference material include art galleries and museums that have contemporary examples. You can also look at movies set in the period, because the costume designers will (or should) have done all the necessary research. Feel free to embellish the designs, but do not add items that did not appear until a future period, unless you can justify them in the story.

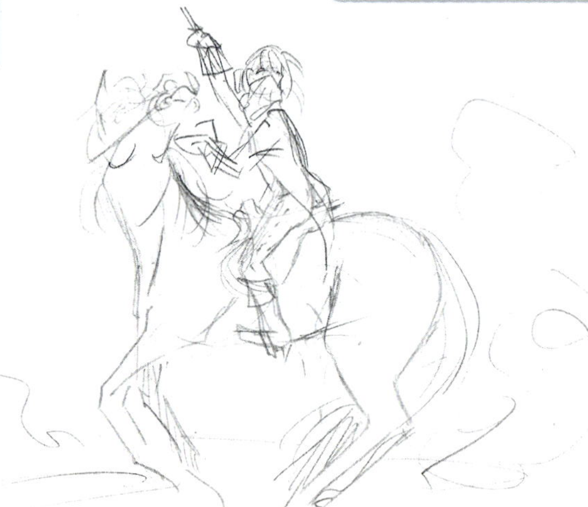

◄ Drawing animals
Extending your drawing skills beyond human characters is vital if you want to be a professional comic artist. Animals, particularly horses and dogs, will appear in all manner of stories. Then there is architectural and scenic illustration to consider as well.

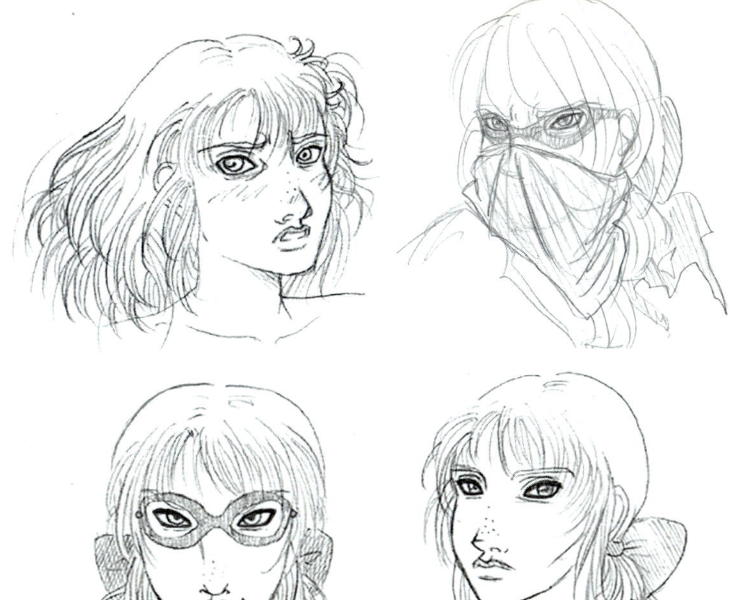

◀ Over the line

Pencil sketches are used to explore poses, and to get the proportions right and the clothing to fit. Because the images are created in clearly defined stages, previous work can be "discarded" and corrections made as your work progresses. To ensure clothing fits naturally to the character's anatomy, it is possible to draw the clothes over the body and remove the "hidden" lines at the inking stage.

▲ Masked man?

The head, or more specifically the face, is the most telling part of a character. In Rose's case, she has two faces, that of the dutiful daughter and that of the masked highwayman. Making as many diverse sketches as possible helps to establish the two different personalities. To hide Rose's gender, experiments with hairstyles and more obvious disguises, such as masks, were tried.

▼ Layers

Using the linework of the pencil drawing for the finished picture gives it a more natural look, especially when combined with coloring style. Excessive or redundant lines can be erased from the scanned image, and the gray of the pencil colorized, in keeping with the overall tone of the image. Each element or article of clothing should be colored on its own layer.

▼ Brushes

To achieve the painted look, you have to set up options for your brushes. Apart from those in the drop-down panel, you will need to set the brush's opacity. This will let you work in a similar way to using watercolor, adding layer upon layer of color to achieve the shadows and highlights necessary for giving your character form.

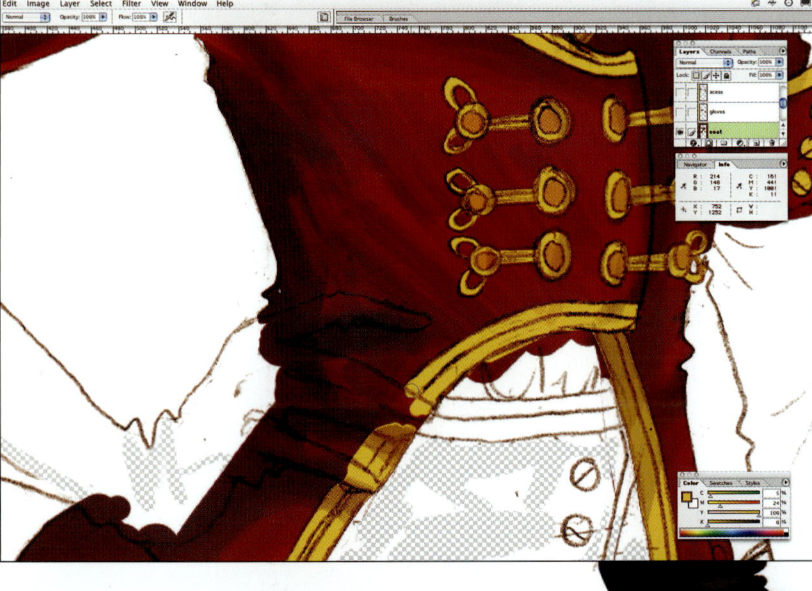

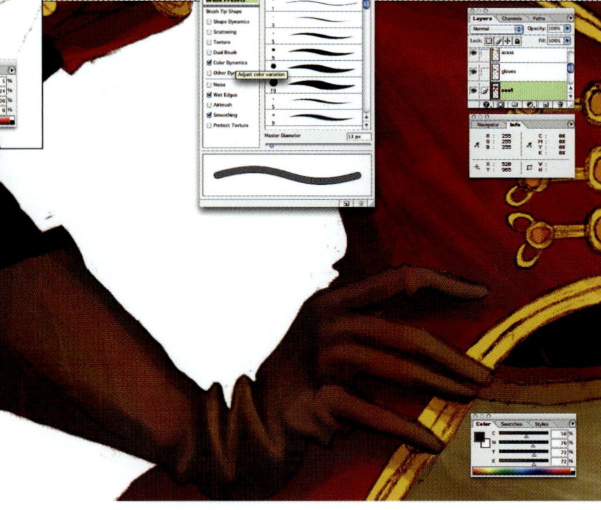

You will need

- Bristol board or drawing paper
- Pencil and eraser
- Black marker pens with various tips
- Macintosh or Windows PC
- Scanner
- Graphics tablet and stylus
- Adobe Photoshop

Who is she? After her mother died and May discovered there was no inheritance, she understood what her mother meant when she said she was "sitting on a gold mine." **What does she wear?** May has a passion for beautiful silks. She finds them very comfortable and very seductive, showing her legs in all their glory. **What does she do?** Part vigilante, part hired assassin, May works for the Corporate Affairs branch of the Justice Department as a freelance operator. Hers is not an exclusive contract, and some jobs she does for free, when proper justice is not meted out.

WORKING GIRL

How does she do it? Her targets are usually high-level business tycoons with a weakness for beautiful young women. Their motives are always self-serving, so they make easy targets when they think the reward is self-gratification. May never lets herself be compromised, however, and never misses a target.

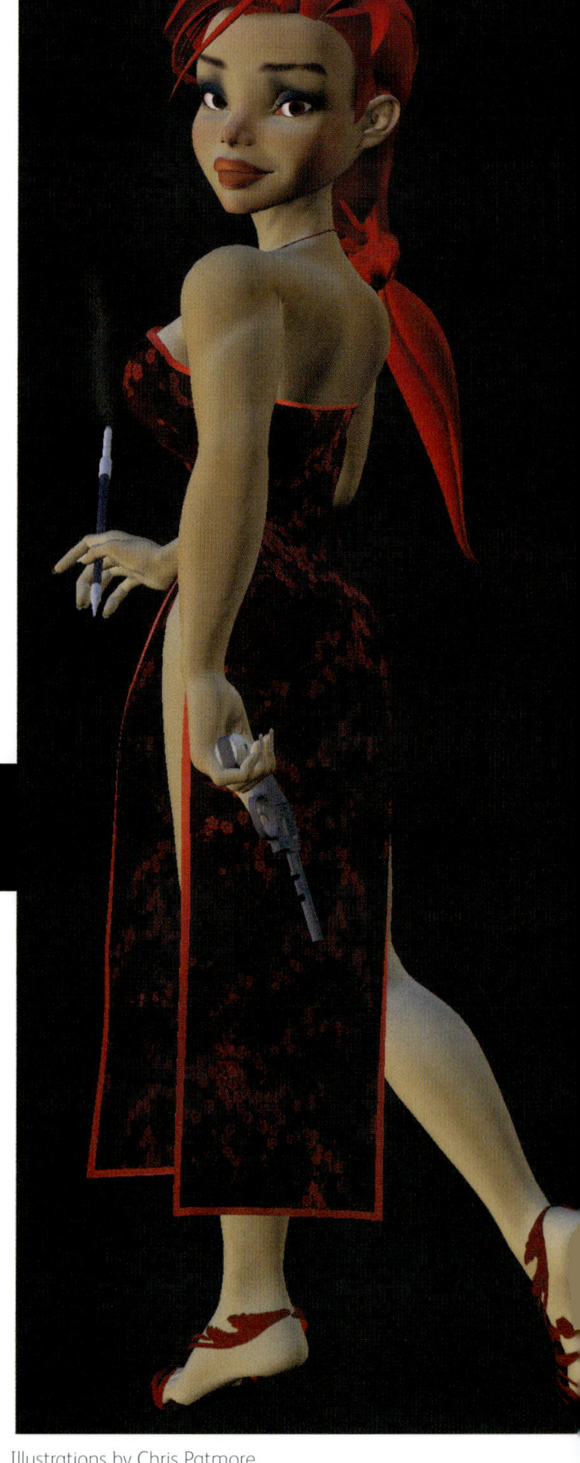

Illustrations by Chris Patmore

Making your own character

DAZ Studio was developed as an alternative to Curious Labs Poser software, by the company that makes the very popular Victoria and Michael characters. Studio was designed to work with DAZ's huge collection of Poser content and integrate with the popular landscape generator Bryce, also produced by DAZ. Studio can be used to produce still images and animations and is offered as a free download. Its approach to creating images is similar to Poser's, but in a less graphically enhanced interface. It's a great way to start learning 3D.

▶ Starting point
Begin by adding your chosen model to the scene, by selecting the appropriate one from the Figures list in the Content palette—in this instance, DAZ's The Girl. A small preview image helps with the selection.

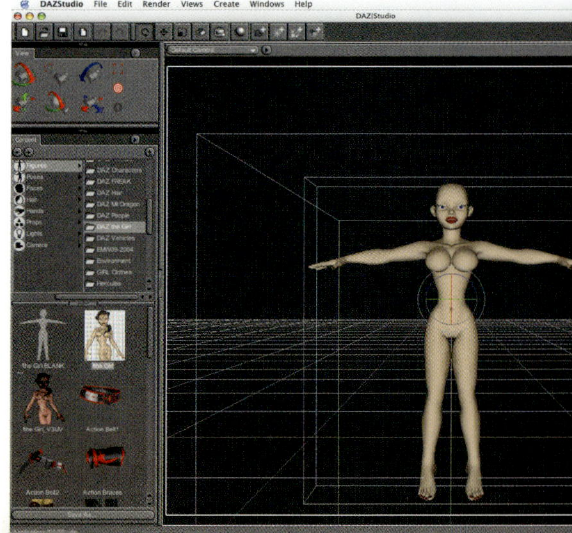

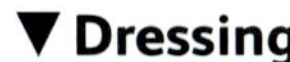

▼ Dressing
Choose Conforming clothes from the Figures list. Conforming clothes are those that can be attached to the main figure so that they move together.

Controls the cameras for different views and movements in animation

Lists all the available content; automatically finds content from Poser, if you have it on your computer, and includes it

Preview of selected content

Controls the movement of the figures

Lists all the available cameras

Menu for preview styles and changing background color

▶ Skin tone
In the Poses menu, choose the textures for the clothes and skin. These are all purchased separately. Building up a collection of props and textures will let you add more individuality to your characters.

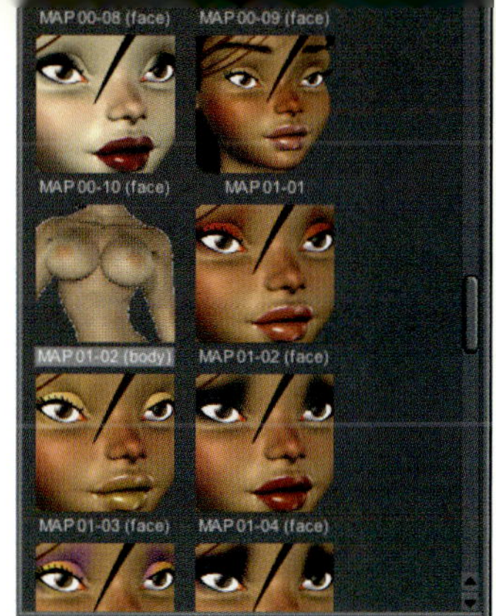

Alternative method of moving cameras

Parameters and Scene palette for selecting and adjusting all the elements in the picture

Move the figure parts manually using the appropriate tool

Pop-up menu for conforming clothes and props to figures

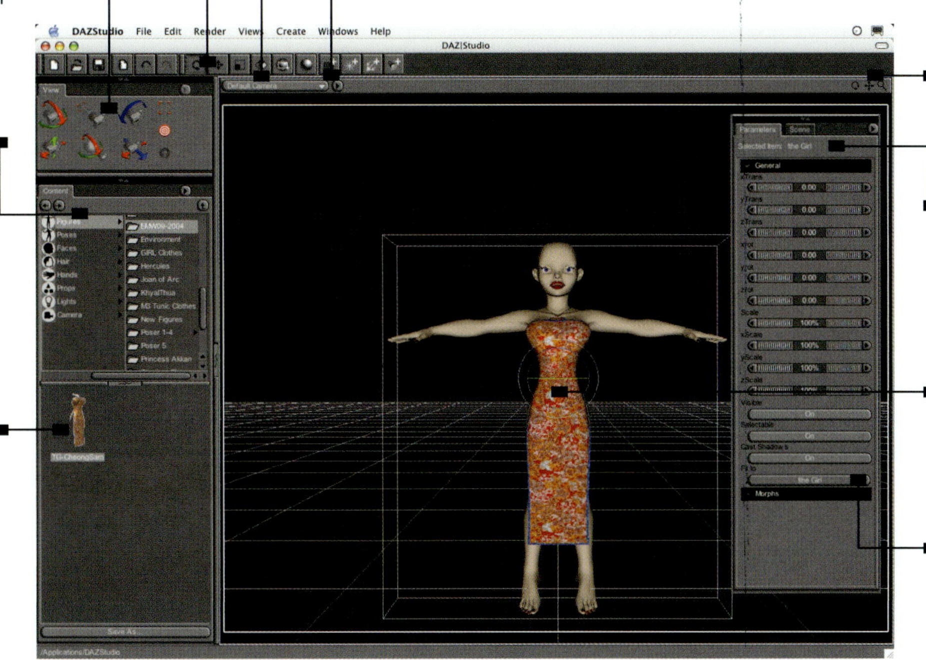

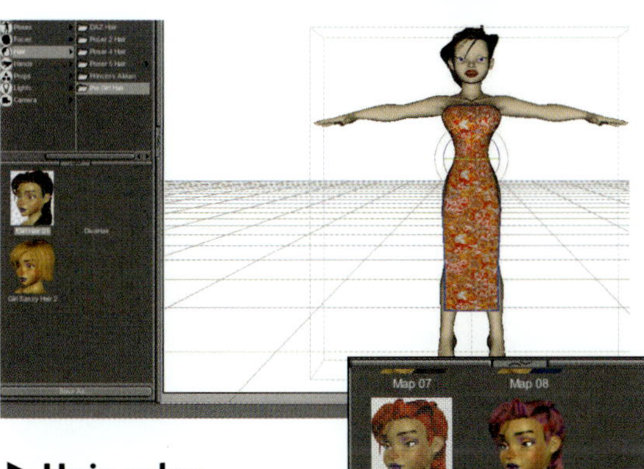

◀ Hair
Choose hair from the Hair menu and add it to the character. A variety of styles are available to buy from the DAZ web site. Change the background to white to make it easier to see what is happening as the character is built up.

▶ Hair color
By clicking through the hierarchical menu of the Scene palette, select the hair, then choose a hair color MAT file from the Poses content menu.

▼ Fine-tuning
Most figures come with a selection of preset poses that can act as a starting point. Once you have set the main pose and added props, such as the gun and cigarette, you can fine-tune the pose. Getting the hand to hold the gun realistically can take lots of small adjustments to each section of each digit, as well as the positioning of the prop itself. Facial expressions also have to be altered into one that is appropriate to the character or the moment being portrayed. You can then add a suitable background and render the finished picture. The cigarette smoke was added afterward, using Photoshop.

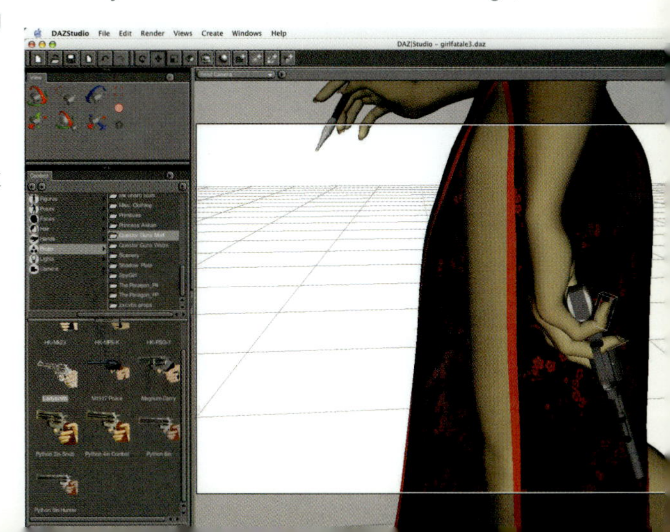

Who is she? Isabella Delarosa was born outside Udine, in northeast Italy. The only child of a merchant, she was determined to carry on the family business, even against social traditions. During her first visit to Venice, as a trader, she met Giorgio Parkhov, a Romanian traveler, which changed her life forever. **What does she wear?** Her taste in fashion has changed over the years, but she always favors clothes that will attract men and impress other women. Her preference is for red silk. **What does she do?** Even though her family's business died with her father, she has retained a strong business acumen, and acquired a storehouse of objets d'art that she can sell when she needs money to fund her decadent nightlife. **What happens to her?** As the years have passed and travel has become easier, her taste in men has become more varied. She arrived in New York in the early 1960s, and was rumored to have appeared in Andy Warhol's *Dracula*, although she cannot be seen in the final film.

VAMPIRESSA

Making your own character

Creating a character with two similar, yet distinctively different, faces is a great exercise in exploring the aspects of facial anatomy and ways of diversifying features. In this case, to what extent you change the face, beyond the obligatory fangs, will depend on which version of the vampire stories you subscribe to.

▼ Turnaround
Developing familiarity with your characters is very important if you have to draw them for a whole comic, or series of comics. Even if you just do them as pencil sketches, draw as many different angles and poses as you can.

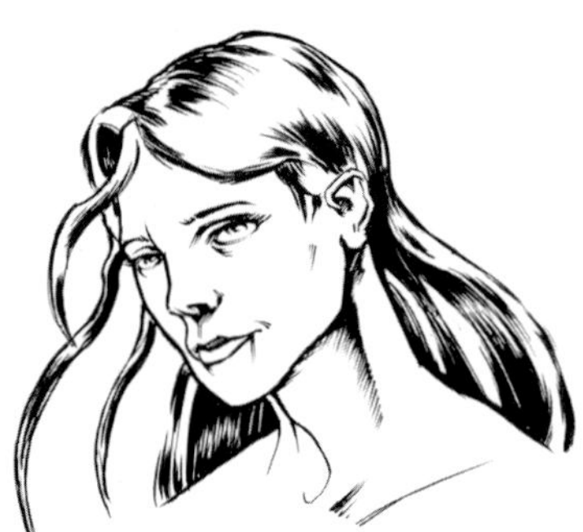

▲ Lines on her face
Because vampires have two distinct faces, and perhaps stages in between, it is particularly important to make sketches of them. These can be done in pencil only or inked and/or colored. This version of Isabella is clearly very close to her manifestation as Vampiressa.

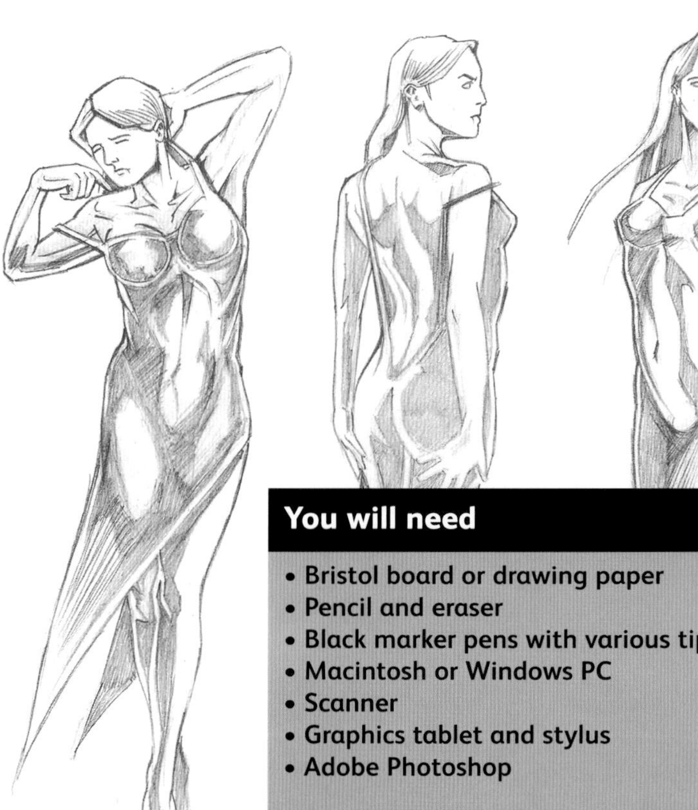

You will need

- **Bristol board or drawing paper**
- **Pencil and eraser**
- **Black marker pens with various tips**
- **Macintosh or Windows PC**
- **Scanner**
- **Graphics tablet and stylus**
- **Adobe Photoshop**

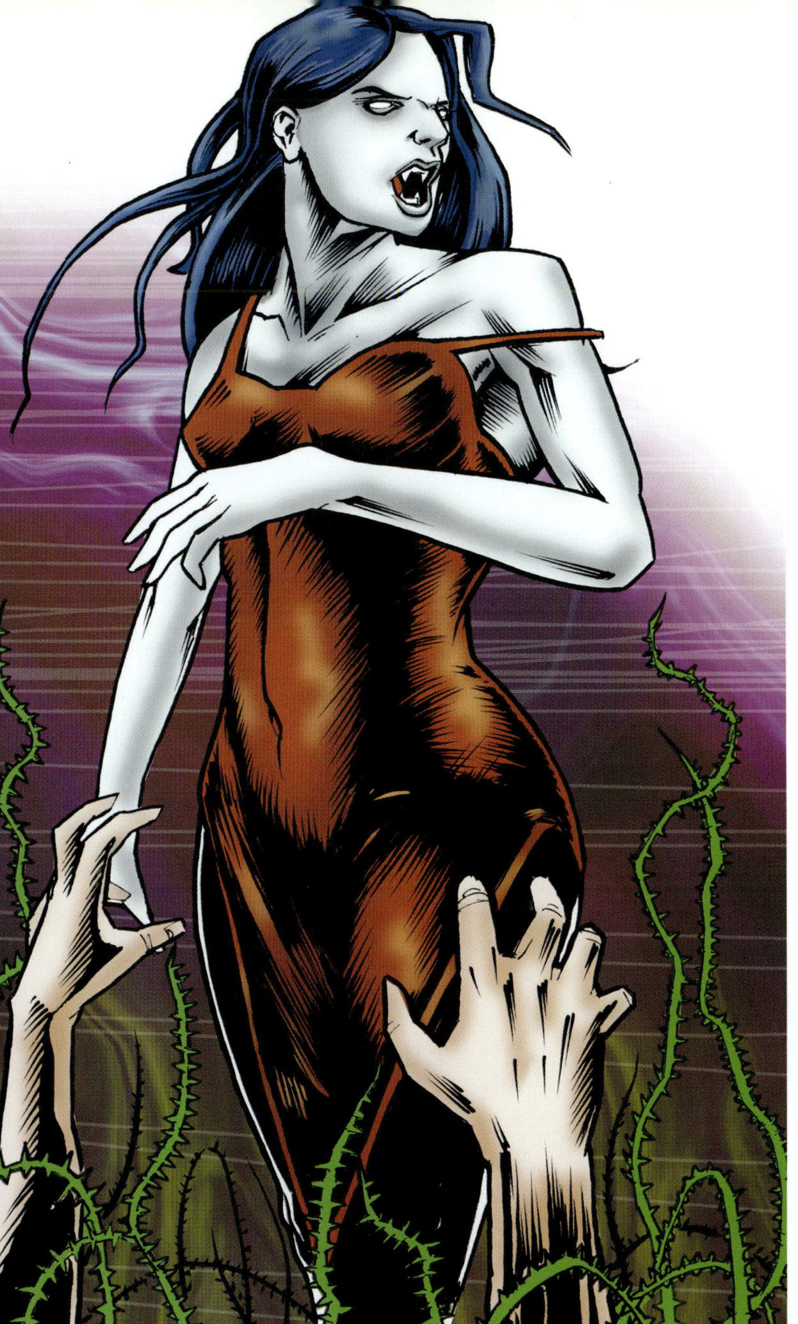

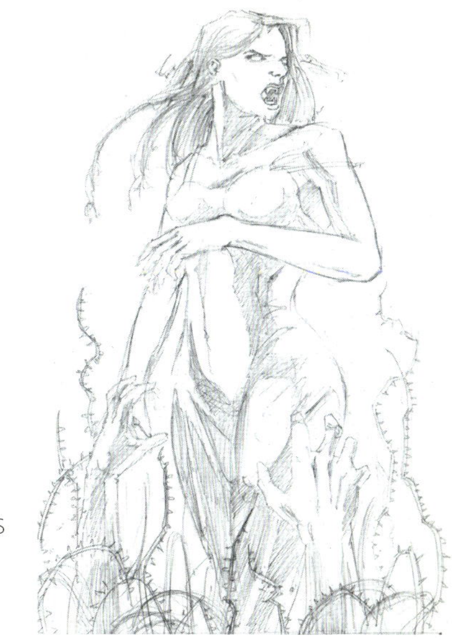

► Pencil pushing

Never underestimate the importance of producing good, accurate pencil drawings. Thanks to erasers, you can experiment with shading and linework until the drawing is perfect (or at least the best you can achieve). Inking gives you the chance to fine-tune the details, but the pencils have to be perfectly clean if you are giving them to someone else to finish, or the desired result may not happen.

◄▼ Mono line

Trying various inking techniques and equipment to achieve different results is always a good idea, especially if you know you will be doing lots of black-and-white work. Practice using hatching and cross-hatching as a way of shading.

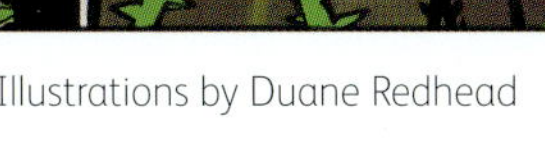
Illustrations by Duane Redhead

► Another angle on coloring

Normally, when color and shading are added to a drawing digitally, they are applied using a graphics tablet and stylus to create smooth, flowing curves, even with toon shading. In this picture, areas of solid color were created using the Polygon Lasso tool in Photoshop and built up over various layers. Some were softened by using Layer Opacity and/or by applying Gaussian Blur. The intention was to create a hard, angular look.

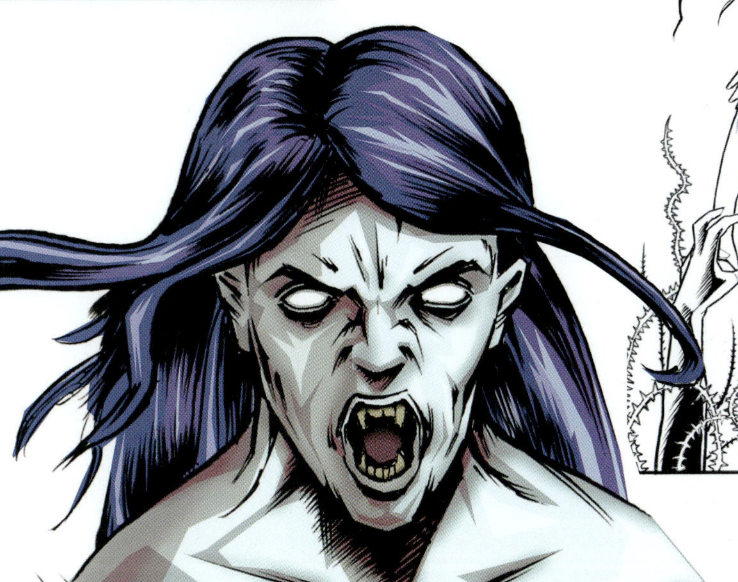

Who is she? Zhi-En Szeto is a brilliant neurologist and robotics surgeon who works within, but not for, the Canton Commercial Empire in the year 42 PC (Post Chaos)—that is, 2054 AD. She could be described at best as mercenary. **What does she wear?** Her pragmatic personality is not overly concerned with the fripperies of wardrobe. Instead, she prefers something more utilitarian, such as trousers and a lab coat, given that most of her life is consumed by her work. However, she is not averse to revealing a little flesh to keep her male colleagues and clients enticed. **What does she do?** Zhi-En's particular surgical skills are greatly in demand among the private clinics of the CYB Organization, whose clientele want the type of cybernetic enhancements that allow them to function with greater efficiency and evade the law enforcement agencies.

RISQUÉ BUSINESS

How does she do it? Zhi-En's ambitions exceed those of simply being a well-paid consultant—she wants to control the empire's underground crime network, so she fully employs her feminine wiles to entice all levels of criminals to her own private clinic, built with funds from her consultancy work. Women who are both attractive and intelligent are often seen as a threat by men, especially those lacking in those departments. They are also seen as a challenge, and this is how she is able to capture and enhance them, to become obedient troops in her battle to overthrow the more resistant criminal factions.

Making your own character

It is very easy to fall into the trap of using clichés when designing intelligent and attractive women. The common Hollywood device is to put nerdy spectacles on them and give them frumpy hair-dos that are later discarded to reveal a stunningly beautiful woman underneath. Try to avoid such obvious devices, especially if the character is supposed to be as self-assured as this one, unless of course she is using her appearance as bait for her trap.

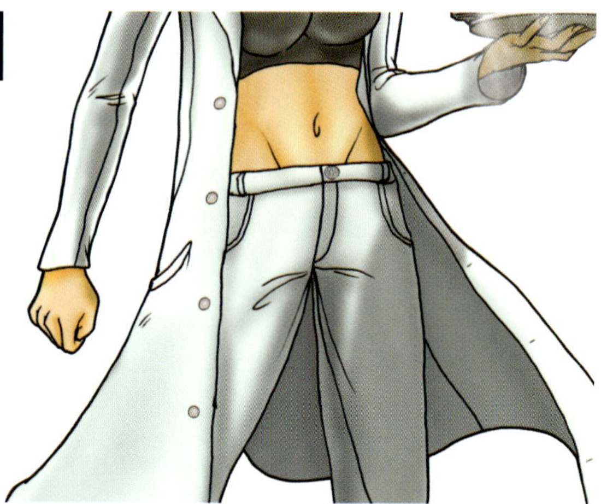

◀ Quick fix

One of the great advantages of working with multilayered digital files is that amendments can easily be made to "finished" artwork. Here, the artist realized that the lines for the hip bones were in the wrong place, so it was simply a matter of deleting them from the black line art layer and resubmitting the file.

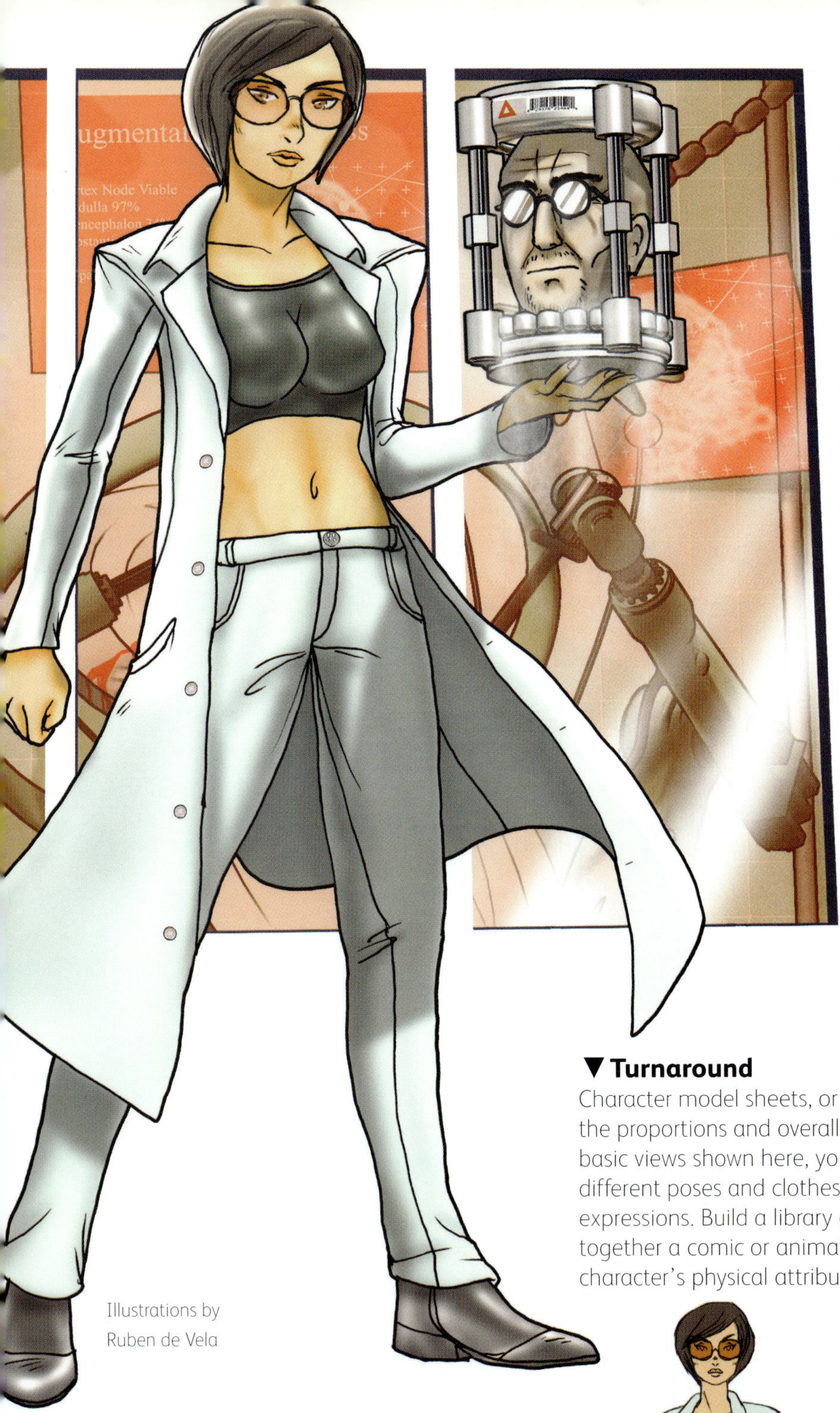

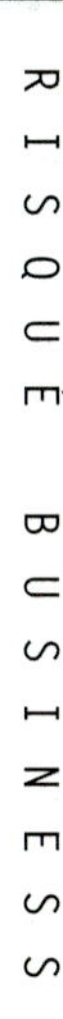

▼▶ Spot the difference

More complex amendments can be made to colors and shading by hiding layers and adding new ones, or saving a duplicate copy of the file and altering that. Having the freedom to make nondestructive alterations will encourage you to experiment with coloring and also to get into the habit of fine-tuning your work.

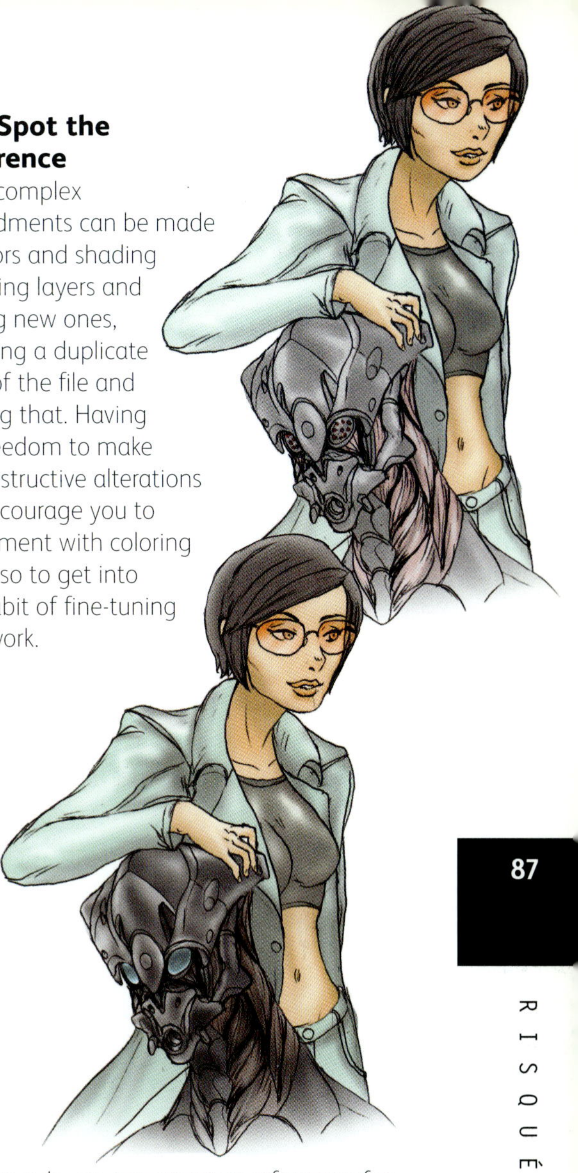

▼ Turnaround

Character model sheets, or turnarounds, are important as references for the proportions and overall look of the character. In addition to the three basic views shown here, you should add three-quarter and top views. Try different poses and clothes at a variety of angles, then concentrate on facial expressions. Build a library of these sheets so that when you come to putting together a comic or animation, you will be completely familiar with the character's physical attributes.

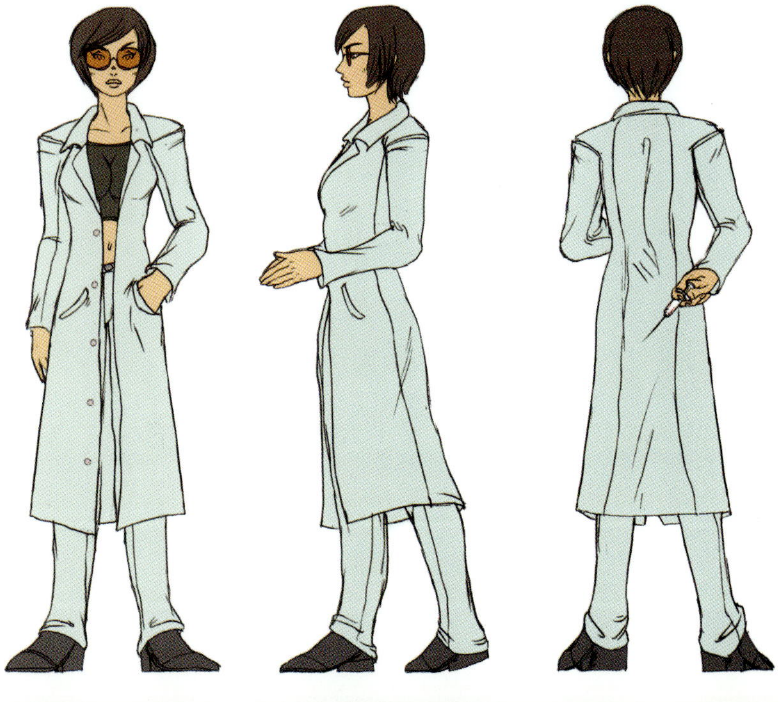

Illustrations by
Ruben de Vela

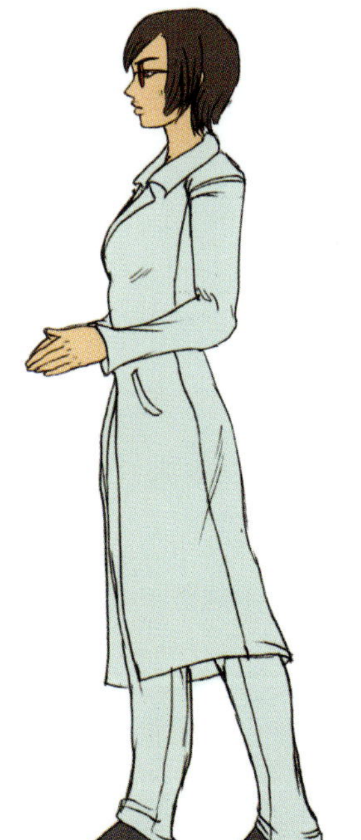

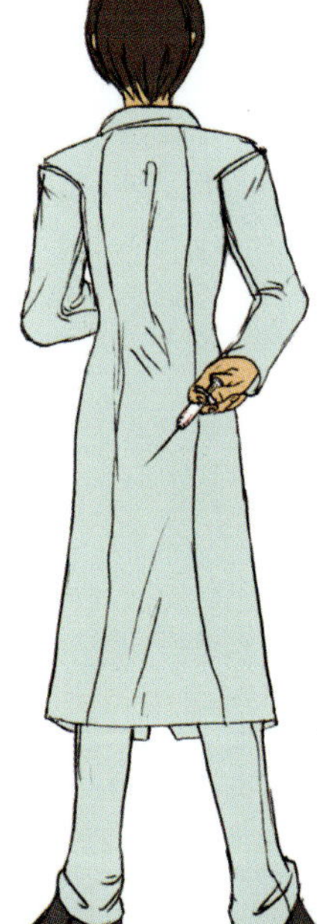

You will need

- Bristol board or drawing paper
- Pencil and eraser
- Black marker pens with various tips
- Macintosh or Windows PC
- Scanner
- Graphics tablet and stylus
- Adobe Photoshop

Who is she? Sirena lives in the memories and imaginations of eons of mariners—a mystical creature seen in all the oceans and seas of the world. **What does she wear?** She is neither human nor fish. Freed from the bonds of human morality and living almost entirely in the water, Sirena has no need of clothes, although she has been portrayed wearing a top made from shells for modesty. **What does she do?** Sirena enjoys the freedom of the ocean. She has often been accused of enticing men to their death, but it is men who pursue her and not the other way around. **How does she do it?** Sirena's curiosity often draws her toward ships, but like her friends the dolphins, she only wants to play. She has no interest in humans other than that, as they cannot live in her world nor she in theirs.

SEA DREAM

Illustrations by Silvia Fusetti

Making your own character

Mermaids appear in the mythology and stories of diverse cultures and regions of the world, from the icy waters of Scandinavia to the Mediterranean and throughout the tropics. All agree on their appearance as having the top half of a woman and the bottom half of a fish. This is the starting point for exploring the design of the character. Her appearance should also take into consideration the region in which you choose to set the story. Would she have a different look if she lived in cold northern waters rather than in the tropics?

▶ Squid ink

This is an experiment at creating a mermaid based around an octopus. This produced a more sinister type of mermaid whose intentions are less than fun. The idea was never taken beyond the sketch stage because it was considered too much of a break from tradition. The ink wash was created in Painter.

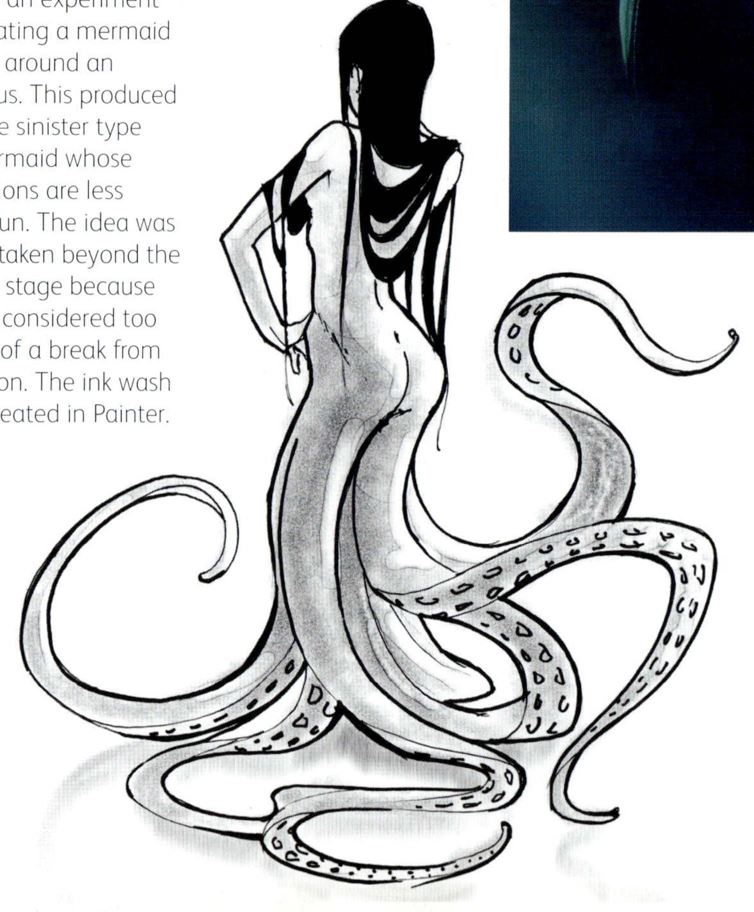

You will need

- Bristol board or drawing paper
- Pencil and eraser
- Black marker pens with various tips
- Macintosh or Windows PC
- Scanner
- Graphics tablet and stylus
- Corel Painter

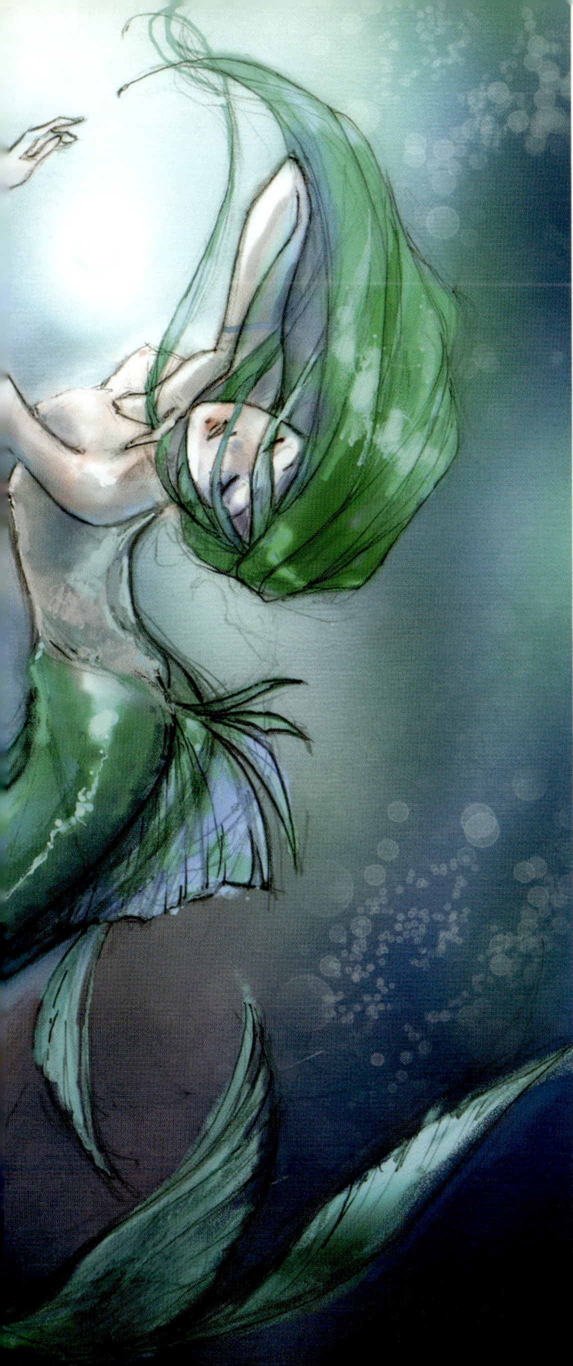

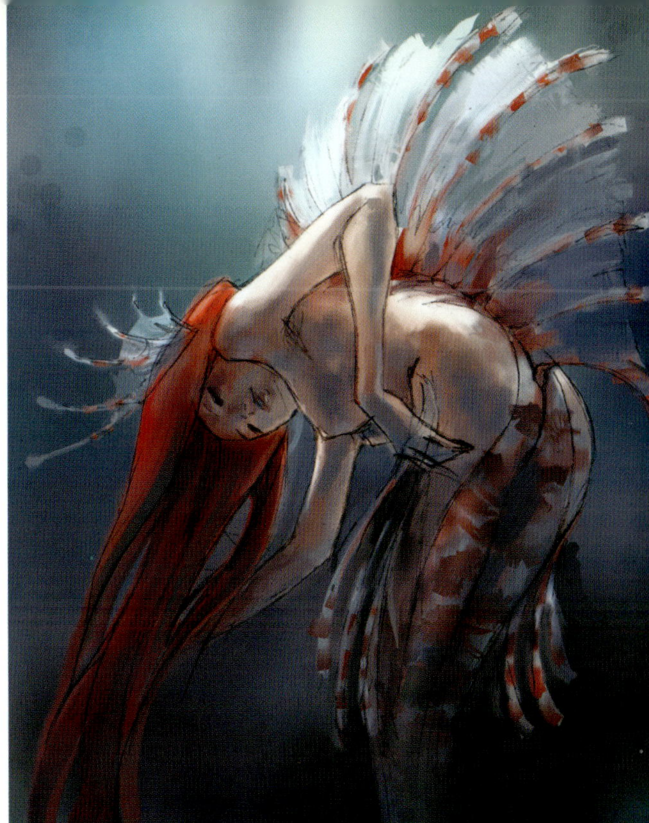

▶ Tropical

Working on a more traditional look, this tropical version of a mermaid is based on a lion fish, using its warm colors to enhance the tropical feeling. Because the lion fish is poisonous, and the dorsal fin is not very attractive, the drawing was rejected as the main character, but not completely discarded because its story possibilities were very good. This was colored in Painter.

▼ Traditional

After a lot of experimenting, the most traditional form was chosen for the character. The initial image was drawn on paper, scanned, and then imported into Painter, where its range of "natural media" brushes were used to create the watercolor effect. A paper texture was also added to the background area. The hair was colored green, like seaweed, with the whole image taking on an aquamarine color.

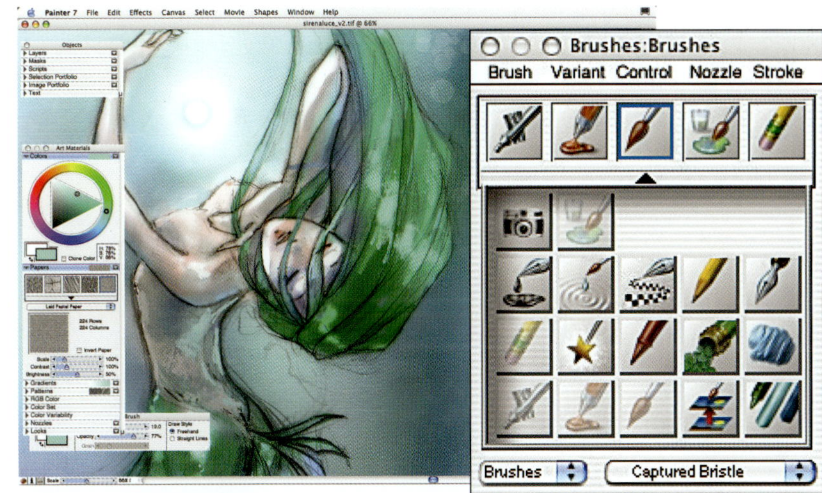

◀ Deco style

For comic use, a simple style often works well because it will not detract from the story. This Art Deco–influenced drawing was created directly in Painter with a graphics tablet and stylus. The black lines were produced on one layer, with the color on a different layer below it. The gray area was selected using the Lasso tool, then filled with 50 percent black. The hair was painted using the Pen tool at varying widths. It was purposely painted out of register.

Who is she? Ashla is an only child living on the Florida coast with her mother. She grew up not knowing anything about her father, and her mother never spoke of him. **What does she wear?** Ashla lives for the beach and the ocean. The weather is hot, life is simple, and her clothes reflect this: bikinis, surfing shorts, T-shirts, and sarongs. **What does she do?** Surf! Since she was very small, Ashla has had an affinity with the ocean. She could swim before she could walk, and surfing seemed to be a natural thing to do. Her mother encouraged her in this; she herself had been a great windsurfer before having Ashla. **What happens to her?** On her 18th birthday, Ashla is told that her father is an Atlantan prince who rescued her mother after a windsurfing accident. They fell in love and conceived a child, but mother and daughter were banished from Atlantis until Ashla came of age. Now she has to choose whether to visit her father or not, and see if she will be accepted as the heir to Atlantis.

QUEEN OF THE WAVES

Illustrations by Jon Sukarangsan

Making your own character

Coming up with new characters is often best done in brainstorming sessions, where ideas can be bounced back and forth, usually between a writer and an illustrator. Someone may have a loose concept that the illustrator can expand with quick visuals that help to stimulate the writer's imagination.

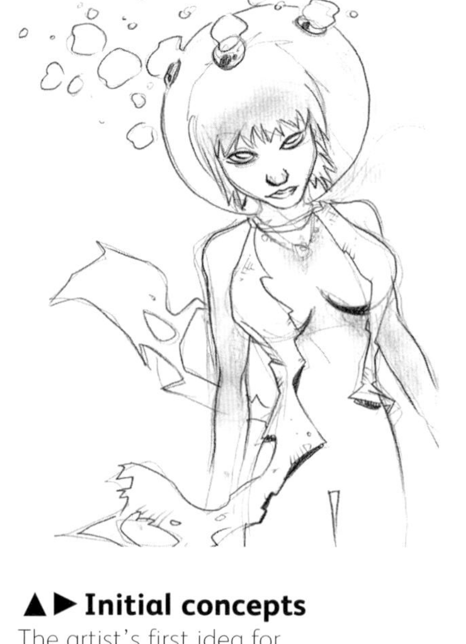

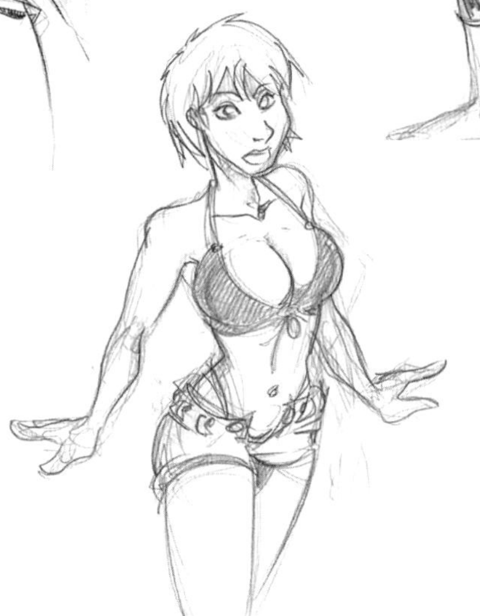

You will need

- Bristol board or drawing paper
- Pencil and eraser
- Black marker pens with various tips
- Macintosh or Windows PC
- Scanner
- Graphics tablet and stylus
- Adobe Photoshop

▲▶ Initial concepts
The artist's first idea for an ocean girl produced the "bubble-head" figure above, but the suggestion of creating a surfer led to the other two sketches. The ideas were then amalgamated to become the story of Ashla.

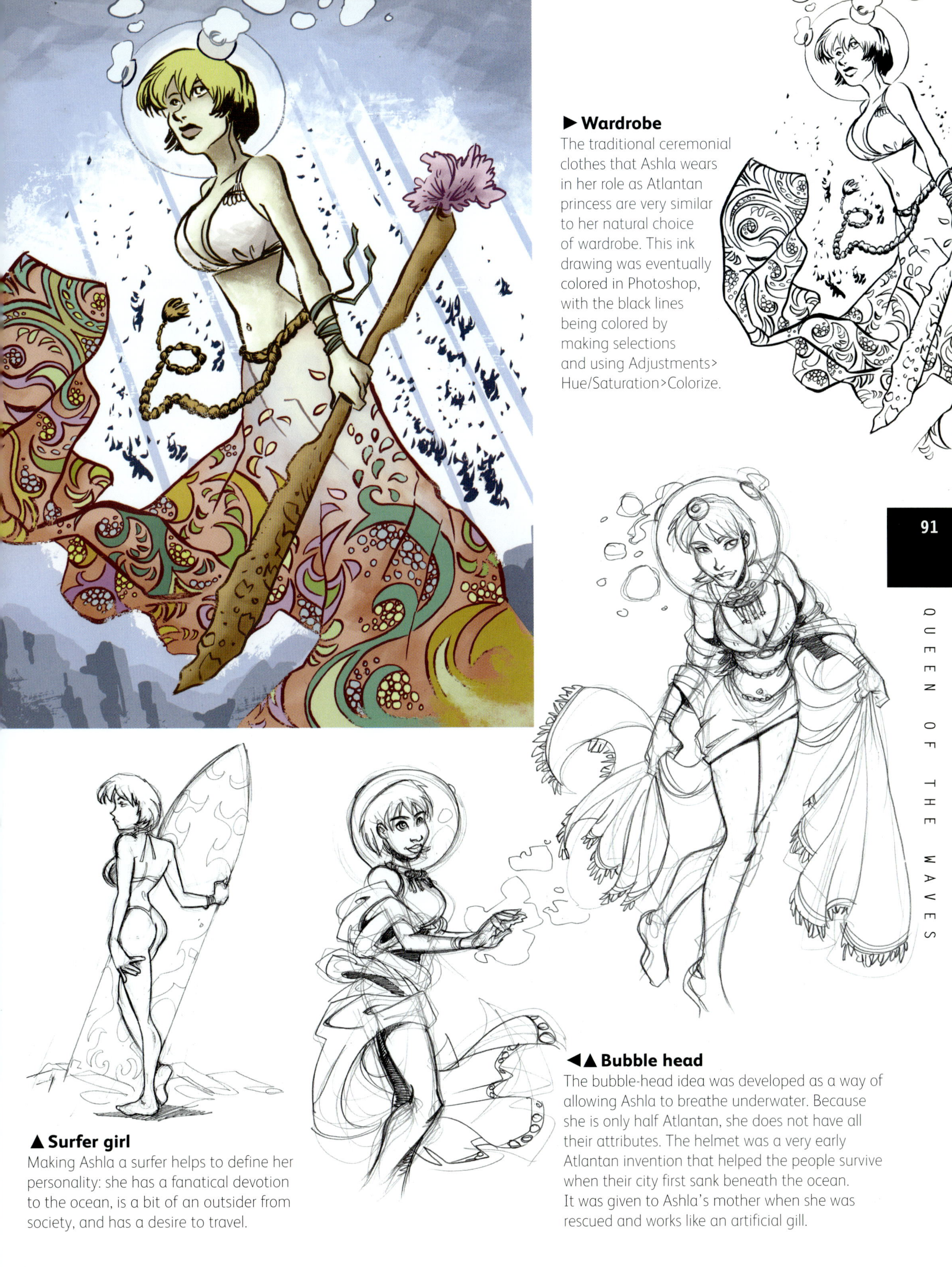

▶ Wardrobe

The traditional ceremonial clothes that Ashla wears in her role as Atlantan princess are very similar to her natural choice of wardrobe. This ink drawing was eventually colored in Photoshop, with the black lines being colored by making selections and using Adjustments>Hue/Saturation>Colorize.

▲ Surfer girl

Making Ashla a surfer helps to define her personality: she has a fanatical devotion to the ocean, is a bit of an outsider from society, and has a desire to travel.

◀▲ Bubble head

The bubble-head idea was developed as a way of allowing Ashla to breathe underwater. Because she is only half Atlantan, she does not have all their attributes. The helmet was a very early Atlantan invention that helped the people survive when their city first sank beneath the ocean. It was given to Ashla's mother when she was rescued and works like an artificial gill.

Who is she? Mohini lives in the equatorial and tropical waters of the Pacific. Warm water and an abundance of fish and fruits suit her needs and temperament. **What does she wear?** Beads in her braided hair and sometimes a shell necklace, but clothes are of no use to her. She has never understood why humans cover their bodies when they are in the water—it certainly does not make swimming any easier. **What does she do?** Mohini has a fascination for humans who venture into her realm, especially surfers who seem to understand the ocean. When she meets them, she tries to entice them to stay in her world. **How does she do it?** Her beguiling looks always work, but it is people's curiosity at seeing a supposedly mythical creature that makes them take the risk. Some people believe that the kiss of a mermaid will allow them to breathe underwater, and some surfers are convinced that this is how they have survived wipeouts on big waves. Mohini will never kiss and tell.

Ocean Temptress

Illustrations by Chris Patmore

Making your own character

With Poser's ability to control every aspect of the character, the creative possibilities are limitless. Because of the huge number of 3D artists creating content for Poser, and in particular Victoria, you will be able to find something to match your vision without needing any 3D modeling skills, such as Mohini's tail.

▶ Environment
Start the picture with a background setting, in this case DAZ's Heart of the Ocean Cyclorama, a specially designed photographic backdrop that gives the impression of three dimensions.

▶ Introducing Victoria
Place the blank figure into the scene. DAZ's ever-popular Victoria 3 is used here, primarily because of the extensive library of clothes, textures, and props available for her.

▶ Hidden scene
It is sometimes useful to hide the background. This allows the program to work faster because it does not have as many elements to redraw. This is not the same as making it invisible, as is done with the legs (see opposite). Simply select the element you want to hide and choose Hide Figure from the Figure menu.

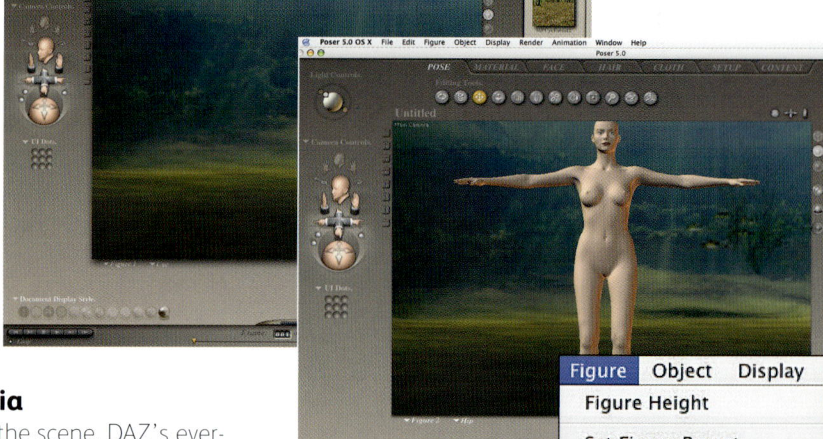

You will need

- Macintosh or Windows PC
- Curious Labs Poser or DAZ Studio
- DAZ's Victoria
- Clothes, props, backgrounds, etc.

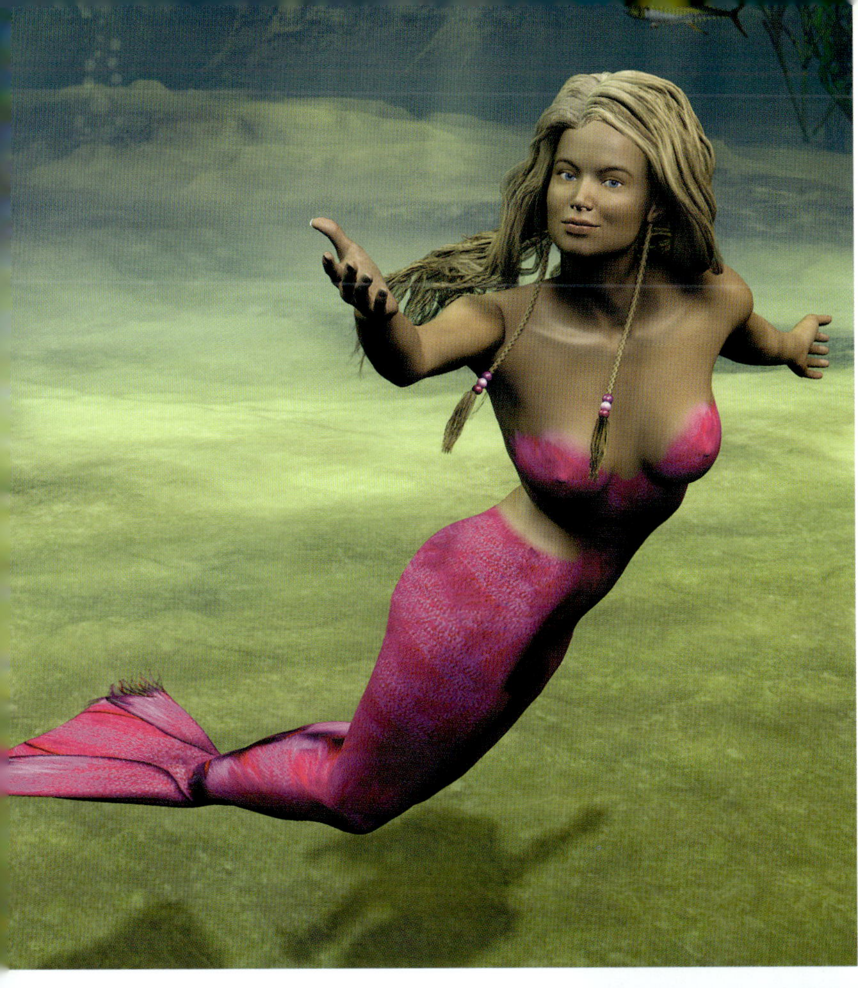

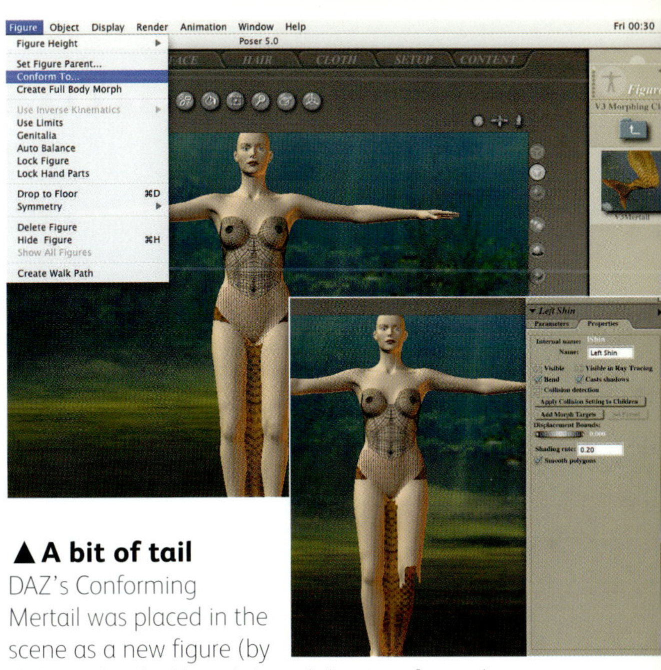

▲ A bit of tail

DAZ's Conforming Mertail was placed in the scene as a new figure (by clicking the double ticks), and then conformed to the main figure, making Victoria and the tail into a single item. Victoria's legs need to be hidden to let the tail be independently visible. Choose Windows>Parameter Dials>Properties and deselect the Visible check box by clicking on it. This has to be done for all the elements (toes, feet, shins, thighs, and so on) until only the tail and torso are visible.

▼ Hair and face

Adding the hair (DAZ's Wild Braids) and creating a unique face is where the character takes on her individuality. Using the Victoria Morph Pack, every aspect of the face can be altered. For Mohini, different Pacific-region ethnic types were mixed to create a unique face. A tempting expression was created, with all the fine-tuning done using the Parameter Dials, because they offer far greater control. The Face Camera lets you get close without having to adjust the main camera's perspective.

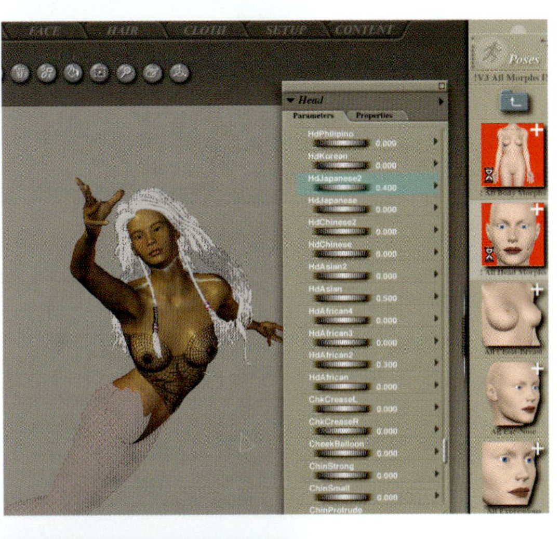

◄ Posing

There are many preset poses available that serve as excellent starting points for creating your own. The one used here is from a set of belly dancer poses, adjusted to allow for the lack of legs. The hands were fine-tuned to get a more alluring feel to the overall pose.

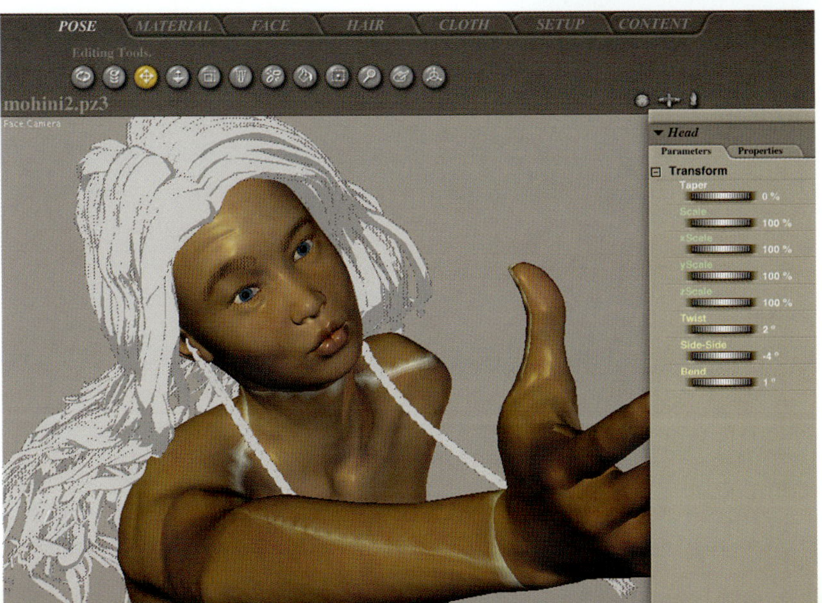

► Texture template

A texture template for Victoria 3. Either photos or digitally painted skin textures can be overlaid in Photoshop or another image-editing program. It is best to do this on a separate layer, keeping the template locked.

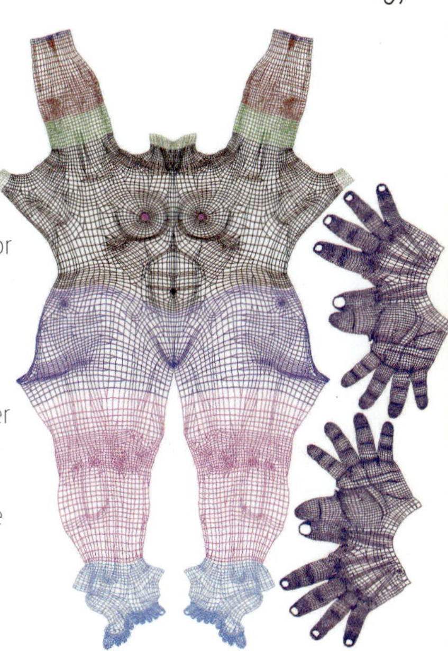

Who is she? Keiko is a remnant of the Asian white collar families that were the cornerstone of consumerism in the two decades that spanned the second millennium. Her personality is dictated by marketing and advertising campaigns and the whims of youth fueled by too much financial indulgence from their parents.

What does she wear? The latest fashion items, and the more original the better. In her quest for recognizable individuality, Keiko often persuades her friends from the fashion college to create something outlandish from the synthetic fabrics the industrial mega-corporations donate to students. Whatever she wears has to be accessorized with the latest gadgets and gizmos, and color-coordinated, of course.

GIZMO GIRL

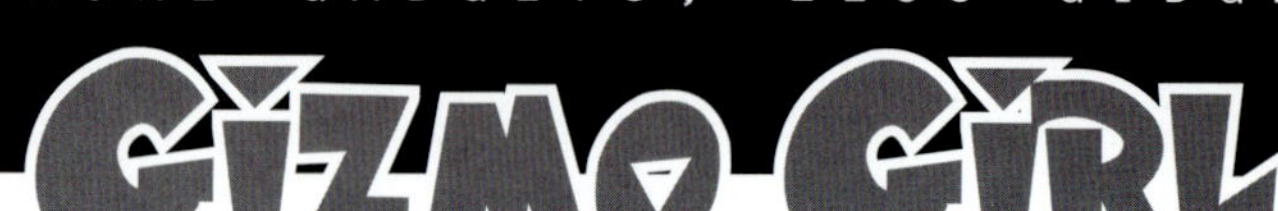

Illustrations by Dock

What does she do? Hanging out with her friends and gossiping takes up most of her spare time. There is so much to talk about—who's wearing what, which color is "now," what the best thing on the video link is. **How does she do it?** Even she wonders how she finds the time to do so much and still go shopping. With all her youthful exuberance, and her daddy's money, she somehow manages to lead a life free from worldly realities.

Making your own character

Endowing your characters with realism means spending time observing people. If, for example, you want to create superficial girls, you will have to frequent the places they gather, such as shopping malls, and listen to their conversations (but without looking like a stalker). Try using snippets of their chatter, because you could probably never make it up. Depending on the ethnicity of your characters, you may have to make cultural adjustments, but people around the world are essentially the same.

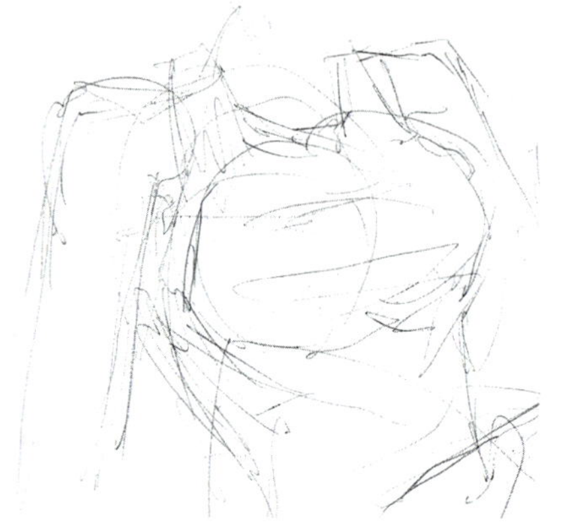

◄ Body building
Before making a final drawing, make lots of pencil sketches. Familiarity with the character's form is vital for maintaining consistency over a series of drawings. The sketches do not have to be facial or full figure. They could be of torsos and breasts (as shown), or the all-important hands.

▶ Facial studies

The face is the most expressive part of a character, and creating distinguishable, individual facial features for each character in the story means making lots of sketches. Remember that you can never have too much practice at drawing.

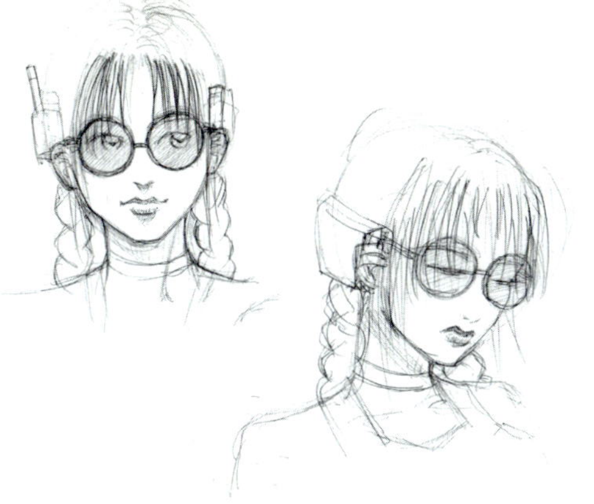

▼ Get in line

Finding the type of pen you feel most comfortable with will take some trial and error. For consistent lines, technical pens, such as Rapidographs, are the best, although some people prefer working with brushes or dip pens. Digital inking with a stylus has many advantages, but it takes time to get a feel for it.

◀ Style and structure

There are many different styles of manga and anime art, just as there are with Western comics and cartoons, although some have recognizable characteristics, such as disproportionately long legs and the more familiar large, round eyes. Look at a variety of manga to find a style that suits you and your story. Once you have decided in your mind how you want the character to look, sketch out the basic structure and proportions with a non-repro blue pencil. This can then be drawn over with a pencil, graphite or red. Try to keep the linework as clean as possible, with the minimum of overdrawing, although this can be corrected at the inking stage.

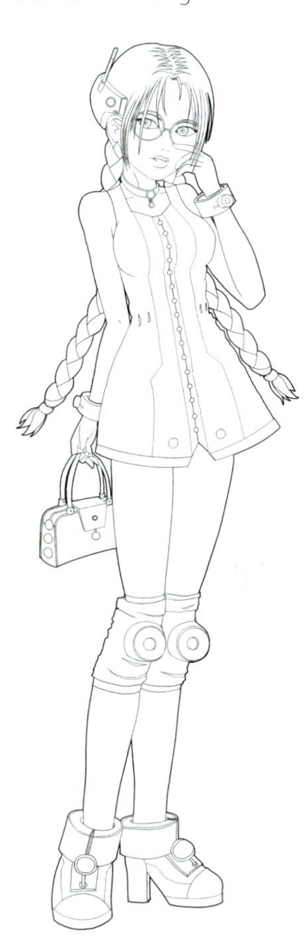

◀ Shades and flats

A lot of colored manga art uses toon or cel shading. Digital coloring is ideal for this because you can get consistent and even colors. It is also easy to add graduated shading and highlights, using the Airbrush tool, to give the image both depth and softness. By adjusting the opacity of layers, you also have great control over shadows.

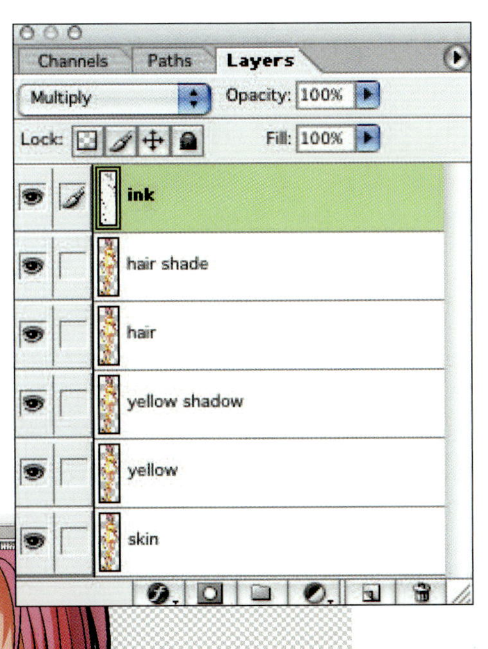

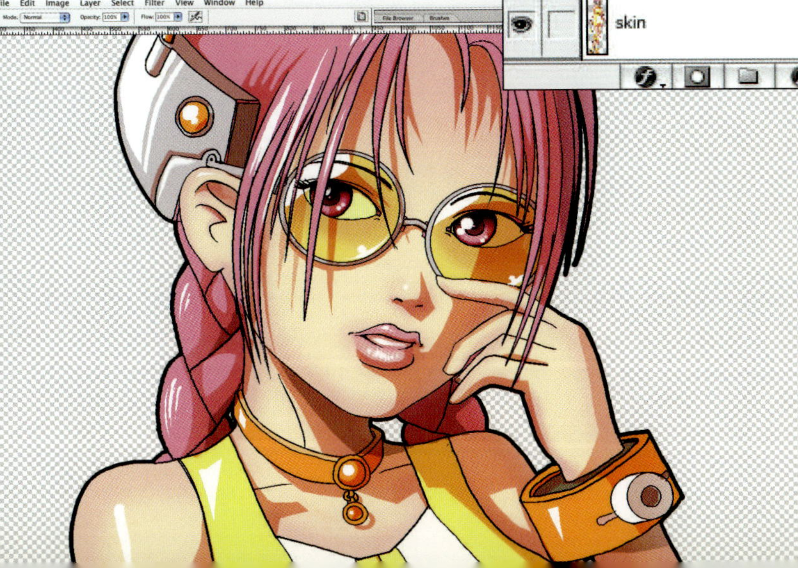

You will need

- Bristol board or drawing paper
- Pencil and eraser
- Black marker pens with various tips
- Macintosh or Windows PC
- Scanner
- Graphics tablet and stylus
- Adobe Photoshop

Who is she? Nadesico is a 23-year-old graduate of the Bunka Fashion College in Tokyo who is struggling to make a name for herself as an international designer. She works in an animation studio, using her drawing skills to earn a living, until she can sell her fashion designs. **What does she wear?** Naturally, she makes her own clothes, which this year are mostly based around the traditional kimono. She is currently wearing a modified kimono complete with an elongated obi and tabi socks under her platform tatami sandals. The modern interpretation also has broken sleeves at the shoulder and a short-cut dress. She wears her hair up, reminiscent of a geisha style, but with strands falling loosely around her face.

FASHION VICTIM

What does she do? Designing clothes using traditional styles with a modern interpretation has made it difficult for Nadesico to earn money. The conservative older generation is shocked by what she does to Japan's heritage, and her peers are more interested in Western-style clothes. **What happens to her?** She keeps trying to interest people in her designs but without much success. Out of frustration she starts writing a diary, as a manga, which becomes more popular than her clothes.

Illustrations by
Emma Vieceli of
Sweatdrop Studio

Making your own character

If you intend to work with cross-cultural images and stories, it is a good idea to do lots of research to ensure accuracy. The best method is to visit the country or area, because nothing can surpass firsthand experience. Full sensual immersion will bring your drawings and story to life, and do not forget to take a camera to photograph everything for reference. If you cannot actually visit a country, try to find an ethnic enclave in a nearby city.

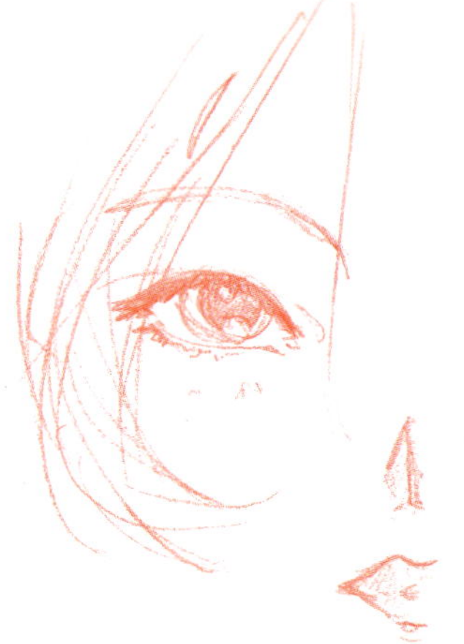

◄ Shojo face

Manga drawing styles range from very simple to extremely detailed, and are determined by the type of story or the audience they are aimed at. Nadesico is drawn in a shojo style, used for girls' comics. Practice will add confidence to your pencil strokes, letting you get the most from each one.

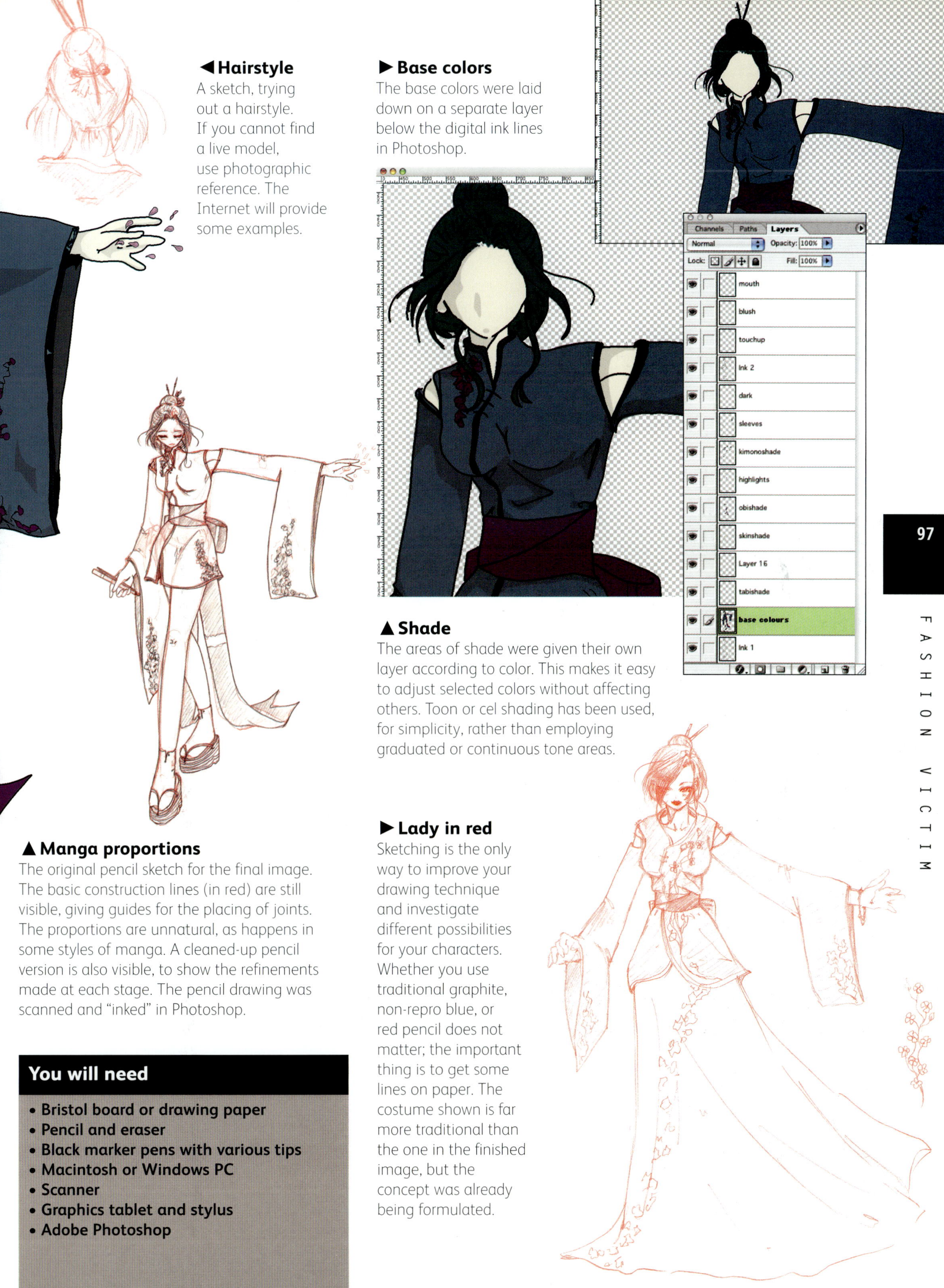

◀ Hairstyle

A sketch, trying out a hairstyle. If you cannot find a live model, use photographic reference. The Internet will provide some examples.

▶ Base colors

The base colors were laid down on a separate layer below the digital ink lines in Photoshop.

▲ Shade

The areas of shade were given their own layer according to color. This makes it easy to adjust selected colors without affecting others. Toon or cel shading has been used, for simplicity, rather than employing graduated or continuous tone areas.

▲ Manga proportions

The original pencil sketch for the final image. The basic construction lines (in red) are still visible, giving guides for the placing of joints. The proportions are unnatural, as happens in some styles of manga. A cleaned-up pencil version is also visible, to show the refinements made at each stage. The pencil drawing was scanned and "inked" in Photoshop.

▶ Lady in red

Sketching is the only way to improve your drawing technique and investigate different possibilities for your characters. Whether you use traditional graphite, non-repro blue, or red pencil does not matter; the important thing is to get some lines on paper. The costume shown is far more traditional than the one in the finished image, but the concept was already being formulated.

You will need

- Bristol board or drawing paper
- Pencil and eraser
- Black marker pens with various tips
- Macintosh or Windows PC
- Scanner
- Graphics tablet and stylus
- Adobe Photoshop

Who is she? Natsuki is a student, of Japanese and English parents, who has just started at another college, in yet another country. Despite the constant moving, new situations still overwhelm her, causing her to appear withdrawn or anxious. **What does she wear?** Her wardrobe is fairly nondescript, tending toward the utilitarian rather than the decorative. Her favorite sweater is an oversized one she borrowed from a male student at another college and forgot to return. Not particularly comfortable with her still gangly figure, she hides it under baggy clothes. **What does she do?** She compensates for her reticence by trying to be studious, which further alienates her from her peers.

DREAM STUDENT

What happens to her? At the new college, Natsuki meets James, a bit of a dreamer, to whom she feels inexplicably attracted. She soon finds that James's reserve hides a more complex and troubled personality.

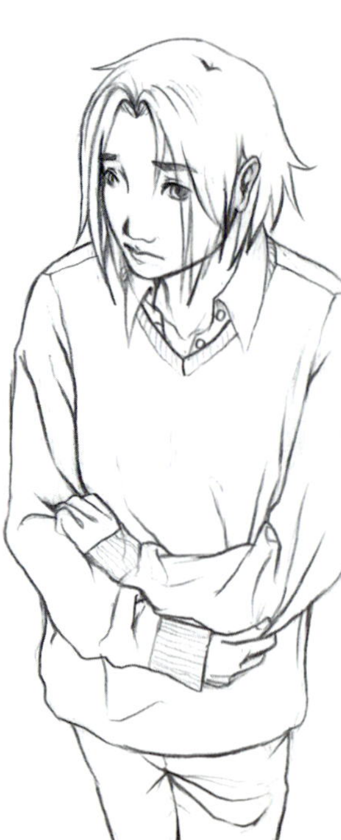

Illustrations by
Paul Duffield

Making your own character

When you want to make your drawing very accurate, it is often easier to work from photographic reference. For the main picture of Natsuki, using a photo served a twofold purpose. First, the unusual angle would be difficult to portray accurately without reference. Second, because the oversize fit of the sweater is a vital part of the character, it was important for the folds to be correctly rendered.

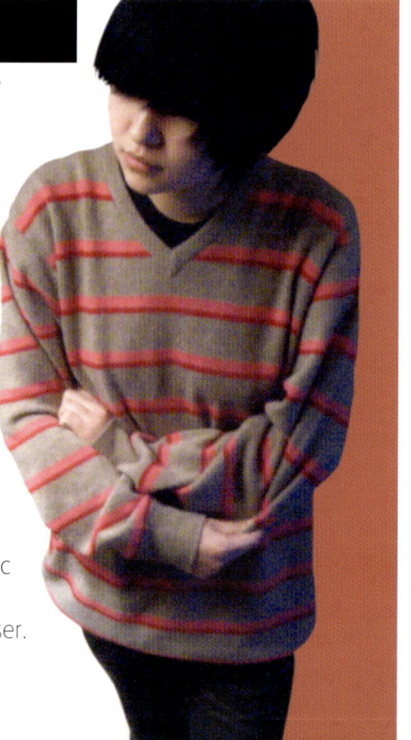

▶ Reference photo

If you need a specific pose, ask a friend whose shape is similar to the intended drawing to act as a model. For more generic poses, there are plenty of books filled with multi-angle shots, or use a program like Poser.

▶ Pencil drawing

Developing good drawing skills, like everything else, requires practice. Understanding anatomy and perspective are two vital elements for figurative drawing. As you are developing your technique and personal style, it is quite permissible to trace your photo reference as a starting point.

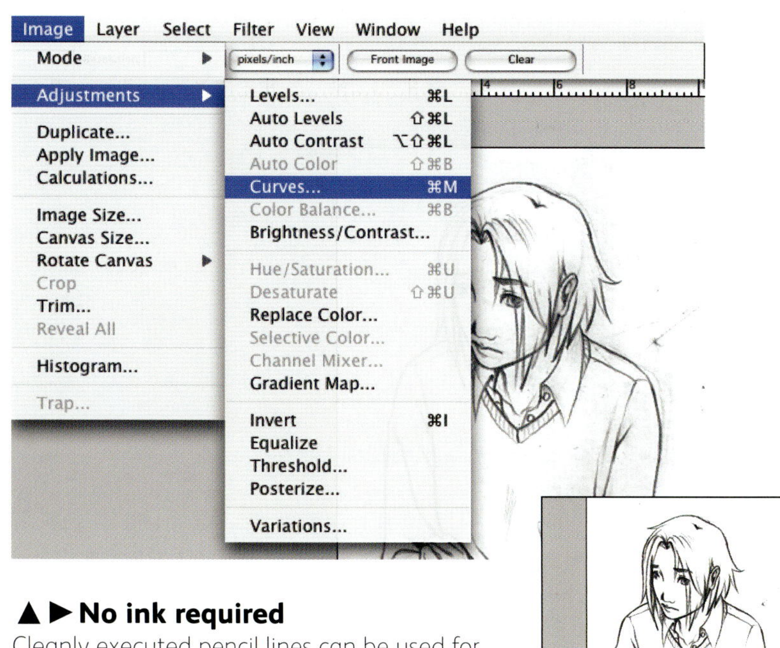

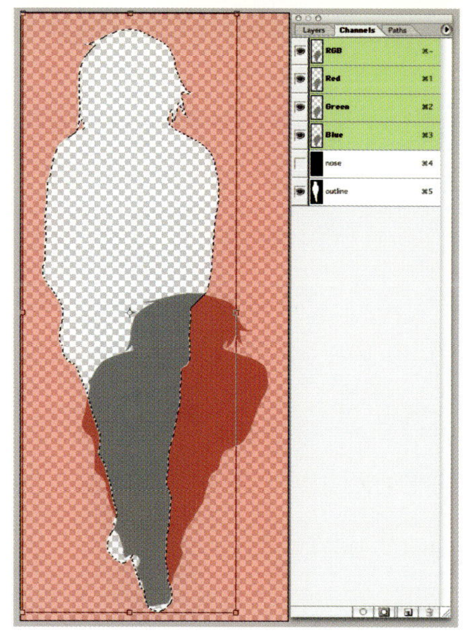

▲ ► No ink required

Cleanly executed pencil lines can be used for your finished image, without the need for inking. This will give a slightly softer look to your picture that can be used to emphasize personality. To darken the pencil lines of the scanned drawing, make adjustments to the Curves. This gives you more control over the tone than simply altering the Contrast. It is best to scan your drawing as grayscale and make the adjustments before converting it into RGB or CMYK for coloring.

▲ Shadow play

To create a shadow, use the Magic Wand tool to select the white background of the drawing layer and invert the selection to give you an active outline of the character. Create a new layer for the shadow, ensuring it is active. Fill the selection with a shade of gray. Use the Transform tool (Select>Transform Selection or CMD [CTRL]-T) to distort the shape by holding down the CMD (CTRL) key and dragging the corner of the selection. You can finish it by adding some Noise (Filter>Noise>Add Noise), as shown on the main picture, or add some blur to create a softer effect.

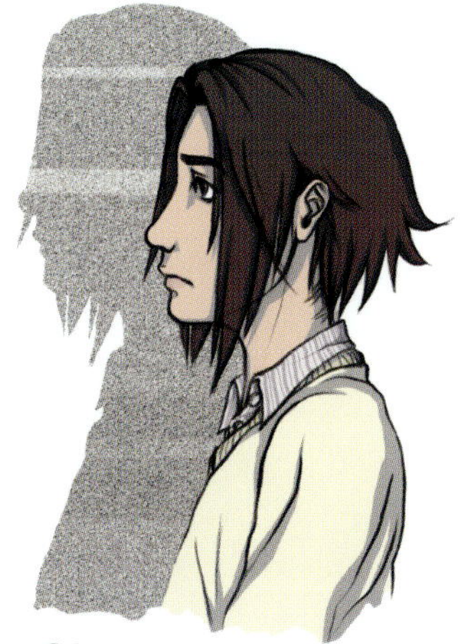

▲ High profile

Although a reference shot was used for the main image, the head was drawn from the artist's imagination, using his knowledge of anatomy to get the correct proportions.

▼ ► Layers of color

Give each clothing item and color its own layer in Photoshop to make editing much easier. Place the original drawing on the top layer. In the Layer Style palette (double-click on the layer in the Layer palette), set the General Blending mode to Multiply, to allow the underlying layers to show through while retaining the linework on top.

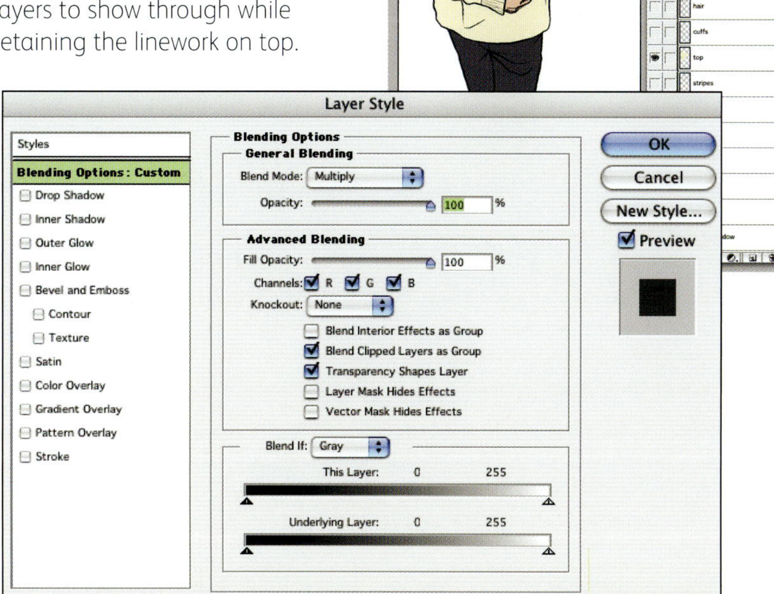

You will need

- Camera (film or digital)
- Bristol board or drawing paper
- Pencil and eraser
- Macintosh or Windows PC
- Scanner
- Graphics tablet and stylus
- Adobe Photoshop

Who is she? Twink is a fairy who lives in a land where the boys will not grow up, and the men no longer want to have fun. She is shunned by most of the other fairies because of her overdeveloped physique and libido. **What does she wear?** She has given up on flimsy gossamer gowns and floral frocks in favor of a more robust terrapin-shell bikini of her own design. **What does she do?** Twink wants to meet a real man, because she is tired of hanging around with a bunch of fairies. "No wonder they call it Neverland," she keeps saying to herself. **How does she do it?** Being only six inches tall, she finds it difficult communicating with men who are too narrow-minded to acknowledge her existence, but she has magic powers and can enter their dreams. In that nether land, they are on equal terms. The best ones even fly with her and never forget their encounter.

FeistyFairy

Illustrations by Monte Moore

Making your own character

Not everything is computer generated, with some artists still working with a range of traditional materials. There is a certain pleasure in the tactile nature of paint and brushes on paper or board, although there is not the same room for error that the multiple "Undos" digital artwork allows. Even if you intend always to work only digitally, it is still a good idea to use some "natural" media to get a feel for how it works, so that you can emulate it with your graphics tablet and software.

▶ Concept

First, a rough concept sketch was drawn to establish the best pose, figure, and personality. This remained essentially the same as the finished character, although some minor changes and refinements were made. Years of experience and practice of drawing females meant the artist could easily sketch an almost finished image without resorting to construction lines.

You will need

- **Bristol board or CS10 board**
- **Pencil and eraser**
- **Colored pencils**
- **Watercolors and acrylic paints**
- **Airbrush**
- **Frisket masking film**

▶ Pencil on board

The character was redrawn in pencil and any necessary changes were made. The drawing was kept very clean and relatively simple, to emphasize the cartoon look.

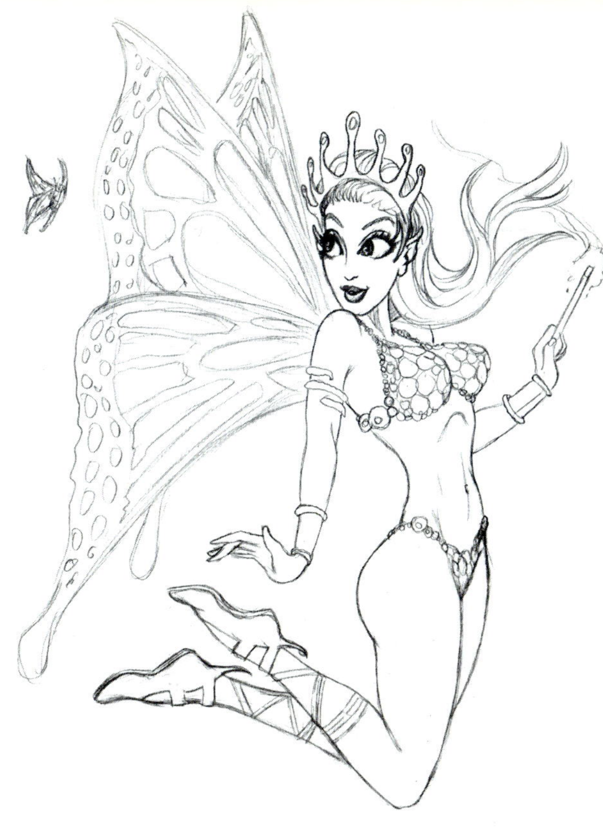

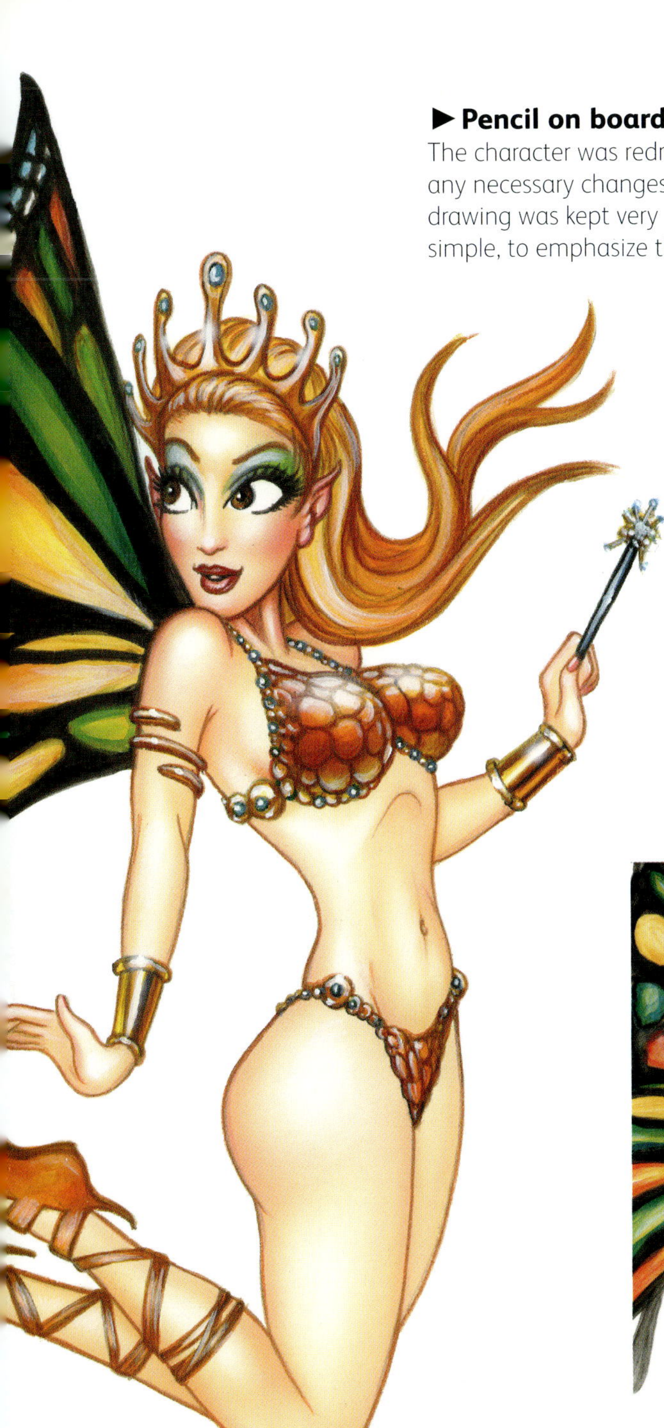

◀ Hand painting

For the initial painting stage, acrylics or watercolors were used to get a base of solid color. Hard outlines were painted in and color choices made. Hair, eyes, and other details were first illustrated at this stage, but skin tones and shading were not tackled because they are best done with an airbrush.

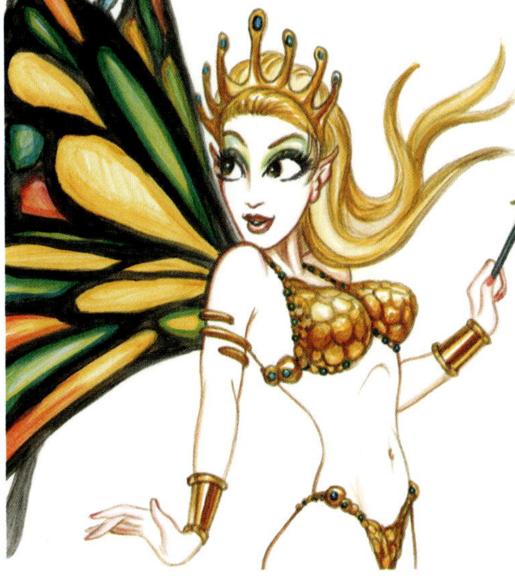

◀ Airbrushing

Airbrushing produces soft, graduated tones. It is often used freehand, but if a more defined line is required, the image is covered with a removable masking film, called frisket. The required shapes are cut out, and color is sprayed into the image. The mask stops the airbrush spray from bleeding onto the white area, and keeps the edges well defined. Highlights and shadows were added to the final picture using more hand-painted acrylics. Colored pencils were also used for precise details, especially for cleaning up the linework to give it a cartoon feel.

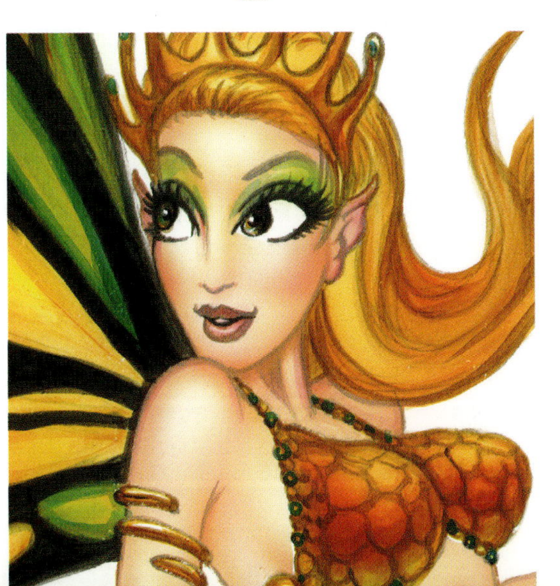

Check this out

Books published by Monte Moore:
Maidens (Vol. 1 and 2)
Maginique
Mystica
Majesika

Who is she? Safiye is a mythological figure of Karkistan, who serves as the narrator of that country's myths and legends. **What does she wear?** Her clothes are made of the finest silk brocade, embellished with gossamer-thin silver threads. Her shoes and accessories are made from the tanned skins of rodents, to produce the supplest leather, and the raised heels are fashioned from the branches of local cedar trees. **What does she do?** She tells the stories and legends of heroes of the past and present, the most beloved of which is Emperor Adham I of the Phantom Noir, whose image adorns her coat (one of Adham's bodyguards is featured on page 54).

STORYTELLER

How does she do it? It is said that Safiye searches for receptive scribes to whom to relate her tales, so that they may be written down for all to enjoy, and the smoke from her pipe puts the writers into a trance so that they can hear her. The finished texts are then copied and distributed to the seats of learning throughout the land. She is often a character in the stories herself.

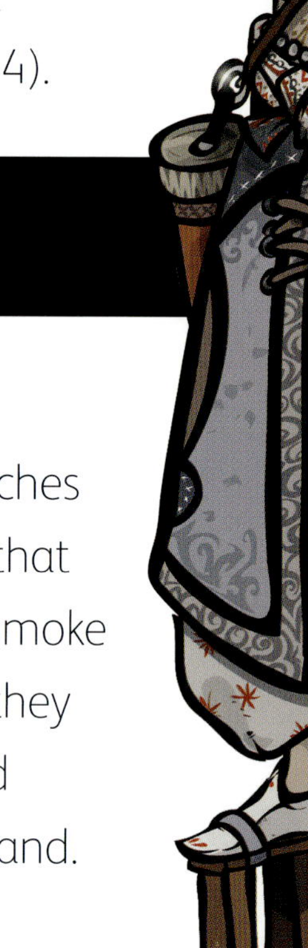

Illustrations by
Nic Brennan

Making your own character

One of the most important factors of storytelling is point of view—that is, who is recounting the story. These are usually first person (I) or third person (he/she), which is sometimes known as the god view. Introducing a character to act as narrator adds a touch of realism, especially when he or she is integrated into the story. If illustrating a comic from a narrator's point of view, take this into consideration when designing the panels, because they should be composed as if through the storyteller's eyes.

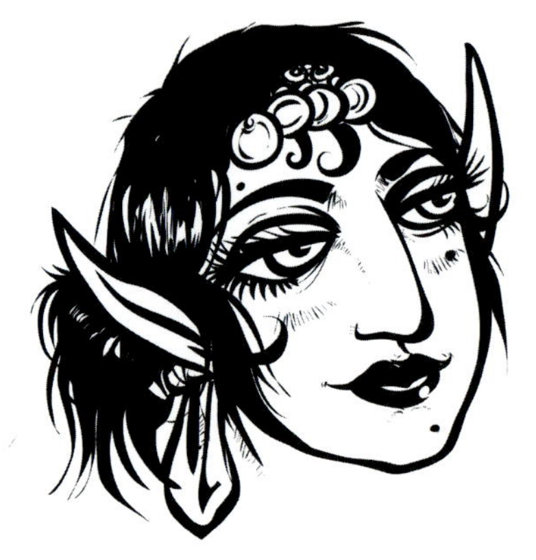

◀ Head lines

Although you are developing your own style of drawing, the tools you choose will affect the way your pictures look. For example, all the images shown here were created in Illustrator. Because it is a vector drawing program, the lines it produces are very crisp and sometimes more angular than those made in a pixel-based program such as Photoshop, giving them the appearance of a linocut or similar graphic style.

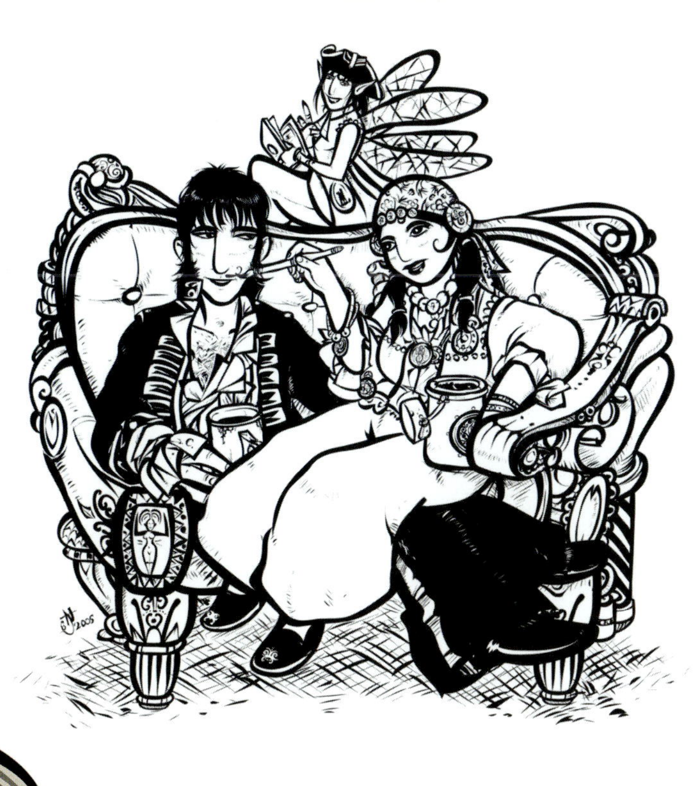

◀ Point of view

Establishing a narrator's place in the story will help the reader suspend disbelief. By showing Safiye in a scene with the protagonist, it helps to establish in the mind of the reader that she actually witnessed the events she is recounting. It also has the added advantage of giving a sense of scale to the character.

▶ Making alterations

Apart from making a graphically identifiable image, Illustrator files have the advantage of remaining editable through all stages. All lines can be changed and colors easily altered. For example, shadows and highlights can be lightened or darkened simply by altering the transparency settings.

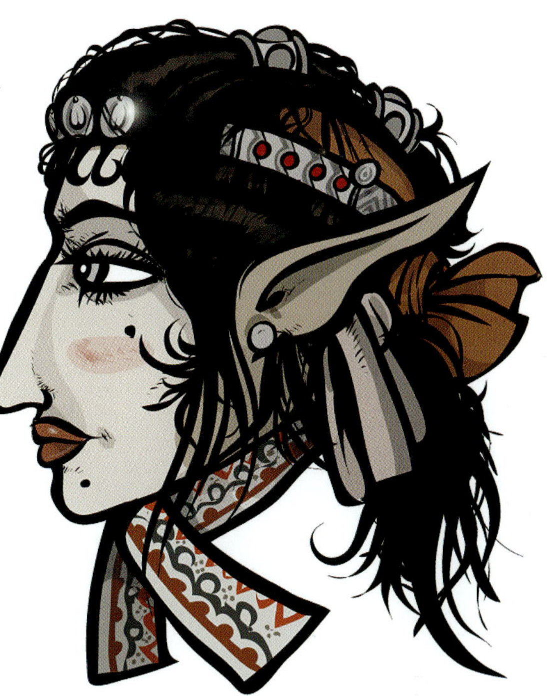

▶ Detail

This illustration is a detail from Safiye's coat, representing the Emperor Adham and his wife, Sophia. It is drawn in the imagined style of art of the fictitious country. Paying attention to such details will make the story seem more real for the reader.

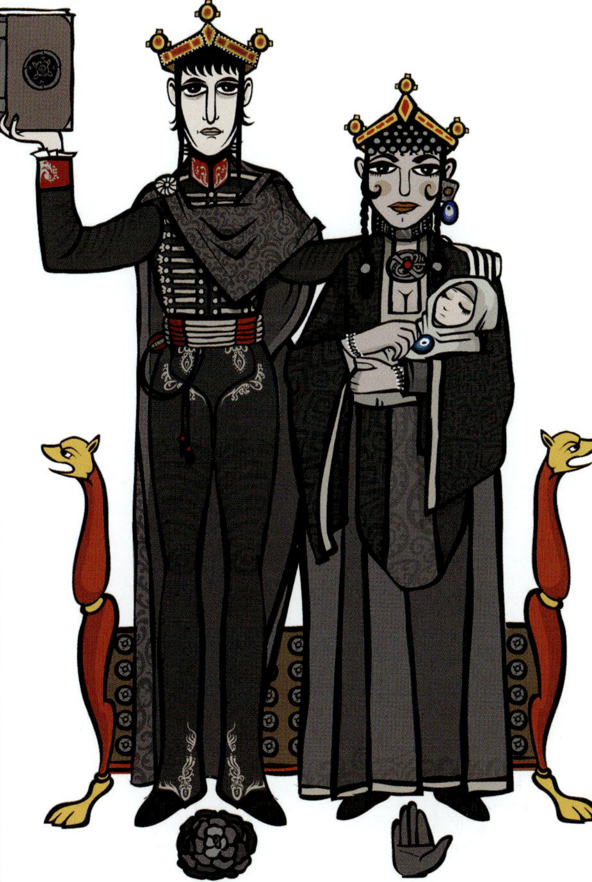

You will need

- Macintosh or Windows PC
- Graphics tablet and stylus
- Adobe Illustrator
- Adobe Photoshop

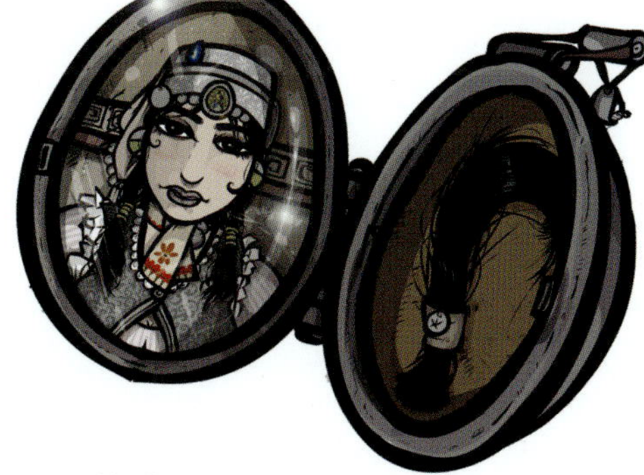

▲ Embellishments

Vignettes, such as this locket containing a portrait of Sophia and a lock of her hair, can be added to the story's page to embellish it, not only pictorially but also by revealing an aspect of the story that might not be expressed in words.

Who is she? Liel is a half-human/half-elf who lives in an elf village at a time of great peace for elves. Despite the utopian idyll, Liel feels marginalized because of her mixed race. **What does she wear?** Her sylvan lifestyle does not require a lot of clothing. The weather is warm all year-round, and being the adventurous type, Liel likes as much freedom of movement as possible. Most of the clothes she does wear are made from the finest leathers that the elfin tanners are renowned for producing. **What happens to her?** Liel is worried by some dark omens, so her friend Gon tricks her into meeting the Swordmaster, a reclusive warrior who lives on the edge of the village. He puts on an impressive display of his martial skills.

A Game Elf

Illustrations by
Simon Valderrama

What does she do? Liel is not convinced about the use of the Swordmaster's martial abilities, as it goes against the elfin ethos. However, events transpire that show Liel that she must learn the warrior's way, so she becomes the Swordmaster's apprentice. Already feeling like an outsider, she has no trouble adapting to the new lifestyle and learns very quickly as the situation darkens.

Making your own character

The character was devised as part of an in-development computer role-playing game called *Genocide*. Different versions were needed for the gameplay, the cut scenes (short movies that segue the game's levels), and for publicity and packaging. The images shown here were created in an anime style as part of the initial character development. The final character used in the game was created in 3D software.

◀ Portrait and profile

Drawn in an anime style, Liel's face has the characteristic large eyes and angular features drawn with minimal line detail. The hair is angular, too, and drawn as large units rather than strands. The coloring is toon or cel shading, which involves using flat areas of color in various tones. These images incorporate some blended tones to give the impression of sheen. Some of the shadows were created using the transparency/opacity function of Photoshop.

▶ Night lights

Using the portrait as a starting point, darker tones of the original colors were used to give a sense of nighttime. Highlights and shadows were given more contrast, and blending was used to add extra softness to the areas, as would happen with the softer night light.

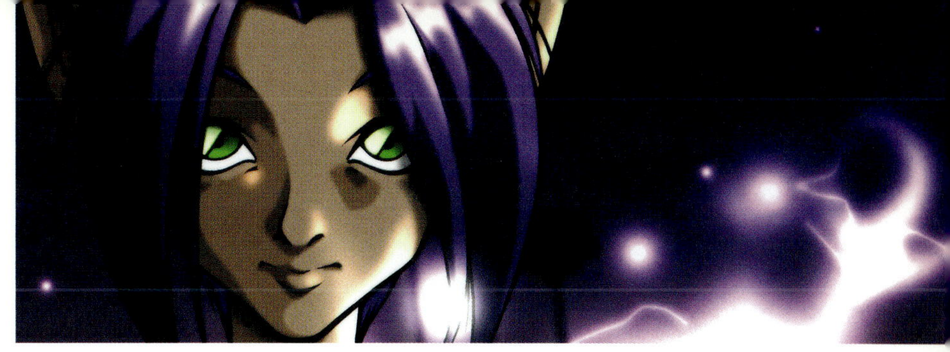

◀▶ Tree shader

Using the portrait picture again, patches of green were painted onto a separate layer in Photoshop and had a Blur filter applied to make them appear out of focus. On another layer, this time on top of the main image, the shadow areas were drawn and the layer Opacity reduced until the desired effect was achieved.

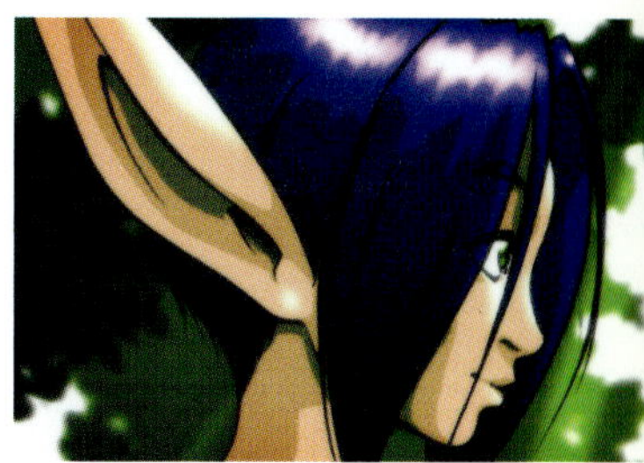

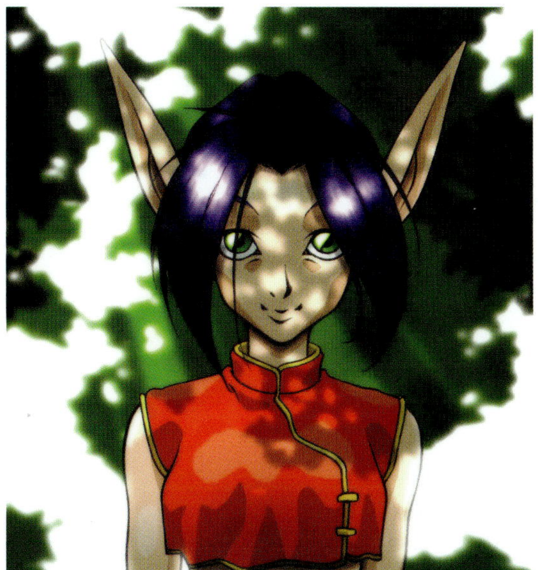

▶ Storyboard

A page from the storyboard for the cut movie shows Liel's first encounter with the Swordmaster. It is very important to storyboard every scene and shot, because the time and expense involved in creating animation does not allow for the experimenting and reshooting that live-action films do.

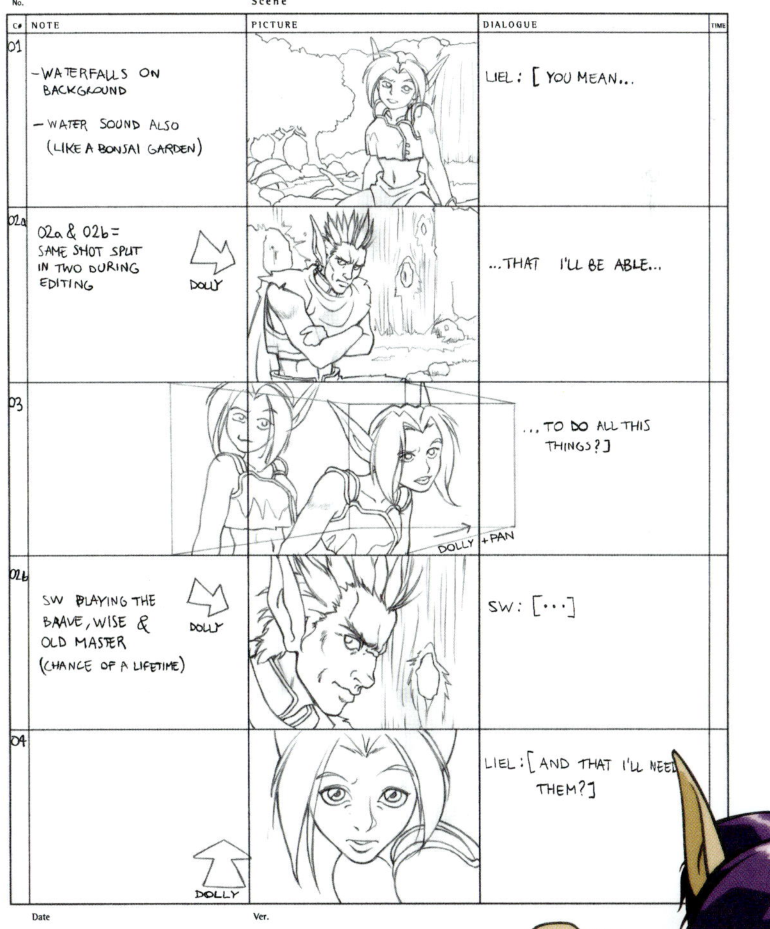

▶ Chibi

As part of the game's development, SD (super deformed) or chibi versions of the characters were created. Chibi (Japanese for child) is a style of manga/anime where the proportions of the characters are similar to those of a child. It is also called super deformed because the features are extremely simplified and exaggerated.

Who is she? No, she is not the cash-carrying benefactor eagerly anticipated by gummy, smiling little children, who is expected to put a coin under their pillow in exchange for a lost tooth. In fact, rewarding children for losing their teeth is the last thing she would do. **What does she wear?** A strappy little mini dress, the color of the pinkest, healthiest gums, and black stockings that reinforce her image as someone not to be messed with. Not all fairies are gossamer and goodness. **What does she do?** Did you ever dream that all your teeth were falling out? That was her work. Her motives and actions are obscure and guarded, and not of the mortal realm.

TOOTH FAIRY

How does she do it? Because no one is really sure what she does, no one knows what her modus operandi is. It is parents who put the money under pillows, so children stop believing in the Tooth Fairy once their cash source of first teeth are gone, and she prefers it that way. After all, she has a reputation to reclaim.

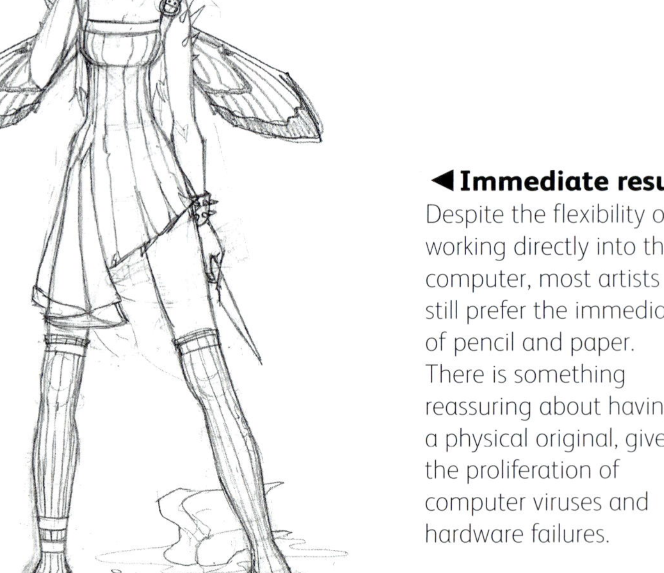

Illustrations by Liz Powell

Making your own character

Making new interpretations of popular icons can be a lot of fun, especially if they challenge people's established concepts. Playing around with religious deities can lead to all sorts of problems with fundamentalists, especially if the boundaries of bad taste are pushed too far. A certain amount of respect for cultural heritage should be maintained. On the other hand, most fairy tales have been sanitized over the years, losing their dark, Gothic origins, and are ripe for new fantasy interpretations.

◄ **Immediate result**
Despite the flexibility of working directly into the computer, most artists still prefer the immediacy of pencil and paper. There is something reassuring about having a physical original, given the proliferation of computer viruses and hardware failures.

▶ Digital inking

Scanned pencils are inked in openCanvas in much the same way as in Photoshop. The advantage of digital inking, especially when beginning, is that you get a second (or third) chance at a line if you make a mistake, without having to resort to Wite-Out or other corrective methods. However, you need a lot of practice with a stylus to produce great lines.

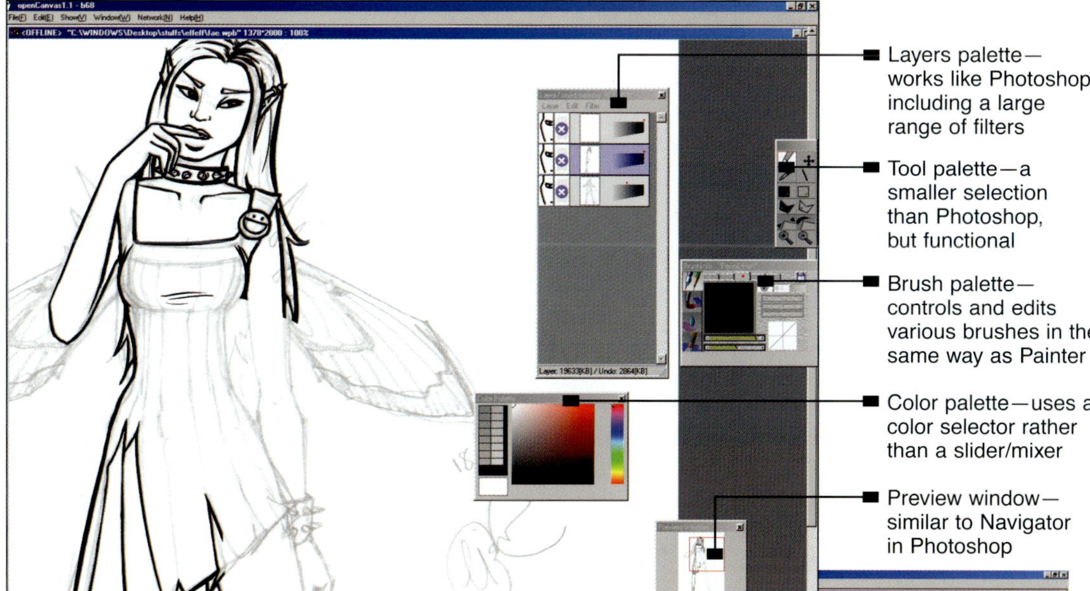

- Layers palette—works like Photoshop, including a large range of filters
- Tool palette—a smaller selection than Photoshop, but functional
- Brush palette—controls and edits various brushes in the same way as Painter
- Color palette—uses a color selector rather than a slider/mixer
- Preview window—similar to Navigator in Photoshop

▶ Skin art

Assigning layers for each color gives you a lot more freedom with your brushstrokes. Using a Watercolor Brush, the color can be applied in broad strokes, laying different densities one on top of another to achieve the required tone and shade. Even though the color extends beyond the edge of the outlines, it is very easy to clean up afterward.

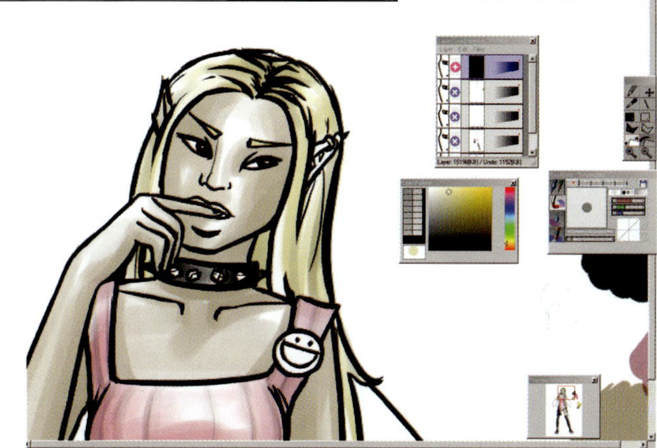

◀ Final ink

The finished "inked" outline is ready to be colored. In openCanvas, the main editing layer is transparent by default, making it easy to paint on the underlying layers.

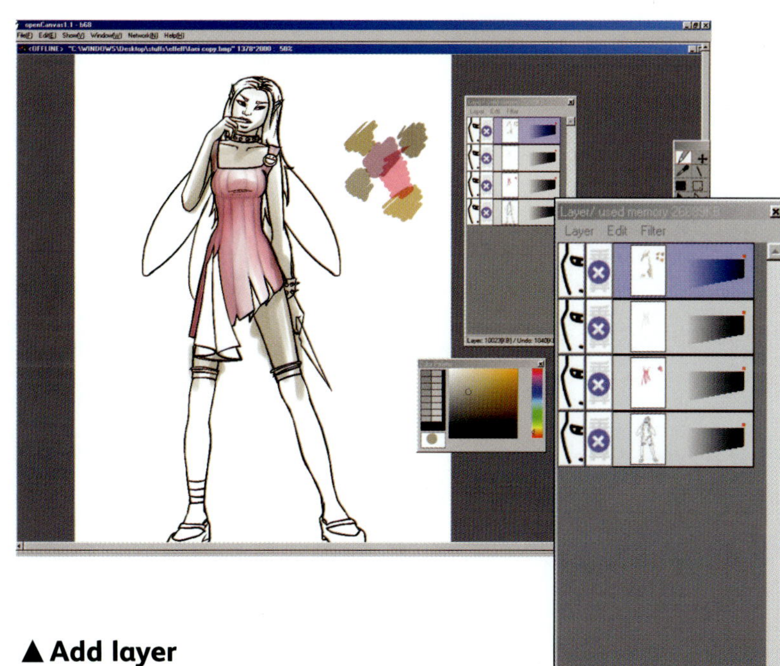

▲ Add layer

In openCanvas, the default layer is called a Multiply layer, where white is transparent, black is solid, and colors have varying degrees of transparency so that colors from other layers show through. Another type of layer is the Add layer (indicated with a + in the Layer palette). Painting on this layer causes the underlying layers to be lightened, similar to using the Dodge tool in Photoshop. It is mostly used for creating highlights and reflections.

You will need

- **Bristol board or drawing paper**
- **Pencil and eraser**
- **Windows PC**
- **Scanner**
- **Graphics tablet and stylus**
- **openCanvas**

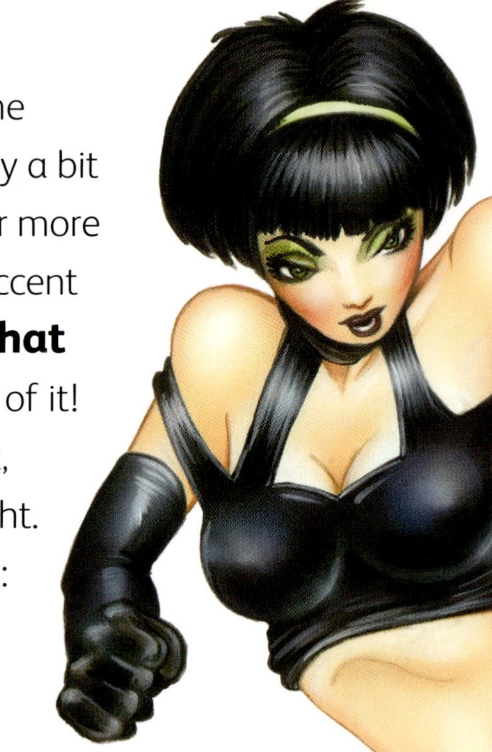

Who is she? Veronique is really Veronica Arnett. She comes from one of those middle-class families that try a bit too hard to be hip and liberal. To make herself appear more exotic, she has changed her name and affected an accent that is a mixture of French and Eastern European. **What does she wear?** It has got to be black, and plenty of it! Her clothes can be made of leather, latex, or spandex, but they have to be black and they have to be skintight. The same goes for makeup. Nail polish: black. Lipstick: black. Hair: black (with a little help). She does use green eye shadow, however, because she does not want to look like she has been in a fight.

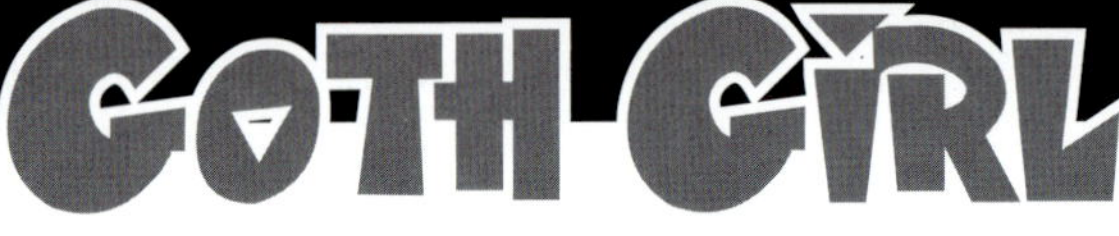

GOTH GIRL

Illustrations by Monte Moore

What does she do? Although she walks around being sullen, brooding, and just too cool to talk, she loves to dance. She pretends to like music that is very esoteric, underground, and on the edge, but in the quiet of her own room, anything with a decent beat will get her moving. **What happens to her?** She really wants to join a goth band, but no matter how well she can fake an accent, she cannot disguise her natural singing voice and it will not develop the raspiness the local bands want. But she's not bitter—much.

Making your own character

In its heyday, pinup art was very popular on saucy postcards sold in European vacation resorts, for decorating warplanes and the pages of *Playboy* and other men's magazines. Although popular tastes change, there will always be a market for this style of drawing. Artist Monte Moore, who to date has had five books of fantasy female art published, created a whole series of images in this and other styles (see also page 100) for a card game called Wench. If drawing fantasy females is your thing, it is advisable to find as many outlets as possible.

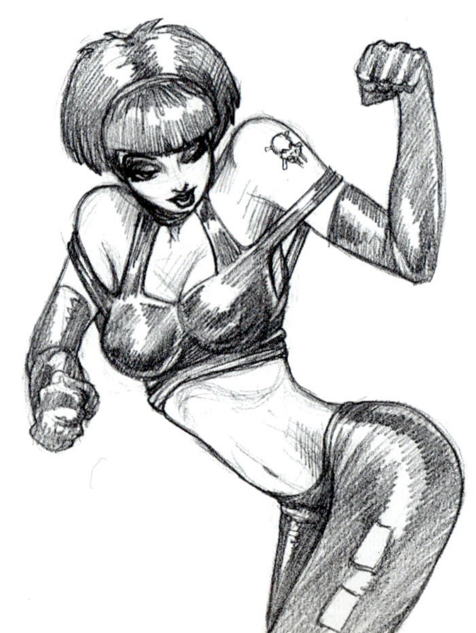

◄ Starting point

As has already been established, sketching is the best place to start your character. If you have a clear idea of what the final image will look like, this can be as simple or complex as you like. This will be affected by the amount of experience you have, your intention for the work, and the techniques and materials you use.

▼ Pencil on board

Making your working pencil drawing is, in this case, best done with a hard pencil (H, 2H, 3H). This will make faint lines that will not smudge or show through the ensuing coloring stages. If possible, keep tonal shading to a minimum at this stage.

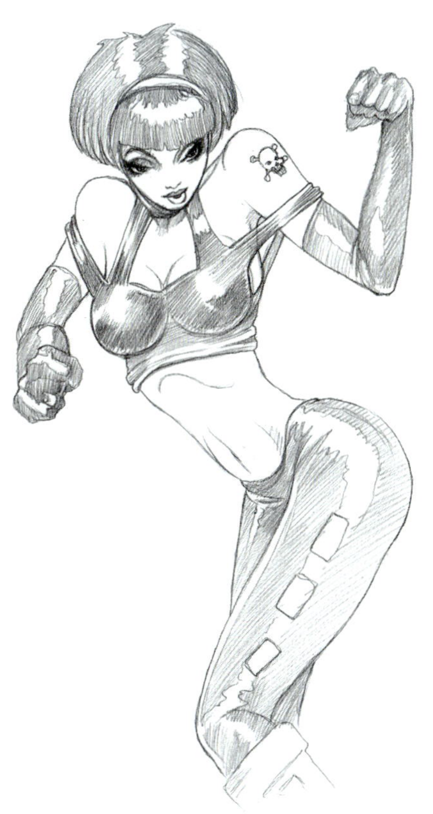

▶ Hand painting

Working with a variety of natural media does require a certain amount of planning to avoid incompatibilities with paints and inks. For example, if you intend to use watercolor washes, these will have to be laid down first so that they can be absorbed by the paper, and to allow stronger colors to be added on top. For this image, a mixture of watercolors and acrylics was used to lay down some basic colors and to paint over the pencil lines.

▶ Airbrushing

Airbrush was very popular in the 1970s and 1980s for all manner of graphic arts, from photo retouching to adding pictures to everything from toys to surfboards to trucks. Although it is still popular for customizing motor vehicles, its use in graphic arts has been more or less replaced by the digital equivalent in Photoshop and other such programs. Most of the coloring in this picture was done with an airbrush. A removable masking film, called frisket, is used to keep colors from bleeding into the wrong places. The inks spray easily off the existing paints, which add extra depth to the new layer of color.

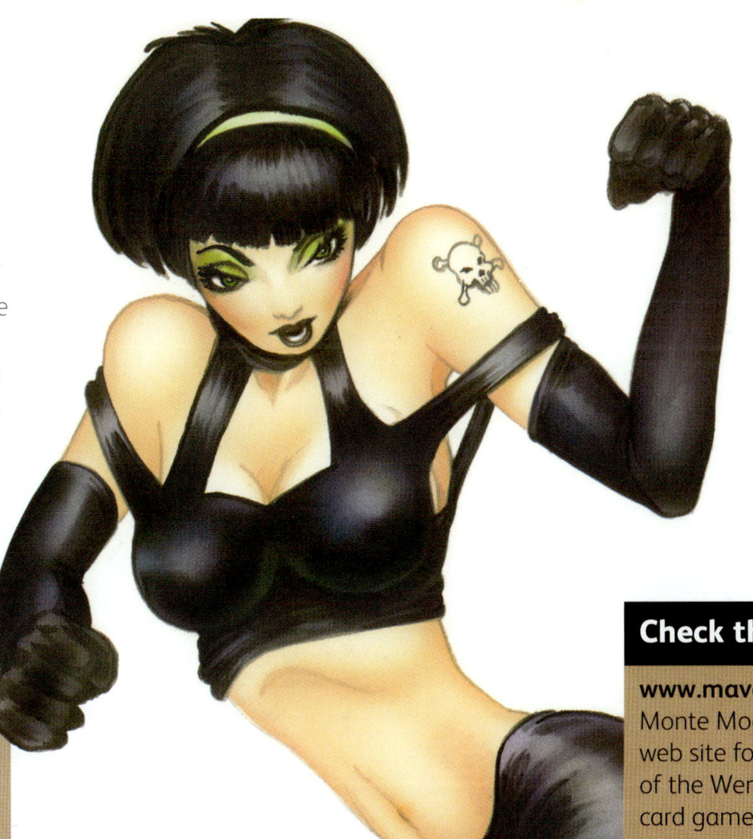

You will need

- Bristol board or CS10 board
- Pencil and eraser
- Colored pencils
- Watercolors and acrylics
- Airbrush
- Frisket masking film

Check this out

www.mavarts.com
Monte Moore's web site for details of the Wench card game.

Who are they? Who would image that one apartment building could house so many fine young women? All beautiful and talented in their own ways, they come from different cultural backgrounds but are united as sisters. **What do they wear?** Whatever takes their fancy, from slinky to kinky and from neat to street, but you can guarantee that they will turn heads when they are out and about. **What do they do?** They sing backup vocals in studio sessions, for the fun of it and to earn some spending money. Alice has been in the business too long and keeps the rest of them down to earth about the empty promises of stardom. Individually, they lead their own lives, trying to do the best they can with their God-given assets. **What happens to them?** Every day is an adventure, from scouring the stores for bargains to fending off advances from all the cocky young men who hope they have a chance at impressing them. They are just having too much fun to want to be tied down to relationships.

BROWN SUGAR

Illustrations by David Bircham

Making your own character

Although every picture can tell a story, it does not have to be a specific one. Comics are not the only outlet for figurative artists. Commissioned illustration is getting rarer, but there is a huge market for stock art that can be bought on CD or over the Internet. All the images shown here were created for DigitalVision. Finding a subject, such as the racial diversity of urban living, and portraying it in a unique style can be very lucrative. Avoiding stereotypes can be difficult, but humor and pastiche can go a long way toward overcoming this problem. Devising a back story for the people in the illustrations will help bring them to life and make them more sellable.

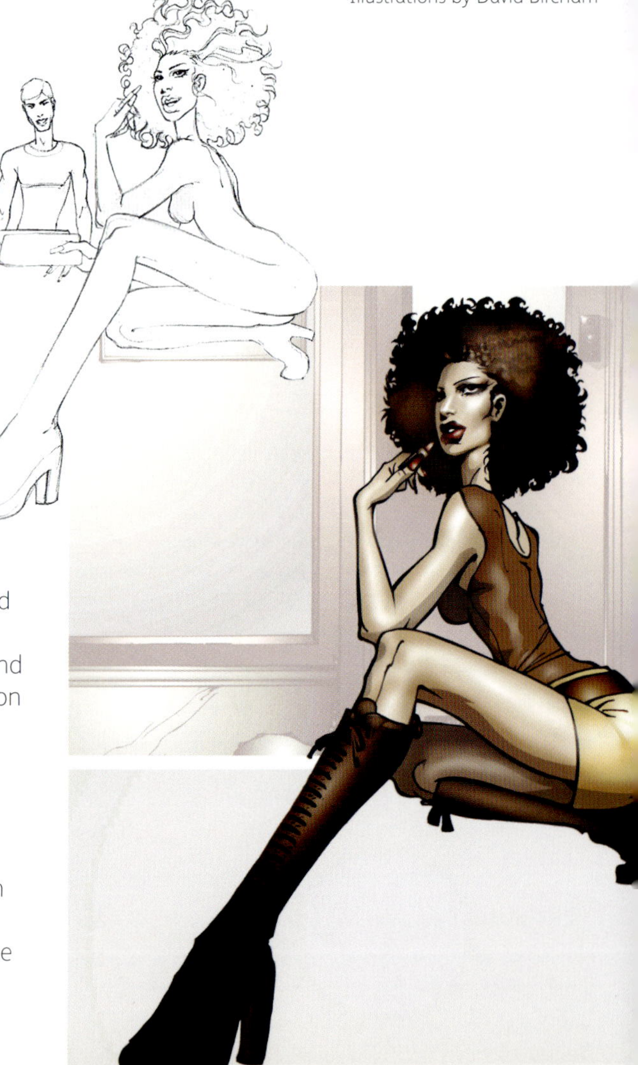

▶ Angela

Angela's earliest memory is of her mother's big hair and listening to her talk about black power and watching *Soul Train* on television. She often yearns to return to those simpler times, which is reflected in the way she looks. Photoshop's Airbrush tool helps the image hearken back to those halcyon days.

You will need

- **Bristol board or drawing paper**
- **Pencil and eraser**
- **Black marker pens with various tips**
- **Macintosh or Windows PC**
- **Scanner**
- **Graphics tablet and stylus**
- **Adobe Photoshop**

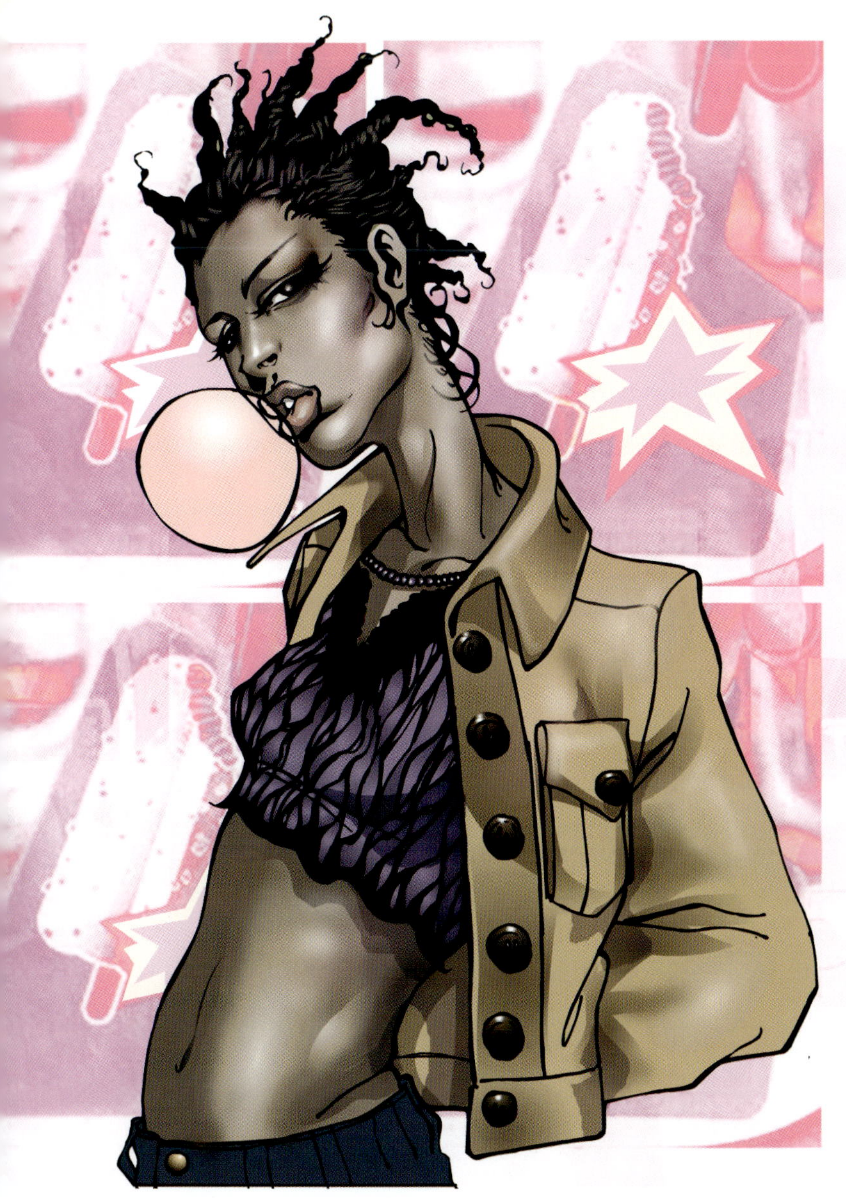

▶ Maria

Maria likes fast cars, and even though she is not so shallow as to let a boy impress her just because he has a flashy car, she will not say no to a ride. Her Latin passion is well tempered by her friendship with Candy.

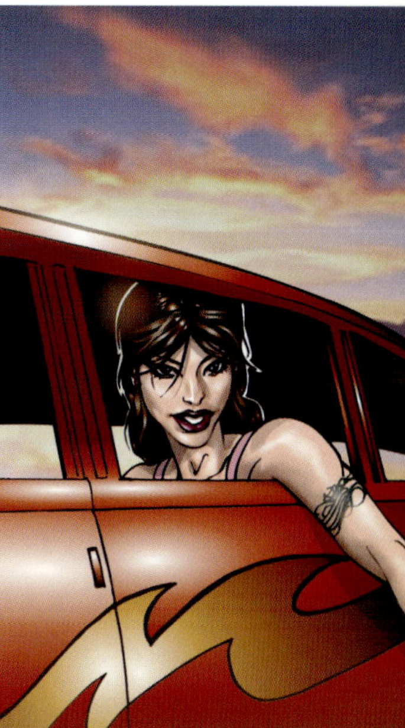

◀ Candy

Candy's lean, lithe body and high-cheekbone looks get her plenty of modeling work, but her real love is video-making. She is developing an idea for a documentary, but will not even tell her friends what it is about.

▶ Alice

The oldest of Candy's friends, Alice has worked in media and publishing for longer than she cares to admit. The fact that she does not need to show a resume when changing jobs attests to this. Alice knows what she wants and how to get it, although she sometimes worries that she is not getting any younger. Using strong, clear linework as a foundation, the Photoshop airbrushing gives the image a high-gloss look that sums up the character's personality.

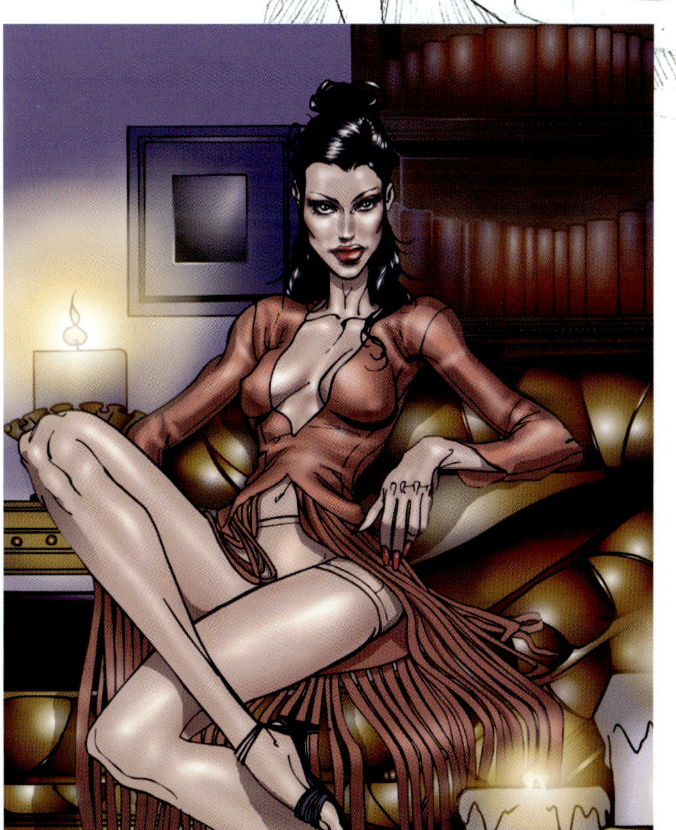

Check this out

www.digitalvision.com Royalty-free illustrations where more examples of Candy and her friends can be found.

www.pulptheatre.com The artist's web site, displaying his latest comics and illustrations.

Who is she? Rachael is just an ordinary girl with good looks and a passion for being in the spotlight. **What does she wear?** Fashion is a big part of her life. Unfortunately, show business has not bestowed its wealth upon her—yet. She is sure it will happen eventually, but in the meantime, she buys cheap clothes and customizes them, and uses a bit of mix and match. Luckily, she has always understood that it is not what you wear but the way you wear it that counts the most. **What does she do?** Rachael tries everything that will help her to get noticed. Well, almost everything. She has sung with bands and in musicals; she has acted on the stage and in movies—even if they are just walk-on parts. She has even modeled—fashion only, though. Unfortunately, that big break keeps eluding her.

PERFORMING ART

How does she do it? With sheer determination and a vibrant personality that is tempered by common sense and a solid moral foundation. It also helps that she has the looks to attract attention. Setting herself certain standards does mean she often misses jobs that girls with less modesty are happy to take, but she knows that her innate talent will shine through in the end, without her having to compromise her values or integrity.

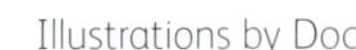

Illustrations by Dock

Making your own character

The idea of creating girl-next-door characters is to take the ordinary and either make them extraordinary, or write stories about everyday life and possibly incorporate moral issues (without being overtly preachy). The advantage of these so-called average girls is that they can be related to in ways other fantasy figures cannot. If truth be known, most boys fantasize about the girl next door more than some unattainable female icon. It worked for Spider-man.

◄ **Explore the possibilities**
No matter how you produce the sketches, make sure you fully explore the character's personality, physique, and wardrobe before you start on any major story project.

▶ Photoshop tips

When drawing sketches in Photoshop, you can easily access the eraser by pressing "E" on the keyboard. To return to the brush, press "B." If you are using a Wacom stylus and tablet, simply turn the stylus upside down as you would with an eraser-tipped pencil.

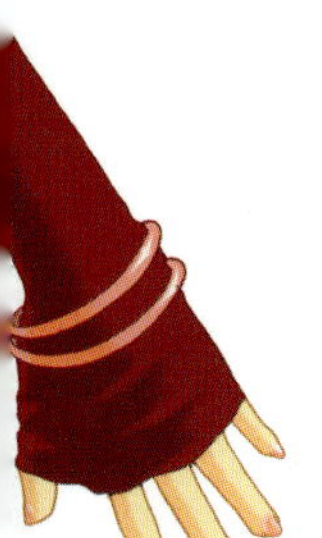

◀ Edited highlights

For the novice artist, one of the hardest things to master is lighting—where the light source is and how it affects the character. This means getting the correct proportion of highlights and shadows and ensuring they are consistent throughout the image. The finished picture of Rachael shows a very strong overhead frontal light source, such as a midday summer sun. If you do not have a model to use for photographic reference, Poser or the free DAZ Studio are ideal reference tools.

▼ Make backups

Once you familiarize yourself with digital tools and feel comfortable with a graphics tablet and stylus, there are many advantages to working directly into the computer. All stages of your artwork, from initial construction lines to the final colored image, can be incorporated into a single, multilayered document—which you will, naturally, rigorously back up.

▼ Blue tablet

Many artists now do their sketching digitally. Although these will never quite match paper and pencil, graphics tablets, especially larger ones, do allow for excellent sketching possibilities. Some artists even prefer to do their "pencils" digitally, print out a "non-repro blue" version to ink by hand, then scan it back into the computer for coloring. If you do your sketching or "pencils" digitally, it is advisable to keep printed copies of at least the final line drawing, on top of a regular digital backup, because you never know what is going to happen.

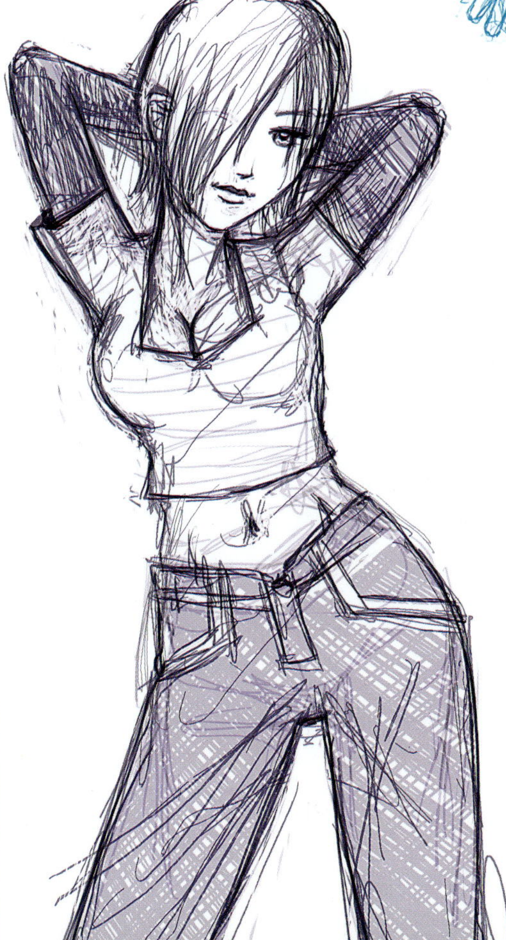

You will need

- **Macintosh or Windows PC**
- **Graphics tablet and stylus**
- **Adobe Photoshop**

Check this out

www.deadpanda.com The artist's personal web site.
www.sweatdrop.com The artist's manga publishing site.

Who is she? Fifteen-year-old Rilla Rosewood is the latest student to start at the mysterious, science-specialized Bourneside School. **What does she wear?** To fit in and look smart, Rilla opts for the school uniform. **What does she do?** Although initially shy, Rilla goes through her last years of schooling at Bourneside with two close friends, who are both completely different personalities. Like most teenagers, she struggles to keep her friendships, studies, and love life in balance, which becomes even harder as stranger and stranger things start happening at the school. Animals appear suddenly in the school grounds, as do doppelgangers of the staff and students.

GIFTED STUDENT

What happens to her? When she first arrives, Rilla is a bit of a blank slate personality-wise, but she soon starts to take on some of the traits of her friends. It turns out that the school is a virtual-reality simulation, and Rilla is the test subject in a scientific experiment.

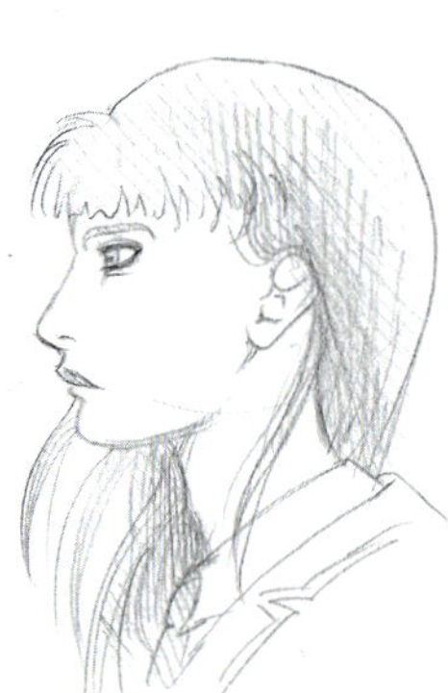

Illustrations by
Kate Brown

Making your own character

Schoolgirls have always been a popular subject for manga, and that influence is clearly visible in this example. Comic artists now have access to a huge variety of styles and cultures, and it is important that these inspire you to develop your own individual style and content, without your art ending up as simple imitation.

You will need

- Bristol board or drawing paper
- Pencil and eraser
- Black marker pens with various tips
- Macintosh or Windows PC
- Scanner
- Graphics tablet and stylus
- Adobe Photoshop

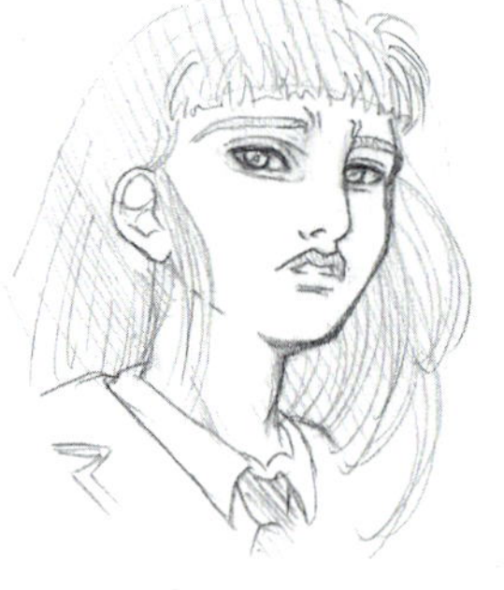
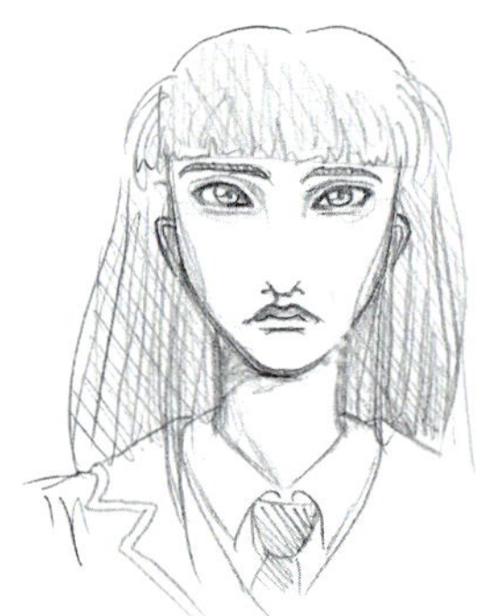

▲ Facial studies
Because the face is going to be the most expressive and distinguishing aspect of your character, it is advisable to do as many varied drawings as you can to establish a good collection of emotions and angles.

▼ Getting in line

Building up a character's pose, starting with a simple single pencil line framework that can be filled out and dressed, ensures that everything is in proportion.

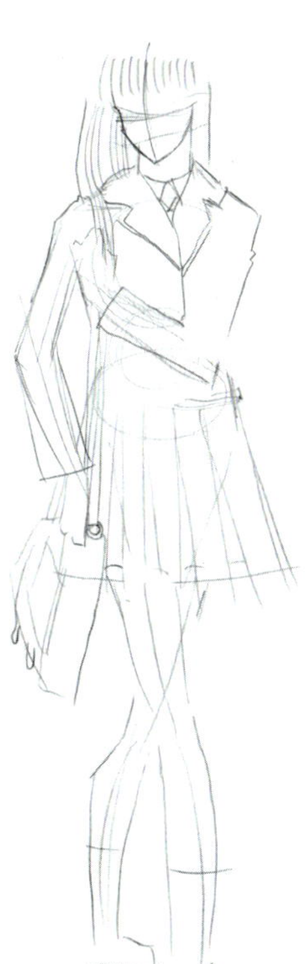

▶ Finished ink

The final inked version, with all the necessary details added to the original line sketch, is ready for scanning and coloring.

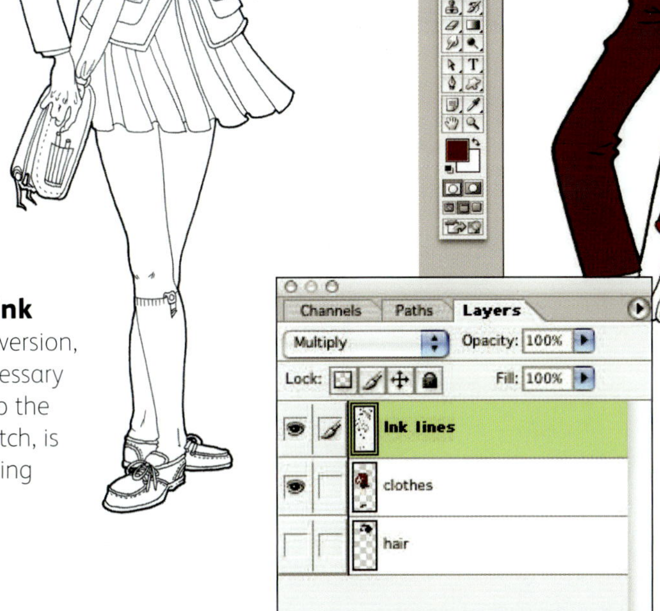

▲ Digital painting

There are lots of different approaches to coloring digitally, and, provided you achieve the effect you are after, there are no wrong ways. Some methods are more efficient than others, such as using Paint Bucket fills, but some artists still like to feel that they are "painting" their images using a brush. The important thing is to take advantage of the Layers palette that most software offers. This can be used for specific items or colors. To color this character, a Brush tool was used with a graphics tablet and stylus. The scanned line drawing was placed on the top layer and set to Multiply, to make the white transparent. On a new layer, brushes of various sizes were used to paint the clothes. Even though the color sometimes went outside the lines, the subsequent layers placed over the top covered these errors, although they could just as easily have been erased.

▼ Portrait

Apart from pencil sketches, detailed color portraits will help you become familiar with the character and coloring scheme.

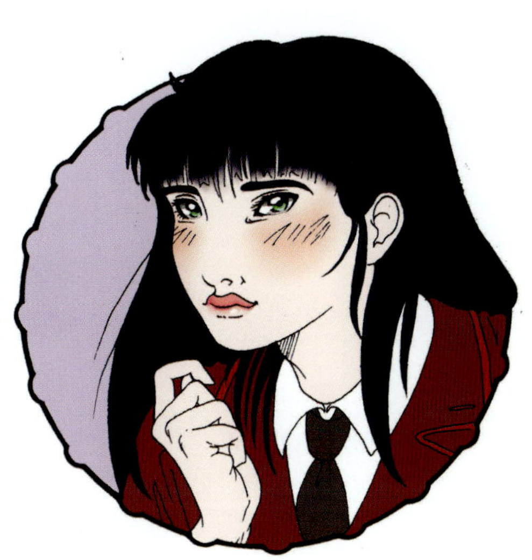

◀ Three-quarter view

Building up a library of different poses and angles will make creating full comics a lot quicker because you will become thoroughly familiar with your character's form. As always, practice makes perfect.

Who is she? Anna is an identical twin. Her sister is Eva. Their mother and father left them when they were 13 and 16 respectively. **What does she wear?** T-shirts and singlets are her favorite. Anna has an "e" tatooed on her arm, and Eva has an "a" on her arm. **What happens to her?** It is believed that when one of the sisters marries, the other will die. On the night before Eva's wedding, a spirit visits Anna and they make love, which makes Anna the first to marry. Eva dies.

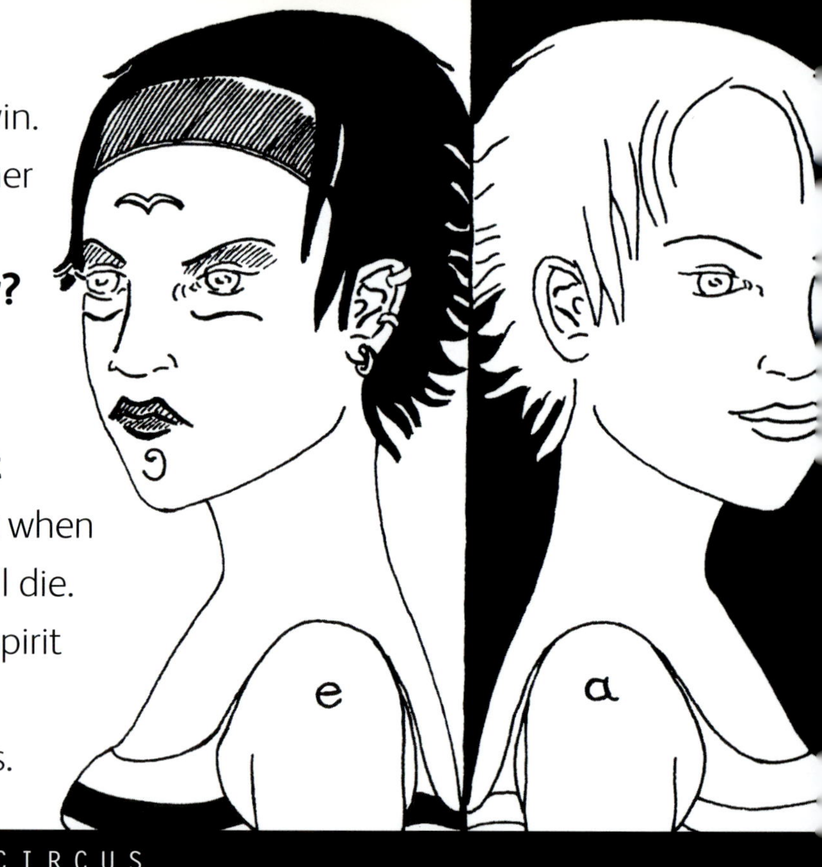

LONELY TWIN

Illustrations by Jennifer Daydreamer

What does she do? Anna owns and runs Circus Zazel, which she took over from her father after he left them. She also likes to dabble in the occult as a way to communicate with her sister.

Making your own character

Confidence in your ability and style can endow your drawings with a certain power that can make them be accepted beyond all perceived conventions of drawing (proportion, perspective, and so on). Once you have that self-confidence, you can draw in a naive, stream-of-consciousness style without fear of derision.

You will need

- Bristol board or drawing paper
- Black marker pens with various tips

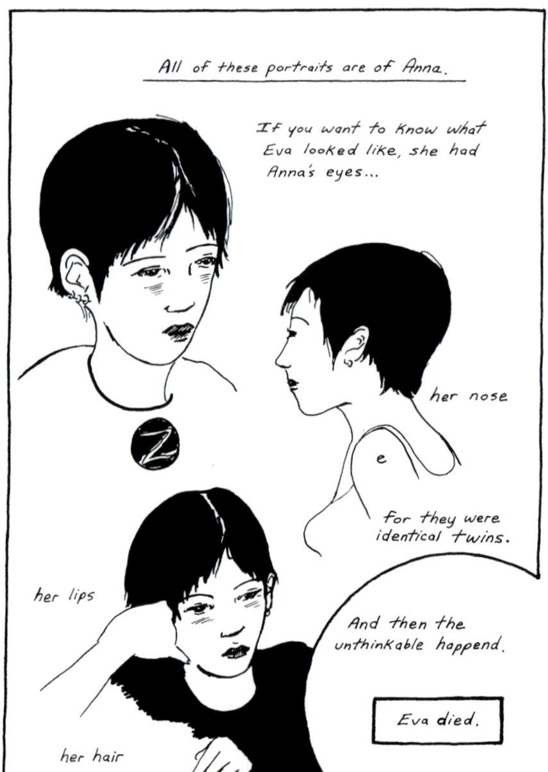

◀ **Portraits**

All the drawings were done in ink, without preliminary pencils or other preparation. Consistency in the character's appearance becomes unimportant because capturing the spirit and personality is the main priority.

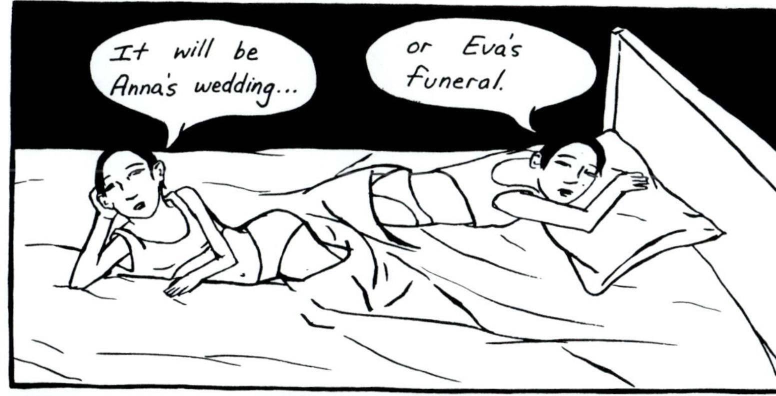

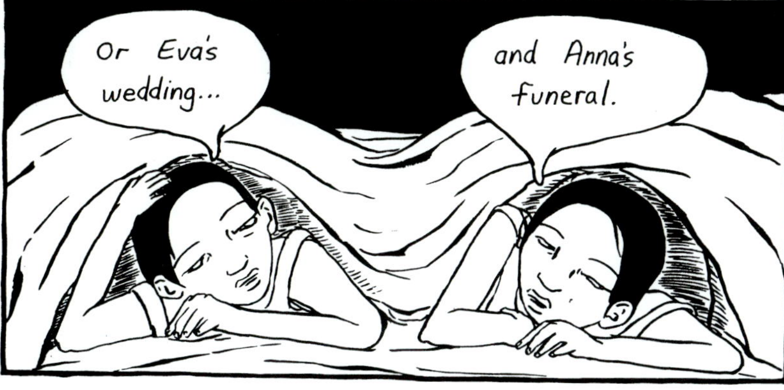

▲ Crisis

The sisters calmly discuss their impending existential crisis. Even though the anatomy is completely wrong, the mind still accepts it because we know what it is supposed to look like—just as we accept the typed symbols ^_^ as a human face. However, this should not be used as an excuse for not learning how to draw anatomically correct figures.

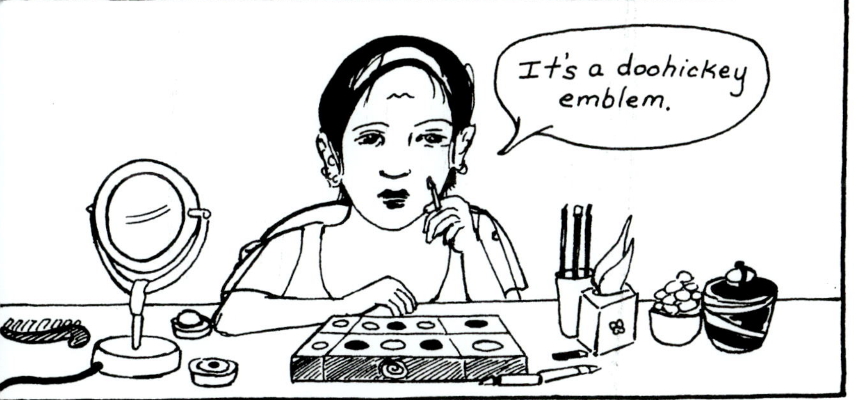

▲ Surreal

The dreamlike quality of the story and illustrations do not always make sense, but they are lucid within their own reality.

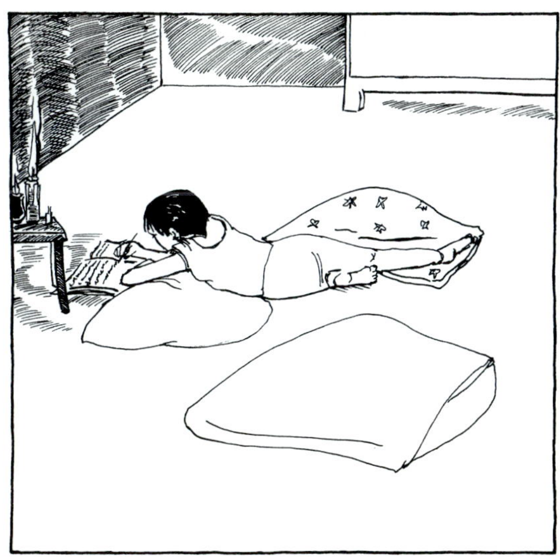

▲ Childlike

This style of drawing is often called naive because it has the innocent simplicity of a child's drawing. There is no thought or hesitation in making the lines, and perspective is not even a consideration. Combining innocence with experience produces striking compositions.

▼ Hatching

Working in pure monochromatic shading can be achieved with hatching (shown here) or cross-hatching (where intersecting lines are used to achieve a denser tone). One of the advantages of working in black and white is the low cost if you intend to self-publish using a laser printer and/or photocopier. The important thing is to achieve solid, rich, consistent blacks. Instant print shops are also economical.

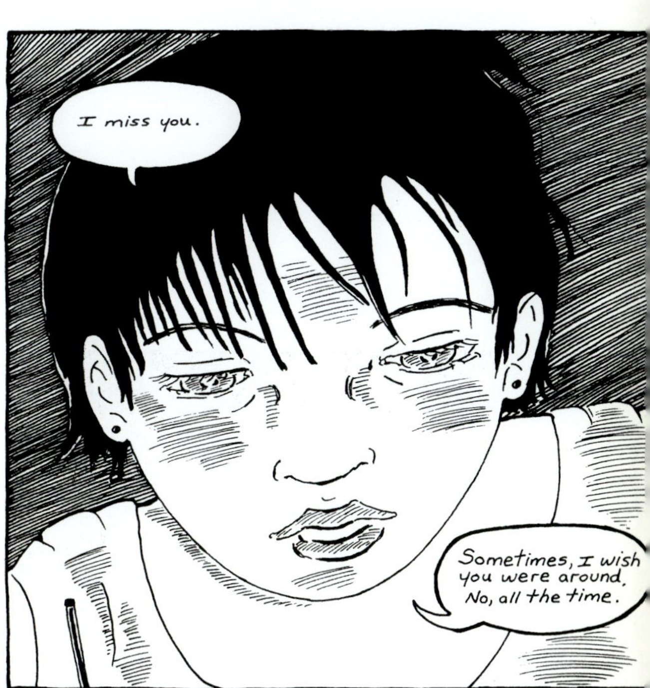

Who is she? Lila is not exactly a tomboy, but she is having trouble adapting to her new body shape and the interest it is attracting. She likes being a girl, but her fiercely independent nature and sense of self are sometimes at odds with the image her gender is expected to portray. **What does she wear?** She mostly likes to hide in looser clothes, but the rush of pubescent hormones has made her reassess how she portrays herself. **What does she do?** Lila is very smart and intuitive, giving her insights that often make her outspoken, but she is not garrulous. She is not affected by the pubescent hormonal rush in the extreme way that her peers are (apart from obvious physical ones) and acts as the (mostly ignored) voice of reason for her friends.

GROWING UP

What happens to her? Lila's freethinking has attracted the attention of the "authorities," who want to use her for a covert project. To snare her, they move a handsome agent, Kyle, into the house across the street, but they have not made allowances for Lila's tenacity…

Illustrations by Emma Vieceli of Sweatdrop Studio

Making your own character

Lila is drawn in the shojo manga style, which lends itself to the portrayal of innocence while allowing room for more interesting aspects to be explored. The long blonde hair, in bunches, and the gangly limbs together with an original dress sense help to convey the feeling of youth—and those pink fluffy slippers scream "homebody."

You will need

- Bristol board or drawing paper
- Pencils and eraser
- Black marker pens with various tips
- Macintosh or Windows PC
- Scanner
- Graphics tablet and stylus
- Adobe Photoshop

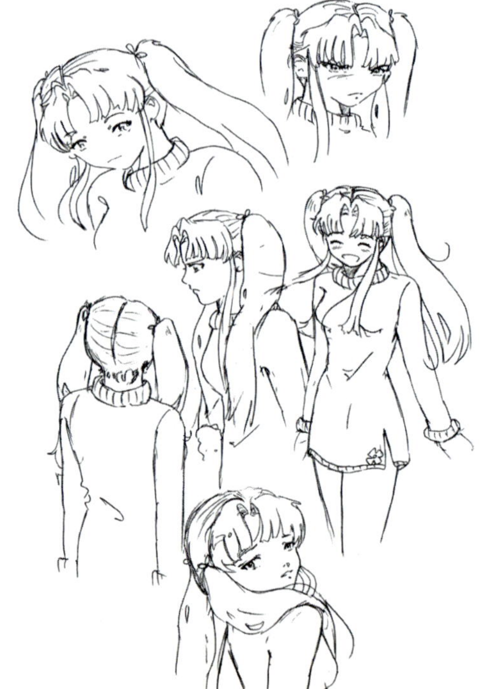

◄ Figure sketches
Apart from creating the initial look, developing a character also involves exploring moods and emotions visually. Because this style of manga uses minimal linework and detail, particularly in the face, most of the expressions are conveyed with the eyes, one of the characteristically dominant features of Japanese comics and animation.

▶ Developing character through sketches

To get the right look for the character, a range of hair, dress, and footwear options were tried before settling on the final combination. Quick pencil sketches make the visualization process much easier, and also leave you with a library of reference material that can be used at a later date.

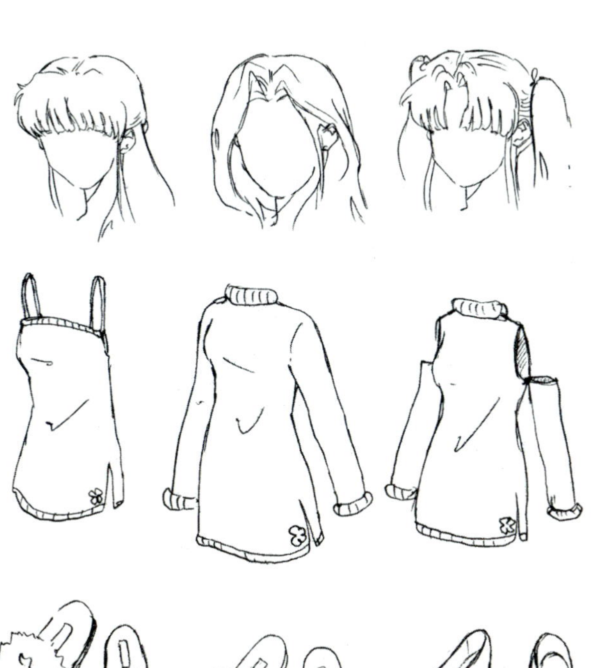

▶ Preparing the final drawing

The final drawing is inked and ready to scan for coloring in Photoshop. Whenever possible, ensure that all paths in your drawings are closed. This means no gaps in the linework. Closed paths mean you can quickly fill an area with color using the Paint Bucket tool. Open paths will cause the color to flow into the adjoining area.

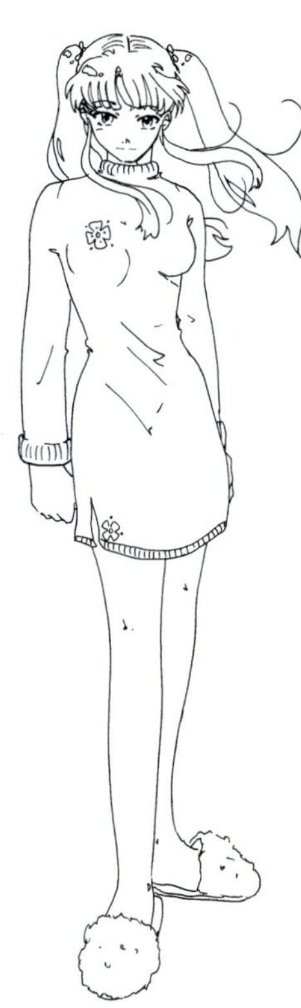

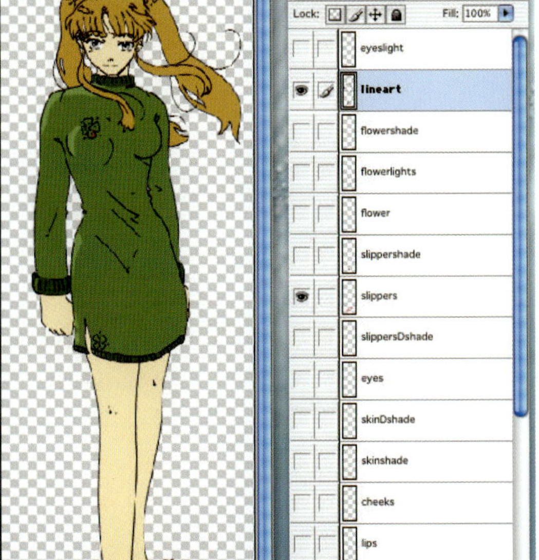

◀ Planning the color layers

The inked drawing was scanned into Photoshop for coloring. Each color was assigned a separate layer, with the main base colors going on first. Shadows and highlights were added using a stylus and Photoshop's Brush tool. By allocating a layer to each color, you can easily make corrections and alterations without affecting other parts of the drawing.

▼ Adding detail

Add detail to the head, one layer at a time, until the desired effect is achieved. Depending on how you intend to use the final image, you can leave the layers or merge them together to export them into a printable format such as TIFF. Either way, keeping a layered file is always advisable.

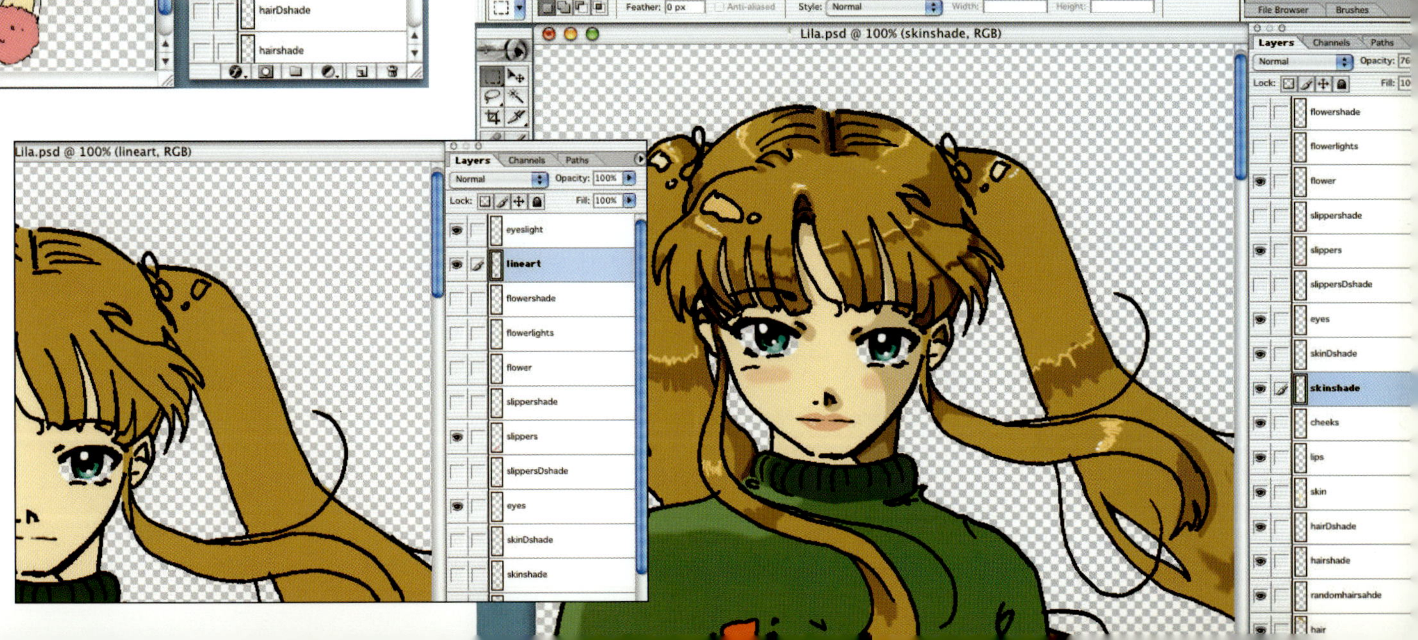

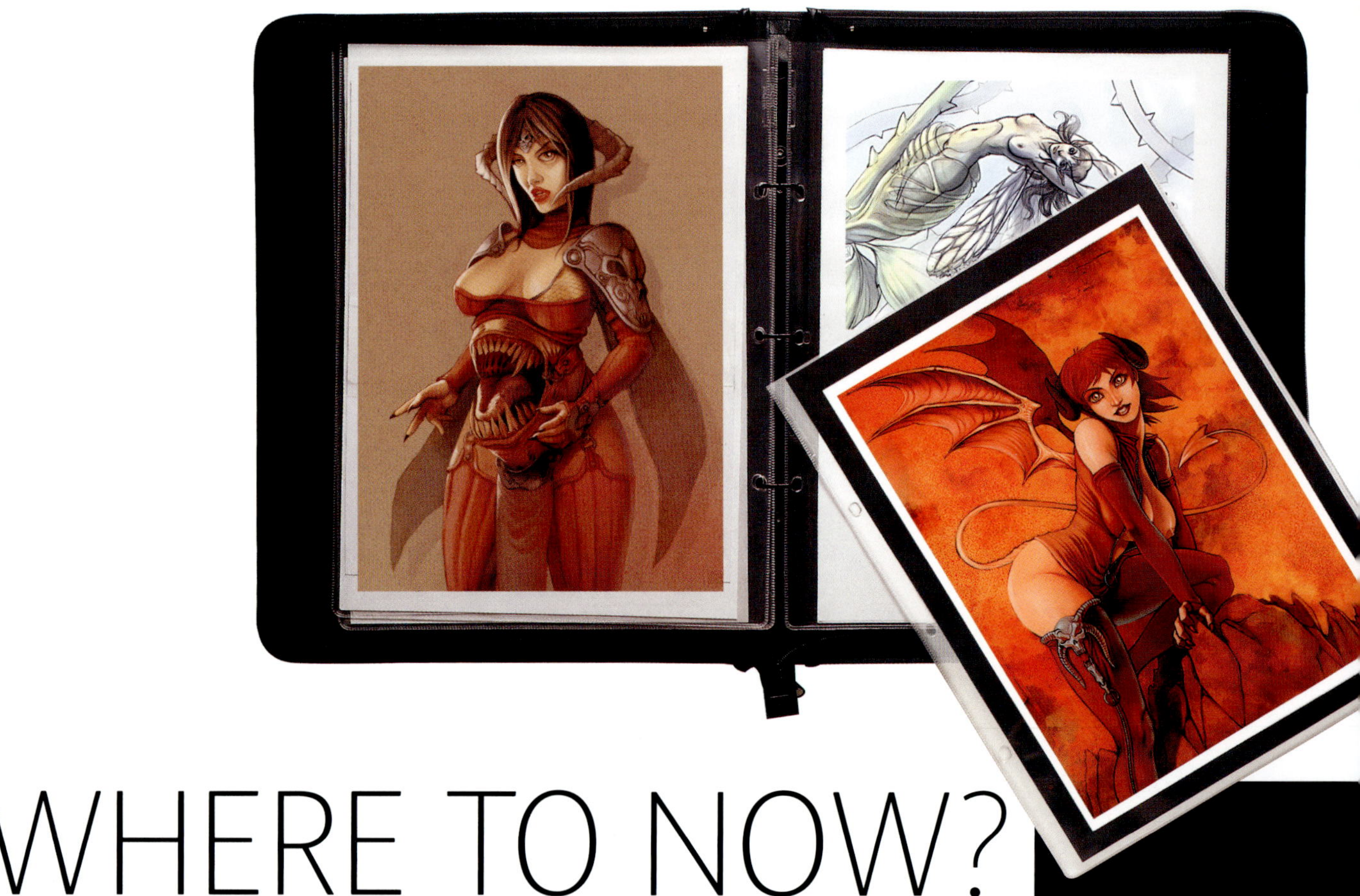

WHERE TO NOW?

This book is an introduction to the basics of drawing and developing female characters. As has already been pointed out, if you are serious about working as a figurative artist, and have not already done so, you should take some formal life-drawing classes. The best way to progress is to be shown the proper techniques and get feedback on where you are going wrong. This does not have to be a full-time course—it could even be just once a week—but the lessons will be invaluable.

PROFESSIONAL PUBLISHERS

Once you are feeling confident and have built a portfolio of characters, and possibly even written some stories to go with them, you will want to share your efforts with others, and put them into some sort of practical format, such as a comic. Be aware that the comics and animation industries are both extremely competitive, with thousands of very talented people vying for slices of a very small pie. The major comic publishers, such as Marvel, DC, Dark Horse, and 2000AD, already have a well-established stable of properties and artists.

If you are happy to work on existing titles, and most comic artists are happy to get any paying work they can, you can try submitting to these companies. The best place to do this is at a comics festival or convention. Web sites such as comicon.com and awn.com list most of the events and who is attending, so you can find one that suits you. Some of the smaller festivals have portfolio sessions, run by editors from comic publishers.

They will look at your work and give you critical feedback, often in a brutally honest way, but it will let you know where you have to improve. These people work with some of the best artists in the world and know what they are talking about.

If they like your work, they may ask you to submit some test panels, but this is still no guarantee of work. Should you be lucky enough to get asked, send only copies of your artwork; if they want to see your originals, make an appointment to show them in person. Of course, if you are working digitally, that is not an issue, and if you do get a commission, you will be sending the printers digital files anyway.

Getting publishers to look at new characters is even more difficult. So what do you do if you want to see your character in print? The first places to try are the smaller, independent publishers that manage to eke out an existence supplying more adventurous comics. There are advantages to these smaller concerns, not least of which is their sense of humanity. They will often give you a lot more freedom to produce your work than large, corporate-owned studios.

SELF-PUBLISHING

If, after lots of "great work but it's not what we're looking for at the moment" rejections, you feel a little dejected, you may decide that the best thing to do is to self-publish. It can be hard work, but it can also be lucrative. Self-publishing has the advantage of giving you total control over your work, but you may want to get feedback from more experienced professionals before putting your money on the line; otherwise it could be your sales figures that tell you how good you are.

If you want to self-publish, it may be worth engaging someone not involved in the creative process to take care of production and business matters. These will use up a lot of time and energy that you should be dedicating to writing and drawing the next issue.

Self-publishing, on however small a scale, is going to take some financial backing to pay for the printing costs. Working in black and white will mean lower costs, and it can even be produced on a desktop laser printer, but the results will look homemade. The price of digital printing and print-on-demand (POD) are continually dropping and are a good option if you want an affordable, professional-looking color job without being left with a garage full of unsold comics (try www.lulu.com and www.comixpress.com POD websites). The other advantage of POD is help with distribution.

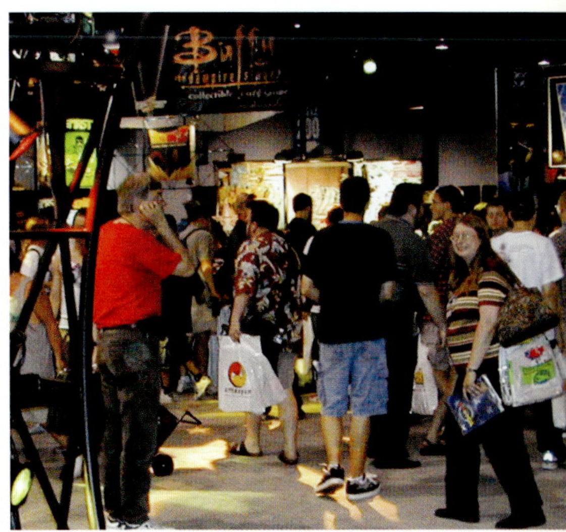

▼ **COMIC CONVENTION**
A comic convention is a great place to show your work to prospective publishers and meet other artists.

GO ONLINE

Another alternative is to go completely digital and put everything on the Internet—this means you will have no printing or distribution costs to worry about, and you will reach a potentially huge international audience. Comics can be saved as PDF files that can be viewed by the free Adobe Acrobat Reader. One of the advantages of PDF is that you can make versions in different resolutions— one for screen (which you can protect so it will not print) and another for printing. You can charge different prices for the different versions, and because your overhead is minimal, you can charge a much lower price and make more from it than with a printed version. There are several reputable online companies that can handle secure payments.

Above all, keep drawing and improving your own style. If you are persistent, you will eventually get a break, but luck and contacts are going to be your best way forward. Try to meet other artists; despite the competition, the comics community is very supportive.

► USING THE INTERNET
The internet is a great place to advertise a portfolio of your work, or you can go completely digital and sell it cheaply with minimal overheads.

Online portfolio

There are many free places on the Internet where you can place your work to show it off and have it appraised by your peers. Here are some of the more popular ones.

www.deviantart.com
www.dragonberry.com
www.renderosity.com
www.voodoochilli.net
www.gfxartist.com/

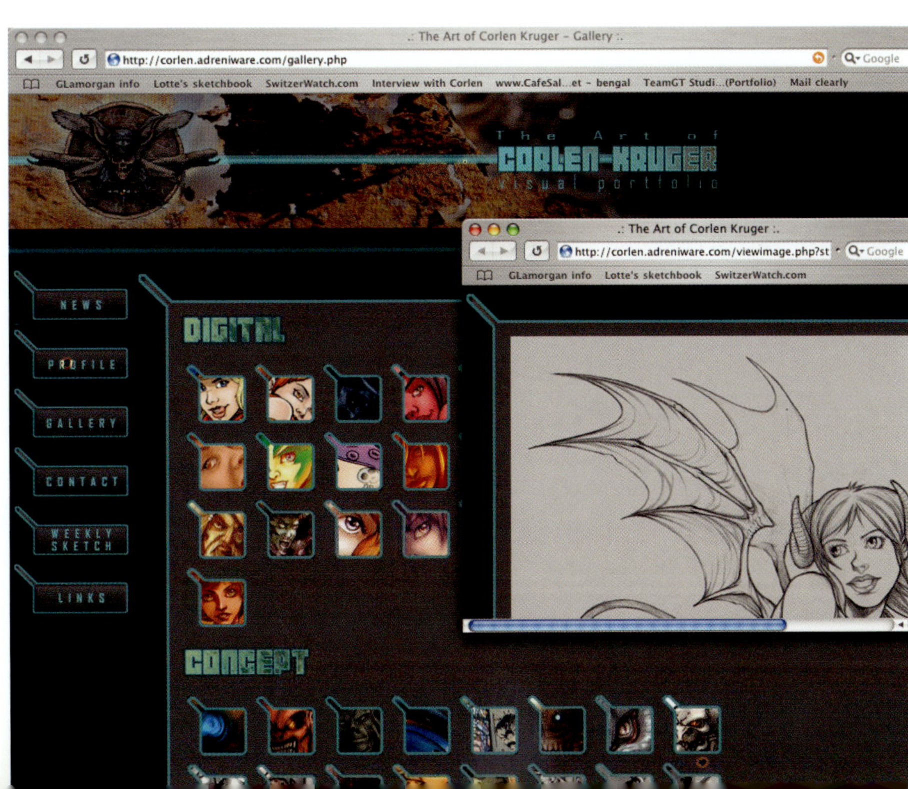

GLOSSARY

Digital: Anything created on computers and other devices using information stored as ones and zeros. Digital information does not deteriorate when duplicated.

Flash: A program by Macromedia for creating vector-based animations.

Gouache: A type of watercolor paint mixed with a whitener, such as chalk, and gum arabic to make it opaque. The pigment dries slightly lighter than it appears when wet. It is sometimes called poster paint.

Graphic novel: A story told as sequential art. These are usually longer than standard comics or a single-volume collection of multipart stories.

Graphics tablet: A computer peripheral that acts as a drawing surface on which you can draw, paint, and write using a stylus. Most are pressure sensitive to give variable lines.

3D SFX: 3D special effects, as used in Hollywood movies. These are usually realistic animations created with 3D software.

3D software: Computer programs that allow you to create models in a 3D space. Poser is a very useful 3D program for character designers.

Acetate: Transparent sheet of cellulose acetate film used for painting and drawing, especially in traditional animation. Also known as cel.

Airbrush: A small, precision spray gun that runs on compressed air and uses inks to produce soft, graduated colors.

Analog: Often used to mean the opposite of digital, but is still concerned with computers, using electrical current rather than numbers. Pen and paper are not really analog media.

Anime: Japanese animation, also known as Japanimation. Any animation created in the style of Japanese animation. There is no one single style.

Archetypes: The ideal form of a personality type.

Bitmap: A text character or graphic image composed of dots or pixels in a grid. Together, these pixels make up an image.

Bristol board: A fine, double-sided, lightweight pasteboard with a smooth, usually unglazed surface intended for long-term use and archival preservation. It is the most commonly used medium for comic art.

Broadband: Fast internet connection. For home users, this is usually either DSL or cable and requires a special modem.

Cel shading: Using flat color to simulate graduated tones. Gets its name from painting flat colors onto acetate sheets in traditional animation.

Character profile: A personality history of a character to help make him or her appear more believable.

Chibi: A style of anime or manga where the characters resemble children and have very big eyes.

CMYK: Cyan, magenta, yellow, and black. The four color inks used in color printing. *K* is used for black so as not to confuse it with blue.

Continuous tone: Where there is no discernable line between different shades of a color, like in a photograph.

Cross-hatching: Two groups of closely drawn parallel lines that cross each other, especially at an angle of 90 degrees, to show differences of light and darkness.

In-betweener: In animation, the person who draws all the movements between different keyframes. The process is known as tweening.

Inker: The person who draws over the original pencil drawings to give clean black lines.

Ink-jet: A high-resolution printer that makes the image by spraying minuscule drops of ink onto paper.

Keyframe: In animation, a drawing that shows the extreme position of an action or movement.

Light box: A box containing a powerful light source, covered with translucent glass or Plexiglas, used for tracing.

Magic markers: Fiber-tipped pens with a variety of nib sizes and huge color range, usually used for visualization art in advertising studios.

Manga: Japanese comics.

Model sheet: A reference sheet to help maintain consistent proportions and appearance of characters for comics and more generally animation. Usually show front, side, back, and three-quarter views, plus other details such as expressions.

Non-repro blue: A very pale cyan blue that does not show up when photographed by a printer's camera.

Pixel (PICture ELement): The smallest unit of a computer image, a pixel is a square of colored light that creates a picture when combined with adjacent pixels. The picture's printing quality is dependent on the resolution or number of pixels that make up the image. Photoshop and Painter are pixel image editors.

Presentation panel: A highly finished drawing or collection of drawings that show a character in action without necessarily telling a complete story. Used when selling an idea to a publisher.

Process colors: The four color inks—cyan, magenta, yellow, and black—used to print full-color images.

RAM (Random Access Memory): Computer memory that stores the working data before it is written (saved) to the computer's hard disk as a retrievable file.

Rapidograph: A proprietary name for precision technical pens invented by Rotring. Now used as a generic name.

Rendering: The process of producing a lifelike 2D image based on 3D data stored in a computer.

RGB: Red, green, and blue. The three colors used to display images on screen.

Scanner: Computer peripheral for transferring printed images into the computer.

Spot color: A single, special-color printing ink made up from a mixture of other colors. Pantone Match System (PMS) is the best known.

Stylus: A pen-shaped input device for a computer that is used in conjunction with a graphics tablet. It simulates working with pens and brushes.

Texture map: A digitized photograph or painting of a texture that is applied to a 3D object to make it more realistic.

Toon shading: An alternative term for cel shading.

Turnaround: An alternative term for a model sheet.

Vector: Illustrations created using lines and colors generated by mathematical equations rather than pixels. This makes them resolution independent.

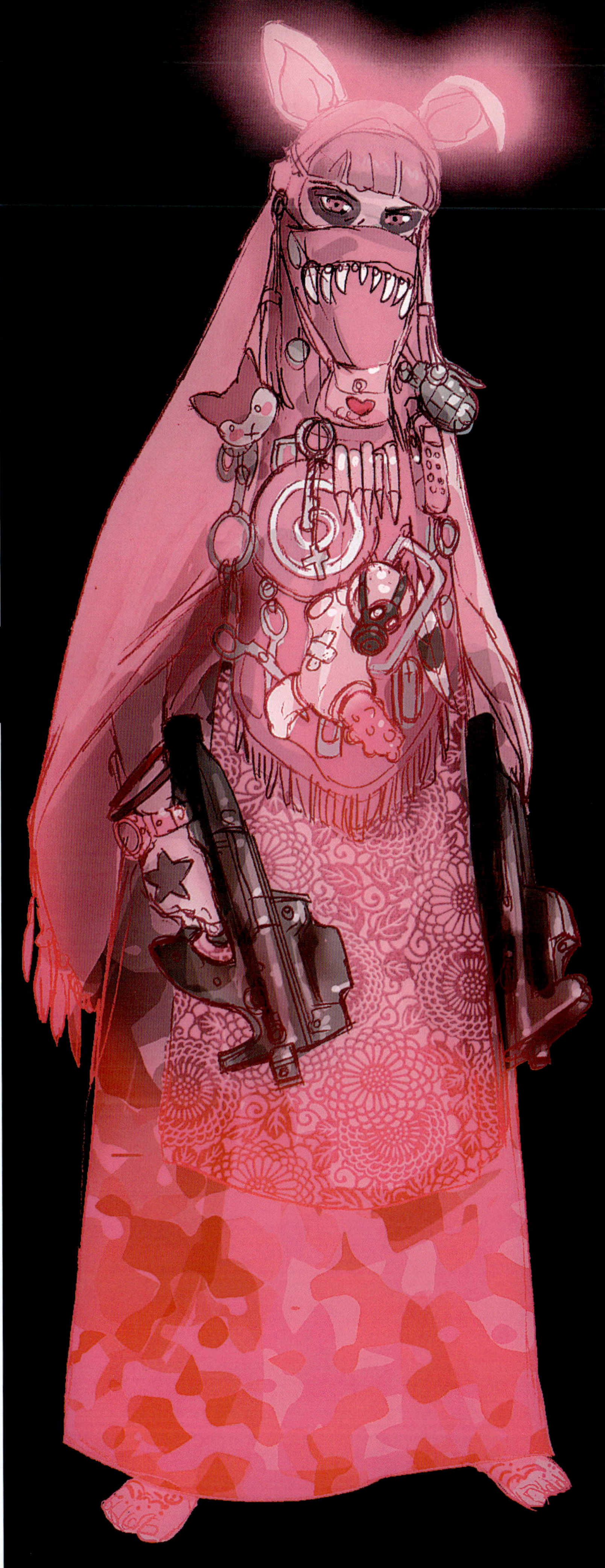

RESOURCES

This is by no means a complete or definitive list, but it does provide a good selection of titles and web sites that you may find inspiring, interesting, or informative as examples of illustrated female characters.

Fantasy art
- *Amazona*—Chris Achilleos (Titan Books)
- *Imago*—Jim Burns (Titan Books)
- *Majestika*—Monte Moore (Paper Tiger)
- *Revelations*—Max Bertolini (Paper Tiger)
- *Titans*—Boris Vallejo & Julie Bell (Paper Tiger)
- *Vargas*—Alberto Vargas
- *Watercolor Fairies*—David Riche (Search Press)

General drawing
- *Bridgman's Life Drawing*—George Bridgman
- *Cartooning the Head and Figure*—Jack Hamm
- *Comic Book Lettering the Comicraft Way*—Richard Starkings & John "JG" Roshell
- *Comics and Sequential Art*—Will Eisner
- *The DC Comics Guide to Coloring and Lettering Comics*—Mark Chiarello & Todd Klein
- *The DC Comics Guide to Inking Comics*—Klaus Janson & Frank Miller
- *The DC Comics Guide to Penciling Comics*—Klaus Janson
- *Graphic Storytelling*—Will Eisner
- *Hayao Miyazaki: Master of Japanese Animation: Films, Themes, Artistry*—Helen McCarthy
- *How to Draw Comics the "Marvel" Way*—Stan Lee & John Buscema
- *How to Draw Manga*—Series by Society for the Study of Manga Techniques & Hikaqru Hayashi
- *Understanding Comics*—Scott McCloud

RECOMMENDED READING
Comics
- *Assassin School*—Phil Littler (AP Comics)
- *Catwoman*—Various (Titan Books)
- *Dark Angel*—Kia Asamiya (CPM Manga)
- *Fray*—Joss Whedon (Titan Books)
- *Ghost World*—Daniel Clowes (Jonathan Cape)
- *G.I. Spy*—Andrew Cosby & Matt Haley (Boom)
- *Grrl Scouts*—Jim Mahfood (Image Comics)
- *Kabuki*—David Mack (Image Comics)
- *Love and Rockets*—Jaime Hernandez (Fantagraphics)
- *Mai the Psychic Girl*—(Viz)
- *Modesty Blaise*—Peter O'Donnell (Titan Books)
- *Promethea*—Alan Moore (Titan Books)
- *Strangers in Paradise*—Terry Moore (Abstract Studios)
- *Supreme*—Alan Moore (Checker Book Publishing)
- *Tank Girl*—Hewlett & Martin (Titan Books)
- *Vampirella*
- *Wonder Woman*—William Moulton Marston & Phil Jimenz (DC Comics)

Crossover—Comics, films, and games
- *Buffy the Vampire Slayer*
- *Ghost in the Shell*
- *Resident Evil*
- *Tomb Raider*
- *Witchblade*
- *Xena—Warrior Princess*
- *X-Men* (Marvel)

Writing and reference
- *Alan Moore's Writing for Comics*—Alan Moore & Jacen Burrows
- *Brewer's Dictionary of Phrase and Fable*
- *The DC Comics Guide to Writing Comics*—Dennis O'Neil
- *Eternally Bad: Goddesses with Attitude*—Trina Robbins
- *From Girls to Grrrlz*—Trina Robbins

- *Hero with a Thousand Faces*—Joseph Campbell
- *How to Self-publish Your Own Comic Book*—Tony C. Caputo
- *Story*—Robert McKee
- *Worlds of Wonder*—David Gerrold
- *The Writer's Journey*—Chris Vogler
- *Writers on Comics Scriptwriting*—Mark Salisbury

WEB SITES
Industry related

- *www.2000adonline.com*—Home of Judge Dredd and an excellent resource of advice and comic scripts
- *www.awn.com*—Animation World Network site for everything related to animation
- *www.balloontales.com*—A guide to comic lettering and production
- *www.blambot.com*—Comic book fonts (some free) and other info (M&W)
- *www.e-frontier.com*—Creators of Poser (M&W)
- *www.macromedia.com*—Home of Freehand and Flash (M&W)
- *www.microsoft.com/expression*—Vector-based natural media drawing software (M&W)
- *www.portalgraphics.net*—OpenCanvas, an inexpensive image-editing software package (Windows only)
- *www.poserfreebies.com*—Free Poser content
- *www.poserpros.com*—Poser content providers
- *www.renderosity.com*—Poser content and artists' online community
- *www.runtimedna.com*—Poser content providers; lots of free stuff
- *www.sixus1.com*—Sci-fi and fantasy content for Poser
- *www.wacom.com*—Producers of the best range of graphics tablets and styli

- *www.comicbookfonts.com*—Typefaces for digital comic book lettering (M&W)
- *www.comicon.com*—The premier online comics convention
- *www.howtodrawmanga.com*—Suppliers of manga books and art materials
- *www.sweatdrop.com*—UK-based manga publishers and network

Software

- *www.adobe.com*—Home of Photoshop and Illustrator (M&W)
- *www.apple.com*—Home of Macintosh computers, the creative's choice
- *www.corel.com/painter*—The best pixel-based software that emulates natural media (M&W)
- *www.daz3d.com/index.php?refid=577076248&b=6*—Creators of the best Poser models and DAZ Studio software for character generation; lots of free stuff (M&W)
- *www.deleter.com/eng/*—Manga art suppliers, including Comicworks software (Windows only)
- *www.deneba.com*—Canvas is a popular image-editing program that uses pixels and vectors (M&W)

Contributing artists

- Jesus Barony—http://metautomata.com/barony
- David Bircham—www.pulptheatre.com
- Nic Brennan—www.shugmonkey.com
- Al Davison—www.astralgypsy.com
- Jennifer Daydreamer—www.jenniferdaydreamer.com
- Ruben de Vela—www.rubendevela.com
- Dock—www.deadpanda.com
- Mason Doran—www.masondoran.da.ru
- Paul Duffield—www.spoonbard.com
- Jacob Elijah—www.shadowtactics.com
- Thor Goodall—www.thor.goodall.btinternet.com
- Matt Haley—www.gispyonline.com
- Monte Moore—www.mavarts.com
- Liz Powell—www.deviantart.pixieface.com
- Duane Redhead—duaneandjen@pennybridge.fsnet.co.uk
- Jon Sukarangsan—www.fortunecookiepress.com
- Simon Valderrama—www.edlav.com
- Emma Vieceli—www.sweatdrop.com
- Cosmo White—www.underfire-comics.com
- Mary Wilshire—Mwillustr@aol.com

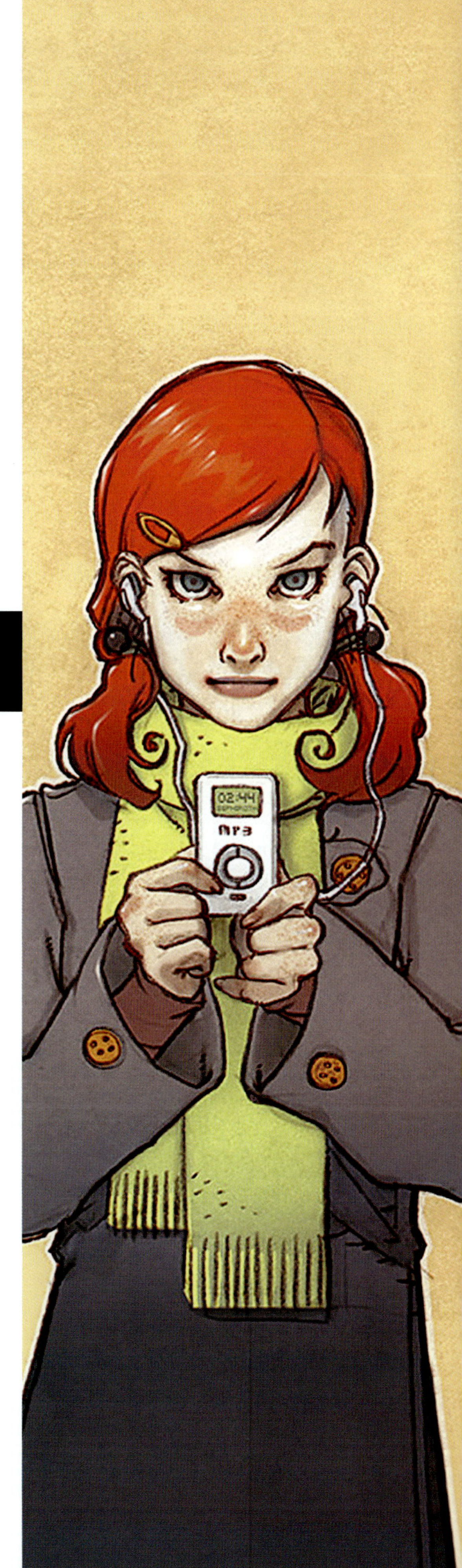

INDEX

126

CREDITS

Quarto would like to thank everyone who contributed characters for Section Two of this book; each contributor has been acknowledged on the page where the character appears. In addition, Quarto would like to thank and acknowledge the following for supplying additional images reproduced in this book:

Key: *t* = top, *b* = bottom, *l* = left, *c* = center, *r* = right

2–3: Francis Tsai © and ™ Privateer Press, Inc. 2005 www.privateer press.com; 4, 6, 7, 13, 14, 15*l*, 15*cl*, 15*c*, 15*r*, 17*b*, 24*t*, 36, 37, 121*t*: Corlen Kruger www.corlen.adreniware.com; 8*bl*, 8*br*: Christie's Images/Corbis; 9*l*: Album/AKG; 9*r*: Touchstone/Amblin/Album/AKG; 10*l*: Hulton-Deutsch Collection/Corbis; 10*r*: Associated TV/Century 21 TV/UA/The Kobal Collection; 11*l*: Warner Bros/The Kobal Collection; 11*r*: Corbis Sygma; 12, 16–17*t*, 18, 125, 128: Matteo De Longis www.kamenstudio.com; 15*cr*: Matt Dixon www.mattdixon.co.uk; 19: Francis Tsai www.teamgt.com; 24*b*: Kai Chamberlain, Monofone www.nervsys.net; 121*b*: Alex Faurote www.dangerousuniverse.com; 123: Tek! www.poompee.be.

All other illustrations and photographs are the copyright of Quarto Publishing plc. While every effort has been made to credit contributors, Quarto would like to apologize should there have been any omissions or errors—and would be pleased to make the appropriate correction for future editions of the book.

AUTHOR'S ACKNOWLEDGMENTS

This book is dedicated to Sri Adi Shakti Mataji Nirmala Devi, the source of all creativity and the epitome of female power. Without her love, none of this would exist.

I also want to thank all the women who helped bring this book to fruition: my wife and daughter for their love and support; and the editorial and design staff at Quarto, who brought it all together. In *The Picture of Dorian Gray*, Oscar Wilde wrote, "Women inspire us with the desire to do masterpieces, and always prevent us from carrying them out." In this case it was less than true.

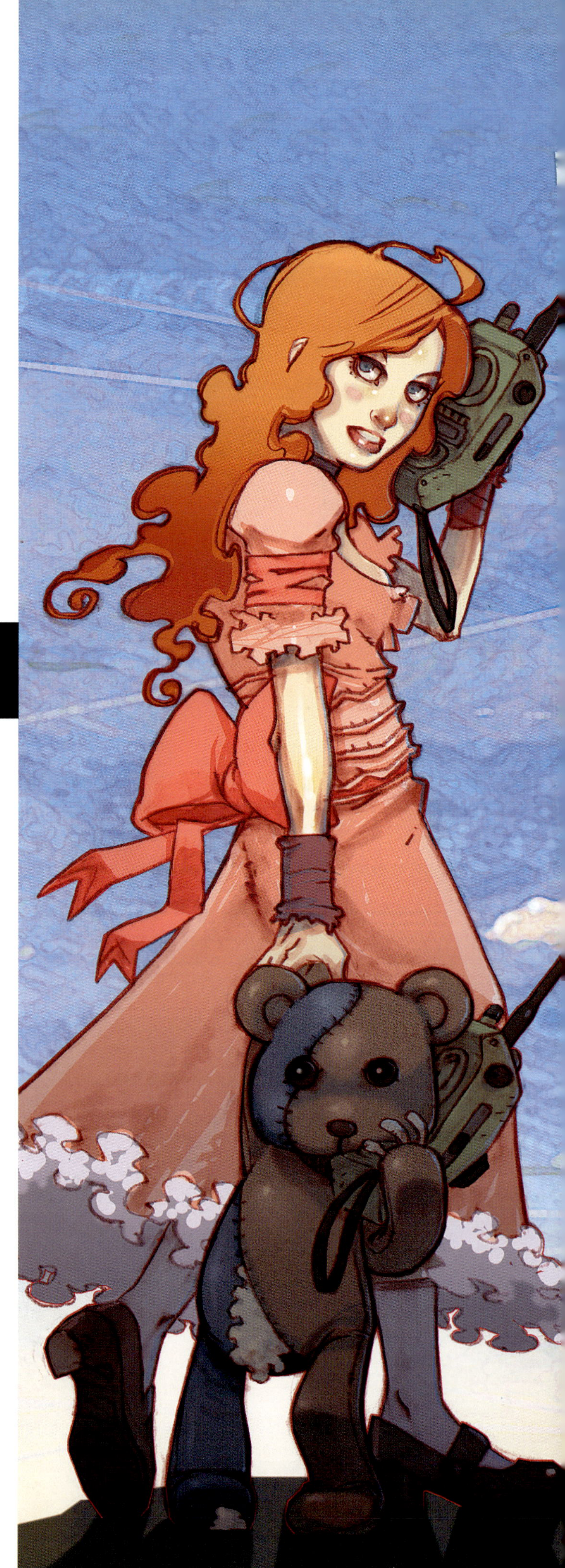